🌸 🌸 🌸 *Textual Studies*
and the Common Reader

Edited by Alexander Pettit

ঞ ঞ ঞ *Textual Studies*

and the Common Reader

Essays on Editing Novels

and Novelists

The University of Georgia Press

Athens and London

© 2000 by the University of Georgia Press
Athens, Georgia 30602
All rights reserved
Set in 10 on 14 Berkeley by G&S Typesetters, Inc.
Printed and bound by McNaughton & Gunn
The paper in this book meets the guidelines for
permanence and durability of the Committee on
Production Guidelines for Book Longevity of the
Council on Library Resources.

Printed in the United States of America
04 03 02 01 00 C 5 4 3 2 1
04 03 02 01 00 P 5 4 3 2 1

Library of Congress Cataloging-in-Publication Data
Textual studies and the common reader: Essays on Editing
Novels and Novelists / edited by Alexander Pettit.
    p. cm.
  Includes bibliographical references and index.
  ISBN 0-8203-2226-1 (alk. paper)—
  ISBN 0-8203-2227-X (pbk. : alk. paper)
    1. Editing.   I. Pettit, Alexander, 1958–
  PN162.T43 2000
  808'.027—dc21   99-462176

British Library Cataloging-in-Publication Data available

Contents

🐾 🐾 🐾

Acknowledgments

🖤 🖤 🖤

As always, my most heartfelt thanks are reserved for Jacqueline Vanhoutte, friend, partner, and wife.

Margo Collins selflessly assumed many responsibilities associated with this book, which is much better for her contributions. She is in many ways a collaborator. Dr. Collins joins me in thanking the contributors for their hard work and their patience as well as for their fine scholarship. Albert J. Rivero deserves particular notice for his almost superhuman accommodation of our various and extravagant claims on his time.

David Greetham assisted in many ways, tactfully and generously; he was instrumental in shaping this collection. As usual, Kevin Cope was a source of encouragement and endless geniality.

The essays by Peter Shillingsburg and James L. W. West III first appeared in a special issue that I edited for *Studies in the Novel* (27.3 [1995]); the contribution by S. W. Reid appeared in that issue in slightly different form. These essays are reprinted with the permission of the journal.

The contribution by Susan J. Rosowski, Charles W. Mignon, Frederick M. Link, and Kari A. Ronning appeared first in *Studies in the Novel* (27.3 [1995]) in substantially different form, under the title "Editing Cather"; several paragraphs first appeared, in somewhat different form, in Susan J. Rosowski, "Willa Cather Editing Willa Cather," *Studies in the Literary Imagination* 29.2 (1996). The new essay is published with the permission of both journals. I am indebted to the editor and the administrative assistant of *Studies in the Novel*, Scott Simpkins and Charlotte Wixom, and to the editor of *Studies in the Literary Imagination*, Murray Brown.

Warm thanks also to Haven Abedin, Diann Ainsworth, Jerry Beasley, Barbara Benedict, Kristine Blakeslee, Jim Springer Borck, Julia Briggs, Marilyn Butler, John Dussinger, Jay Halio, Melanie Hawkins, J. Paul Hunter, Alfred Hurley, the late Gerald Kirk, Jane Kobres, Donald Mell, Karen Orchard, Monica Rais, Sidney, Brenda Silver, Daniel Simon, Gwen Smith, L. Robert Stevens, the late Florian Stuber, James T. F. Tanner, Paul and Jacqueline Vanhoutte, Jeanne Claire van Ryzin, Eugene Wright, and Paul Wright.

Introduction

Textual Studies
and the
Common Reader

🐾 🐾 🐾

Alexander Pettit

This is a collection of essays by editors of literary texts and theorists interested in the implications of what such editors do. Textual studies—"the study of the genesis, transmission, and editing of texts," in the words of one of the contributors[1]—provides the basic organizational principle. But as the book's title suggests, I and my contributors have attempted to extend the debate about textual studies beyond the small circle of professional academic textualists who define and promulgate its terms. Although the essays vary in complexity, all should be comprehensible to educated readers without training in textual studies. The animating assumption is that many people read literary *works,* but far fewer do so with a steady sense of their constructedness as *texts*—that is, of the ways in which their "genesis, transmission, and editing" have shaped them as conveyors of meaning. These essays variously demonstrate that the experience of reading is more rewarding for this sort of awareness.

As befits a collection with a populist approach, the contributions focus on the literary genre most familiar to most readers and, as it happens, most frequently discussed in current literary scholarship: the novel.[2] There is much hand-wringing these days about "postliterate culture," some of it warranted, some of it hysterical, and much of it tending egotistically toward the aggrandizement of those of us who are unashamed of our bookishness. But publication lists, sales receipts, and the less precise data supplied by passengers on trains and buses suggest that a good many people still actually read the novels of Willa Cather, Joseph Conrad, Theodore Dreiser, William Faulkner, D. H. Lawrence, William Makepeace Thackeray, and Mary Shelley, to limit the list to some of the novelists discussed in these pages. It

1

stands to reason that smart discussions of widely read novelists will help guide the debate about textuality past disciplinary boundaries, toward people who read novels because they consider doing so a meritorious or simply an interesting activity.

The practical and theoretical complexities of the trade paperback or non-specialist edition have been discussed ably by other scholars elsewhere,[3] so I have favored essays concerned with critical editing, if sometimes as a point of resistance. A lengthy discussion of editorial practice would contradict the goals of the collection, but a basic description of critical editing is in order. This one is taken from William Proctor Williams and Craig Abbott's *Introduction to Bibliographical and Textual Studies*: "Critical editing . . . does not reproduce the text of a particular document but produces an eclectic text based on several texts and on editorial emendations. It assumes that though the multiple texts of a work may vary in authority, no one text is entirely authoritative."[4] The critical edition comprises the eclectic base-text—the theoretically "authoritative" amalgam of accepted readings that constitutes the edited work—and "an apparatus that presents the evidence used in the text's construction and that lists the variants of the authoritative states."[5] Obviously the preparation of such an edition calls for the employment of rational principles of selection: when different texts present different readings of the same passage, an editor must decide which reading to place in the base-text, which readings to relegate to the apparatus, and which to disregard as entirely unauthoritative. "Since critical editions are eclectic," Williams and Abbott continue, "their editors must have some principle of eclecticism, some basis on which to judge the authority of the variant readings and states of the text and on which to make emendations." They observe that the "dominant authority" invoked by editors has traditionally been the author's "intention" for his or her work.[6]

Williams and Abbott pitch the discussion broadly; they know, as readers of this collection will know, that there is substantial disagreement among textualists regarding the means and ends of critical editing. The central questions concern how editors conceptualize authorship and "authority," and thus how they conceptualize the source of the "intention" that their editions would preserve.[7] Different responses to these questions result in different texts that enable different ways of reading and interpreting literature.

The upheaval generated by the engagement of these matters is the subject of Peter Shillingsburg's essay herein. Because the essay takes up issues that resonate throughout the volume, I will refer to it often in my introductory comments, fleshing out its background as occasion demands, with a mind toward emphasizing trends and ideas broadly pertinent to the collection. Its placement later in the volume is intended to enhance its utility to nonspecialists who will by then have engaged with some of the more professedly generalist arguments of the earlier entries.

As general editor of the Thackeray edition, which he founded in 1976, Shillingsburg has participated in an overhaul of the discipline. He was trained to believe that a critical edition was "a product that would never have to be done again: a product representing the author's final intentions." Shillingsburg notes that an adherence to this belief characterizes the distinguished line of editors that includes, most famously, W. W. Greg and Fredson Bowers. In the early 1950s, Greg bucked convention by arguing that final authorial intention was best recaptured by an aggressive approach to eclecticism. He agreed with his predecessor R. B. McKerrow that an editor should favor the earliest extant state of a work as copy-text—that is, as the text that the editor emends with authoritative variant readings (most often authorial corrections) in order to produce the eclectic base-text.[8] But he differed from McKerrow by positing a distinction between the "accidentals" of a work—"spelling, punctuation, word-division, and the like"—and its "substantives"—the verbal readings "that affect the author's meaning or the essence of his expression."[9] The distinction justified a far broader eclecticism than McKerrow had practiced. Greg believed that the critical editor should generally follow copy-text with respect to accidentals, because contemporary editors and compositors (typesetters) tended to alter these features without fretting overmuch about the author's own wishes. But the editor had no such obligation with respect to substantives, since authors themselves will tend to alter these, but not accidentals, in later states. The liberal emendation of substantives and the conservative retention of accidentals stood to free editing from "the tyranny of copy-text" and thus to facilitate a more comprehensive recuperation of an author's intentions than McKerrow's more cautious methods had allowed.[10]

Greg's theory registers in Bowers's work as a settled preference for manuscripts over printed states. This is understandable: much of the material that interested Bowers—particularly nineteenth-century American fiction, although his credentials were strong in earlier literature, too—provided more manuscriptal data than the Renaissance plays that had inspired Greg's theory. Armed with examples from texts of Nathaniel Hawthorne and others, Bowers argued that prepublication states were more authorial, thus more authoritative, as being less sullied by the hands of printers and other functionaries who converted works of art into units of sale, often without attending closely to the author's manuscripts.[11] By scraping away the excrescences of time and commerce, the editor restored the work that the author intended to make public, ensuring its integrity and ideally its permanence. Anyone who has seen a fresco being restored will have an analogy close at hand.

Shillingsburg is quick to point out that the Greg/Bowers line is easier to dismiss than to engage. Be that as it may, as a young editor he found it impossible to share Bowers's belief that Greg's theory was broadly applicable to later literatures. Shillingsburg and some likeminded contemporaries came to regard Gregian eclecticism as inadequate to the task of editing, in particular novels, to which their generation accorded a higher status than Greg's had and which therefore tended to play a larger role in their theories of editing. As the textual history of the genre came increasingly under scrutiny (due in no small part to the efforts of Bowers, ironically), it became evident that Thackeray and many other novelists tended not to regard intention for a written work as made "final" by the appearance of its early published states. This distinguished these writers from playwrights working in a performative and textually fugitive genre. And, as Bowers himself had shown, intentionality in later periods is often documentable in ways that it is not in earlier ones: we are far more likely to have the letters, diary entries, and manuscriptal states of a recent writer than we are to have the documents of a distant predecessor.[12] With all these data at hand, an editor perhaps did not need to rely on older theories modeled on the practices of biblical and classical editors, doomed as Greg had been by the lack of authorial manuscripts to work backward through various "witness" states toward a lost "archetype."[13] Modernity provided archetypes, and witnesses, in spades.

The situation is not difficult to illustrate. Samuel Richardson, for example, revised *Pamela* (1740) for four editions published in 1741 and for the subsequent editions of 1742, 1746, 1754, and 1761. Still, his final intentions for the novel were not represented in print until the posthumous edition of 1801. Henry James substantially revised his novels toward the end of his life, in some cases decades after their original composition. In the present collection, Philip Cohen demonstrates that the young William Faulkner recast *Flags in the Dust* as *Sartoris* (1929), agreeing to the demands of a powerful publisher and acquiescing in the publication of a substantially different work than the one he had intended to make public. Charles Robinson shows herein that the documentary tangle of Mary Shelley's *Frankenstein* (1818) disallows assertions about the work's finality. In all these cases ancillary documents record something of the author's thoughts on their work and their intentions for it. The Renaissance offers no parallel.

Each state of *Pamela, The Portrait of a Lady* (1882), *Flags/Sartoris,* and *Frankenstein* presents different data for readerly pleasure and critical interpretation. In one way or another, many states have the sanction of their author. The 1740 and 1801 editions of Richardson's novel, for example, present heroines who appeal to readers in very different ways. Through suggestive dream sequences and postural representations deleted in later editions, the prototype of the heroine, unlike the final incarnation, is shown to be sexually needy and erotically compelling—to the reader, not just to the heroine's often doltish suitor. Generically speaking, the early version tempers its morality with the sexual dynamism characteristic of comedy. The later version does not. Which state does an editor edit, and why? As it happens, the 1740 and 1801 editions of *Pamela* provide the bases of two paperbacks now widely in circulation.[14] Both modern editions are the products of reasonable editorial choices: the original texts are sound, and there is nothing wrong with one editor privileging a less experienced and circumspect Richardson and another honoring the final intentions of a mature craftsman and a renowned moralist. But readers of either edition are compromised if they do not educate themselves about the contingencies that help define the volume they have brought home to read. Different editorial practices produce different literary meanings, and different editorial practices are enabled by an expanded field of documentary data.

Someone trying to settle on a copy-text for *Pamela* or indeed for a great many post-Renaissance works will not receive much guidance from Greg/ Bowers orthodoxy. An editor inclining toward prepublication states of the works that I have listed cannot rely on assumptions about intention like those that have to suffice for editors of works that exist in fewer states and are not attended by much, if any, documentary data. To generalize, a "Greg/ Bowers" editor of a Renaissance play, lacking a manuscript (as he or she almost certainly will), is obliged to deduce final intention from that copy of the earliest extant state that is least infected by shoddy typesetting and so forth. As the editor knows, this is a default position necessitated by a paucity of data; the deduction may or may not square with the compositional history of the work, which is probably not recoverable. But this method need not satisfy the editor of later works. Many of the often contradictory "excrescences" in novels (for example) are demonstrably authorial in origin; and the states that contain them, like the authorial documents that discuss them, are often available. So perhaps one need not edit Thackeray as one might edit Ben Jonson.

Frustrated by the incompatibility of their inherited methods and their preferred material, Shillingsburg and others precipitated a "shift in editorial attention . . . from 'final authorial intention' to 'multiple authorial intention.'" This development, Shillingsburg notes, "resulted from the accumulated weight of discontent with the goal of single end-products experienced by editors of modern texts for which a richness of evidence was still extant and whose investigations more and more revealed that authors had changing, developing intentions and sometimes more than one distinct audience. Multiple authorial intentions provided the impetus for the change in emphasis from product to process." Shillingsburg began to produce volumes of Thackeray that were not "standard text[s]" in the tradition of Greg/Bowers eclecticism, but rather "reading text[s]" with appended "guides to [the] work's development and its alternate authoritative forms." Volumes were meant to be histories rather than episodes, so to speak, because the works they contained seemed themselves to be so.

Because it devalues the idea of the primacy of a single state, process-oriented editing discourages precise rules for the selection of copy-text. An authorial manuscript could no longer be regarded as unambiguously the best choice. Shillingsburg notes that "the manuscript represents, undoubtedly, what the author did but not clearly what he intended to have published; the first edition represents, undoubtedly, what the publisher did but not clearly what the author wanted either." But neither choice allowed the editor "to present both what the author did and what he wanted." Theory and practice were again, or still, at odds. Theories of copy-text were perhaps categorically inadequate to address the problems posed by (to use the term broadly) modern authorship.[15]

Certainly a commitment to reevaluating orthodox beliefs about copy-text was manifest throughout the discipline. Although Shillingsburg has no reason to say so in his essay, by the early 1970s Philip Gaskell and James Thorpe (and a few others) had begun questioning the use of manuscripts as copy-texts.[16] Both pointed out that the textual intrusions of in-house editors and others often completed rather than countermanded an author's intention: the novelists Sarah Fielding, Charlotte Brontë, and Anthony Trollope are among the writers whom Thorpe shows cared (or understood) little about the messy business of accidentals.[17] In cases like these, first editions stood to represent, in Gaskell's words, "the text as the author wanted it to be read," not just the one that he or she "actually wrote."[18] Noel Polk's essay in this collection suggests that Faulkner may stand as a further example, and Robinson shows that many hands participated in *Frankenstein*, with Mary Shelley's blessing. A modern editor who favored Faulkner's or Shelley's fair copies—the autograph manuscripts delivered to the publisher or professional scribe—would be disregarding the author's intentions for his or her own work.

With different emphases, Thorpe and Gaskell—like Shillingsburg, in his interest in plurality of intention—were pressing a point that all editors knew anyhow: the materialization of the creative impulse as a work of literature is an accretive process that includes the history of the text that transmits the work. And this history may involve friends and spouses (such as Percy Shelley), scribes, compositors, and in-house editors, any of whom may be ignorant or learned, drunk or sober, given to censorship or committed to the free exchange of ideas. Such an observation would not have surprised Greg or Bowers. The question, rather, came increasingly to concern whether the critical editor was charged to expunge the taint of commercial culture from a text or whether he or she should acknowledge commercial culture as a valid part of the literary product, or the compositional process, that editing honors. If a publisher's editor alters a passage—or if an author, like the young Faulkner, does so under pressure—is the emended section necessarily a contamination of the text? Or might it represent evidence of a (literally) creative collaboration, if self-evidently a commercial one, characteristic of works produced in accordance with the dictates of market forces different from those of earlier periods? To recast the matter, what authority do we invoke (or promote, or construct) when we refer to the "author" of a text plainly beyond the control of any single person? Who *did* write *Sartoris*? Beyond question, William Faulkner wrote *Flags in the Dust*. But that book wasn't published during the author's lifetime.

A desire to provide theoretical and historical grounding to questions of this sort prompted Jerome McGann to write *A Critique of Modern Textual Criticism,* published in 1983. Shillingsburg's essay attests to McGann's impact on practical editorial matters; but it is fair to regard the *Critique* itself, unlike much of McGann's later work, as concerned more with theories of textuality than with methods of editing texts.[19] McGann's argument in the *Critique* hinges on his belief that authorship is a collaborative social phenomenon, comprising not only the plural compositional processes variously identified by Thorpe, Gaskell, and Shillingsburg but also the cultural and commercial factors that, as Philip Cohen's essay on *Flags/Sartoris* suggests, had come increasingly to participate in the construction of literary works. The McGannian paradigm's "emphasis," Shillingsburg notes, "is not on creative processes but on the meaning of production as a social element." McGann argued that by endorsing "a Romantic conception of literary production" based on "the autonomy of the isolated author," textual studies had mistaken the evidence of cultural processes for textual contaminations; eclectic editors thus created sanitized texts that ignored the historical particulars of "modern" authorship.[20] Charlotte Brontë, Mary Shelley, and William Faulkner are norms, not aberrations.

Shillingsburg observes that the McGannian paradigm "replaces the critical examination of textual evidence to ferret out authorial intentions (with emphasis on their plurality) with the 'critical' sequencing of documents in such a way that each new document is seen as a new version of the work." McGann's theories, that is, contradict both the traditional belief in creating stable editorial products and the more recent enthusiasm for replicating dynamic authorial processes. The goal is to position the text in a "sequence" of relevant data and thus to stress its production (or cultural constructedness) rather than its creation (or isolated genesis and development). Whereas an editor in the Greg/Bowers line "takes all the responsibility to produce the text the author wanted his public to have," the McGannian editor "abjures all responsibilities except that of collecting the evidence and giving a guided tour."

Hans Walter Gabler's "synoptic" edition of *Ulysses* (1984) negotiates between these two models by presenting an eclectic "reading text" of Joyce's novel on the recto pages and, on the versos, a version incorporating variant readings intratextually (rather than in an apparatus). His intention, Gabler would later say, was to chart "the growth of the text through all stages of composition and revision from the fair copies or final working drafts to the first edition."[21] McGann himself has moved farther still from eclecticism. His current project is *The Complete Writings and Pictures of Dante Gabriel Rossetti: A Hypermedia Research Archive,* which, when fully operable, "will hold a digital image of every textual and pictorial document relevant to the study of Rossetti," including "Rossetti's poetical manuscripts, early printed texts—including proofs and first editions—as well as his drawings and paintings . . . in full color as needed."[22] The reader will find ample supplementary data on the poems and paintings and may even, if so inclined and if possessed of the proper hardware and software, visit a "model of Dante Gabriel Rossetti's studio, with paintings and drawings on the wall, to scale." But one will not encounter an edited text of any of Rossetti's poems. This should come as no surprise; McGann's theory has tended consistently in this direction.

On balance, McGann's contribution to the field is threefold. First, as all sound theorists must, he has helped his discipline retain a vital self-consciousness about its methods. Second, he has provided an anticipatory theoretical framework for a medium for "sequencing"—computerized hypertexts—that calls attention to some fundamental limitations of critical editing. Third, his democratizing theories of text, with their theoretical sophistication and their anxiety about loci of authority, have made textual studies attractive to younger academic theorists who previously found little to interest them in the discipline.

These three items seem to me collectively to characterize the disciplinary

Zeitgeist. In an expansive age, each item suggests expansiveness: from assumption to argumentation, from selectiveness to profusion, and from specialization to interdisciplinarity. But for all that, McGann's work has not opened up the discussion as much as it might have. The debate has become less technical (that is, less centrally concerned with the hows and whys of editing texts) but also less accessible to readers unschooled in the arcana of postmodern literary theory. A bright beginning graduate student in the humanities can follow the main arguments of the *Critique;* few nonspecialists could hope to fathom much of the recent scholarship beholden in one way or another to McGann, however meaningful it might be in other contexts. This strikes me as a problem, as well as an irony, given the populist strain of McGann's work.[23]

The present essays accept the invitation to popular debate implicit in the expansionist paradigm that has come to dominate textual studies. "Authorship" and "authority" are the touchstones here as throughout the discipline. And the essays remain true to the state of the discipline by examining critical editing critically, sometimes defending or complicating its methods, sometimes examining its inadequacies, and sometimes rejecting its premises, as when Charles Ross argues that the sequences of hypertext, and not the selections of critical editing, are needed to convey the complexities of D. H. Lawrence's fiction. All the essays share with Shillingsburg's entry a belief in patient explanation. All are mindful of the extradisciplinary community whose interest in reading novels justifies the discipline's interest in editing them.

An explicit commitment to the "general reader" animates the essay by Susan Rosowski, Charles Mignon, Frederick Link, and Kari Ronning, partners in the Willa Cather Scholarly Edition, that leads off the collection. The appeal to expansiveness gains in force when one realizes that Rosowski and her colleagues are among a small group of scholars working to promote women as the subjects and practitioners of critical editing and of textual theory more broadly. The imbalance between male and female editors and "editeds" will be clear to anyone who surveys the field. Equally noticeable is the paucity of critical commentary on women and editing, a stark and surprising disavowal of the terms of the contemporary academic debate. Charles Robinson's essay on Mary Shelley joins the entry by Rosowski and her colleagues in suggesting that the discussion may finally be opening up a bit; evidence elsewhere, albeit scanty, props up the point. One hopes that this work will prove foundational rather than aberrational.[24]

Rosowski and her colleagues opt for a less polemical approach than my comments might lead one to expect. Among much else, the essay is a useful "how-to" outline of conventional editing. One finds, for example, that the edition's copy-texts are selected and emended according to procedures developed by Greg and Bowers and institutionalized by the Modern Language Association's Center (later Committee) for Scholarly Editions (CSE) and its predecessor, the Center for Editions of American Authors (CEAA). This might eventually raise a red flag for some of Shillingsburg's readers, who will learn from his essay that a CSE inspector delayed publication of the "process" edition of *Vanity Fair* for about five years; indeed the CSE's 1977 introductory statement was for a time the favorite whipping-boy of editors dissatisfied with the Greg/Bowers line.[25] But this does not mean that the Cather edition is retrogressive or that the CSE's guidelines are not appropriate for an author, like Cather, who shaped her work into a highly controlled final form. By choosing the right methodology for their author, the editors have transcended the limitations often associated with that methodology, specifically its putative tendency to limit readers' access to texts by favoring the exclusionist strategies of eclecticism to the democratizing practices of sequencing. The Cather edition turns out to be an unconventional attempt to put the yields of textual studies at the service of an inclusive community of readers. An acolyte of McGann would have to applaud its populist orientation, even if he or she might be leery of its methods.

The essay confronts an irony intrinsic to critical editing specifically and to the academic appropriation of literature generally: the works that provide the raw materials for academic study are characteristically written by writers and for readers outside the academic establishment. Cather "explicitly identified *her* reader as someone outside the academy," the essayists note; pitching the volumes to professional academics would therefore be "perverse." The historical essays prepared by volume editors address a broad audience, and the pages of the base-text are set in "clear" rather than annotated form. The appended notes are "fuller" than is usual in editions of fiction; and the textual commentary—in less thoughtful editions the bête noire of many be-

ginning scholars—explains the edition's editorial principles "with a sufficient clarity and extension to meet the needs of the general reader who may
not be aware of their importance."

The effect of such decisions will be clear to anyone who compares a volume from the Cather edition and a good edition produced in the heyday
of the Greg/Bowers paradigm. The latter will be bracingly erudite; the former will be generously so. The benefits of the edition's generosity are mani-
fold. In the apparatus often given over elsewhere to abbreviations, cross-
references, and cryptographic symbols, readers can trace Cather's characters
from their genesis in the pages of census records and regional newspapers
through their various incarnations in drafts and revisions of the novels. The
"community's history" that Cather wrote is broader still: the introductions
and annotations show that Cather had a botanist's familiarity with the flora
of her native Nebraska and a zoologist's familiarity with its fauna. Humans,
plants, and animals take on, or resume, a solidity and resonance—a meaning—that they cannot have in an inferior edition. When Cather wrote about
"breaking sod," she could assume that her fellow Nebraskans would know
that "sod roots extend at least two and a half feet on an unbroken prairie"
and thus that the task was a considerable one. But how many readers now
know this? Cather's intentions for her work hinge on assumptions that time,
distance, and unannotated texts have rendered faulty and that sensible editing stands to reanimate.

Good editing combats shallow stereotypes—probably sexist ones in Cather's case, too, although Rosowski and her colleagues choose not to say so.
One result of their work, they note, is that "fiction once assumed to be transparent and artless is now recognized for its depth and complexity."

Rosowski and her colleagues have corrected an anticritical tendency
among some of Cather's earlier academic readers, who could dismiss Cather's
art simply by preserving their own ignorance of her participation in the textual histories of her work.[26] Readers of this essay will probably have a hard
time imagining a less "artless" author than Cather, who was involved in virtually every stage of the preparation of her books, for example providing, as
Mark Twain did, minute instruction about those vexing editorial sandtraps,
Greg's "accidentals." Faulkner's editor Noel Polk might envy Rosowski and
her colleagues the comfort of working with such an author. For Faulkner,

punctuation and suchlike were "the stuff that don't matter," to borrow the title of Polk's good-humored essay. Cather's editors can sleep soundly knowing that the ellipses in their editions are the ellipses that Cather intended, but Polk has to toss and turn, fretting about accidentals because Faulkner himself spent little time doing so.

Polk's essay is unusual not so much in its approach to editorial method as in its willingness to justify fine points of method in a teacherly fashion. An editor of his stature might have brushed aside the old animus against "comma counting" by pointing out that, since accidentals convey meaning, critical editors must take them into account, even if authors do not always do so themselves. This would not have been a difficult task, rhetorically, but neither would it have been a useful one. Polk takes a different approach, explaining that Faulkner's lack of concern for accidentals is intermittent and thus anything but an invitation for laissez-faire editing. "The rub," he notes, "is that with a modernist author like Faulkner, that stuff matters *when it matters,* and it is the editor's job to discover when it matters and when it doesn't." And Polk has found that Faulkner's early fiction in particular "is filled with instances where punctuation, accidentals, matter very much indeed."

Even so, Faulkner was a bad speller and an indifferent copyeditor; the contrast to Cather is almost comically strong. Polk argues that Faulkner's casual orthography forces an editor to regularize Faulkner's texts, even at the cost of obscuring the author's own "ignorance" about certain matters of usage. To let stand the misspelling "rotundra" in *Pylon* (1935) is to "[impose] a meaning" on Faulkner's work that Faulkner evidently did not want but that he did not care enough or know enough to avoid creating. Unavoidably, however, emendations of this sort misrepresent authors, specifically by making them seem as capable as our cultural myths might like them to be, even if, for all that, they aren't always. Polk is right to consider the trade-off a good one, and textualists wary of critical editing—including some from the present company—will have to answer his apology for eclectic texts. He perhaps tells us more still by reminding us of sometimes uncomfortable consequences of even sound editorial practices.

In a typically lively locution, Polk refers to accidentals as "the designated macadam over which [a work's] larger issues have to travel to reach the reader." But what about the cars and trucks, the stuff that *did* matter to Faulkner? Whereas Polk discusses Faulkner's relationship to accidentals, Philip Cohen discusses his relationship to substantives—the words, not the commas that separate them. Cohen is interested in Faulkner's approval of or acquiescence in emendations that deemphasized his own conflicted sense of masculinity, his habit of representing men as either overt misogynists or "sexually repressed Prufrockian failures with artistic leanings and quasi-homosexual characteristics." When Faulkner agreed to the publisher Alfred Harcourt's demand to truncate *Flags in the Dust,* the result was *Sartoris,* his first best-selling novel. Faulkner himself further shrank the novel a year after its initial publication. In both cases, much of the excised material played up the contrast between the failed lawyer Horace Benbow and other, more aggressive male characters. The author himself participated in the elision of what Cohen calls Faulkner's "crisis of masculinity," making his novel less complex if more palatable to an audience anxious about Oedipal dramas of a sort common in Faulkner's earlier and less successful fiction.

Like the hypertextualist Charles Ross elsewhere in this collection, Cohen suggests that editorial "censorship," social pressures, authorial intention, and the modernist fondness for indeterminate meaning interact in the process of textual production. And Ross would surely point out that Cohen bases his observations on data that would be inaccessible even to readers of a critical edition of *Sartoris,* were such an edition available, since *Flags in the Dust* is a substantially different work from its successor and as such not susceptible to reconstruction from a table of variant readings. The larger point is clear enough, and Cohen makes it emphatically: the meanings of literary works are in fundamental ways closed to readers unaware of the history of the texts they read.

Although Cohen for the most part chooses to leave this aspect of his thesis implicit, his topic has as much to do with biography as it does with critical exegesis. The Faulkner that readers encounter in *Flags in the Dust* is defined by the author's unsettled response to the exaggerated masculinity characteristic of his native culture. The Faulkner of *Sartoris* additionally proclaims the author's ambivalence about revealing this anxiety in print. The two "Faulkners" are, in a very real sense, different. Noel Polk might add that his readers' "Faulkner" is more fastidious than the real one was; Susan

Rosowski and her colleagues could remind us that the "artless" Cather is a biographical misconstrual based in part on careless editing. James L. W. West III and Charles Robinson will be intrigued by these arguments, since they too are interested in biographical implications of textual editing. West expresses a theme common to these five essays when he says that editors "construct in their minds a conception of the author's creative personality that will undergird all that they, as editors, wish to do to the texts." Modern editors, like the publisher in Cohen's essay, create versions of individual genius, reconciling it to the needs of commerce and, as West shows, to the structures of the editor's own mind, however well informed. All five essays address the issue of editorial and biographical "fashioning" and so tap into questions of constructedness that have engaged theorists like Michel Foucault and Stephen Greenblatt.[27] West and Robinson, like Cohen, Polk, and Rosowski and her colleagues, demonstrate that "fashioning" is often a matter of editorial practice and as such a significant factor in shaping the texts through which readers encounter authors and meanings.

West's particular contribution is the illumination of relationships among biographical prejudice, editorial choice, and literary history. His experiences as editor of Theodore Dreiser and editor and biographer of William Styron have taught him that editing is an inductive biographical enterprise, not, as some textualists sometimes believe, an empiricist one. Especially when working with texts from the document-rich modern period, editors employ "preconceptions about their authors, notions taken from biographers and critics who have come before." The habit affects the selection and presentation of copy-text. "One might," West notes,

> choose to depict an author as a young innocent, ignorant of the ways of the publishing industry, powerless in dealing with its bureaucracy, and anxious to make whatever concessions might be necessary to see a work appear between hard covers. This authorial personality would require an editing style valuing early, untainted intention over later compromise.

With Cohen's essay still in mind, we may observe that an editor could take such an approach to justify a preference for the manuscriptal *Flags in the Dust* over the published *Sartoris*. The inclination might be stronger still given that the formulation relies so heavily on the "outsider" persona common in literary myth-making since the late eighteenth century. An advocate for *Sartoris* might reasonably take another approach:

> Alternately one might portray this same young novelist as talented but callow, inclined to produce overwrought and sophomoric writing, grateful (especially in retrospect) for the guiding hand of the older, wiser trade editor, pleased that his excesses were curbed or her writing toned down for public consumption. Such an authorial personality would justify an editing strategy designed to validate the received text and to rid it only of mechanical error.

This editor would prefer a printed edition to a manuscript. Both editors would pitch their introductory and explanatory materials to bolster "their" version of the author. Neither would necessarily err in doing so. Readers of biographies are accustomed to this sort of "fashioning." Readers of editions should be too, West believes.

Styron's case is in some ways similar to Faulkner's. As a young writer, Styron reluctantly agreed to "tone down" a section from *Lie Down in Darkness* (1951) full of references to "genitalia, menstruation, promiscuous sex, and incestuous feelings." Later, however, he came to regard the excisions as "judicious and proper"; he asked West not to restore the deleted readings in his 1992 edition of the novel. Styron and West agree that the work is better, artistically, for this decision. But there is no denying that the recent edition presents an author who is "talented but callow" rather than "powerless" before "bureaucracy"; and in 1951, Styron, faced with something like an ultimatum, was indeed "powerless," as Faulkner had been in 1929. One might even say that West's edition encodes the biography of an older writer—staid and circumspect—not the young author of *Lie Down in Darkness*.

Dreiser's case recalls Cather's. West faced a problem like that encountered by Rosowski and her colleagues when his research showed that Dreiser was often more attentive to compositional detail than his biographers and previous editors had been willing to believe. In reputation, Dreiser reached the late twentieth century as "uneducated and crude," "a writer . . . who needed help with spelling, grammar, style, and even content." Early printed editions propped up this prejudice by declining to incorporate manuscriptal readings that contradicted it. These editions formed the bases of later editions, so the persona endured. But Dreiser could in fact be extremely careful about his work; and his contemporary editors' interventions, to his irritation, sometimes subverted his own carefully wrought intentions for his work. By incorporating early forms of certain labored passages into his texts, West challenges "the standard biographical portrait" of his subject, as the Cather editors have done.

West says explicitly something that the Faulknerians and the Cather editors only imply: editors edit authors as well as texts. Foucault argued that inquiries into the ontology of authorship should not privilege certain types of artifactual data—this is his surprisingly influential "laundry list" thesis.[28] The claim casts editors and biographers as inert functionaries like Don DeLillo's archivist Nicholas Branch, who, in *Libra* (1988), is palsied by a surfeit of data that may or may not have meaning. More subtly, West asks us to confront our own processes of selection and to acknowledge that various editions construct various authors as surely as textual variants construct multiple meanings. Who, or whose version of whom, are we reading when we read Dreiser's *Sister Carrie* (1900) or, again, *Sartoris*? A reader aware of the practical implications of this question will be better equipped to appreciate the flux of meaning in literary works and the texts that transmit them. "Dreiser," like "Faulkner" and "Cather," is a more corporeal but no less complex figure than Foucault might have thought. Perhaps incidentally, West hints at a weakness in the old notion of the "definitive edition," since his "Dreiser" is after all *his* "Dreiser" and as such an impermanent, if substantial, phenomenon.

The question of authorial identity turns out to be particularly knotty in the case of *Frankenstein,* now among the most frequently republished and assigned of English novels. Charles Robinson is well suited for lucubrations on the matter, given his status as one of Mary Shelley's recent editors. In the collection's most demanding essay, he observes a chain of creative energies at work in *Frankenstein:* Shelley wrote the novel using the persona of Robert Walton, himself the editor of the papers of Victor Frankenstein, who in turn was the creator of literature's most famous monster. Furthermore, Percy Bysshe Shelley contributed material to the novel, as to a lesser extent did

William Godwin and other contemporaries. When we read "Mary Shelley," we read many writers, all of them, Robinson says, self-consciously engaged in shaping or "editing" the text.

Granted, everyone involved didn't live and breathe. We know that Shelley isn't Walton, obviously, just as we know that Charles Dickens isn't David Copperfield, even though the latter, like the former, had a tough childhood and grew up to be a writer. But Shelley seems to have placed a permeable membrane not only between herself and her work but, so to speak, between her work and her work's work. Robinson notes that both Shelley and her character Walton "took nine months to write their narratives" and that Shelley was given to "esemplastic fusing of words and images and symbols . . . into the text of her novel." For example, the novel becomes Shelley's "hideous progeny" in her introduction to the 1831 revised edition. Given *Frankenstein's* tortuous history of revision, which "Shelley" an editor presents depends in part on his or her sense of Shelley's affiliation with her characters, her husband, and her (other) contemporary editors. The question, again to anticipate Charles Ross's essay on hypertext, concerns how to free the "voices" that aggregate in the text of a novel.

Robinson began unpacking this biographical and textual problem in a recent diplomatic edition of the novel—that is, an edition that replicates a given textual state or states, with cancellations and additions. *The Frankenstein Notebooks* presents "a type facsimile of the manuscript (with different fonts to distinguish Mary Shelley's hand from Percy Shelley's)" alongside "a literal transcript of the 1818 edition." [29] Shelley and her novel thus assume a biographical and compositional complexity that they could not in a critical edition or a trade paperback. No edition with a single base-text could have accomplished the task that Robinson had in mind.

Robinson is participating in the rebellion against Greg/Bowers eclecticism that also produced Shillingsburg's "process" editions and McGann's "socialized" theories (and the hypertexts they anticipated). Like Shillingsburg and some of the other contributors, Robinson would attenuate the pressures inherent in a textual medium—print—that cannot transmit meaning without circumscribing it, often along lines defined by academic habit or vogue. Diplomatic editing offers this attenuation, intrinsically. But this does not mean that Robinson is proposing a new standard for the old notion of "definitiveness." Rather, like Shillingsburg, Polk, and West, he allows us to conclude that any text-based edition is a record of the editor's interests, including (as Rosowski and her colleagues might add) his or her sense of audience. Editors have points to make about the authors they edit; and Robinson's edition, like the others that I have mentioned, in a sense *is* his point. The idea is central to Shillingsburg's and West's arguments and may be deduced from Robinson's decision to favor diplomatic to critical editing as surely as it may from Polk's decision to gussy up Faulkner and from the Cather editors' assault on Cather's "artlessness."

In Robinson's essay we again encounter the pressures that precipitated the paradigmatic shift from the restrictiveness of eclecticism to the freedoms of diplomaticism—we may wish to recall Shillingsburg's "guided tour" analogy and McGann's Rossetti archive. The anti-authoritarian strain of this phase will no doubt quicken pulses less readily in the future than it does now, but presumably its hypertextual aspect will figure in the debate for some time. Shillingsburg, whose essay follows Robinson's, believes that the current "editorial fashion is attractive for three basic reasons":

> first, it requires no agonizing over indifferent variants (those for which the evidence for intention are equally divided between two or more forms); second, it avoids the charge that emendations made in the text represent nothing more than editorial preference; and third, its ideals can be adequately and elegantly presented in hypertext, multimedia computer forms.

Robinson's work addresses the first two points but not the third, although it would seem to incline in that direction. Shillingsburg himself is optimistic about the application of "computer forms" to the challenges that he enumerates in his history of the Thackeray edition, specifically those posed by the construal of "intention" as a diverse and protean quantity. "Perhaps in the electronic scholarly edition," he writes, "we have a medium with the dexterity, capacity, flexibility, and agility to incorporate multiple editorial intentions and readerly intentions as well as those of the author and producers of books."

There is a tension underlying all this. One could find in Shillingsburg's essay a belief that "computer forms" accommodate the supersession of the eclecticist's search for intervention: they relieve the editor of making choices that stand to circumscribe meaning in the name of assigning it to a certain author at a certain time. On the other hand, Shillingsburg at least implies that the "computer forms" stand to *legitimate* the search for intention, because the very urge to multiply models of intentionality, accessible technologically as it once was not, testifies to the importance of intention in the first place. Among the many rich implications in an essay long on rich explications, the foremost is perhaps the sense that electronic texts have everything to do with the future of editing but that we are just now beginning to consider just what this "everything" might mean or what we ought to do with it.

This inquiry is fundamental to the essays by S. W. Reid, Charles Ross, and Michael Suarez that close out the collection. Like Shillingsburg and several of the other contributors, Reid is a respected critical editor who has seen the successive dominance of the paradigms that Shillingsburg outlines. His call for "digital" editions is interesting in part because it justifies the electronic presentation of "a given text-document as a sociological phenomenon"—the very stuff of McGannian theory—by appealing to a more traditional model of authorial intention and by defending the integrity of critical editing even while he assesses its limitations and seeks to expand its boundaries.

Reid analyzes the textual history of Joseph Conrad's 1921 preface to *The Secret Agent* (1907) in order to argue that "the technology of the printing process and the human agents directly involved in the processes of transmission" kept Conrad from realizing in print his own intentions for his work. Publication thwarted rather than fulfilled the author's intention; the case would seem to support the inclinations of Bowers rather than those of Thorpe or Gaskell. Extant states of the preface include a typescript revised by Conrad; two sets of proofs, one revised by Conrad; and various British and American editions and the reprints that they generated. The author's intentions for his preface may not be perfectly recoverable, but they are far clearer than the printed states suggest. Scribal errors, lost documents, senseless editorial intrusions, and a promiscuous melding of states have conspired to produce what Reid calls a "textual muddle." As often happens, the work of a major writer reaches us as a pastiche of various more-or-less authoritative readings, some of which are all but meaningless.

The critical editor's traditional task is the rectification of such "muddles," and indeed Reid is co-editor of a critical edition of *The Secret Agent*.[30] But Reid finds critical editing limited by several practical factors: the inaccessibility of critical editions to scholars and "general reader[s]" in out-of-the-way places;[31] the interpretive difficulties posed to nonspecialists by the apparatus of critical editions; and—again we think of Shillingsburg's rebellion against the Greg/Bowers line—by the inability of the critical edition clearly to present a history of an author's intentions. Reid's critical edition cannot benefit people who cannot find it or understand it. And however responsible it might be editorially, such an edition only "represents a novel at one stage of its development—say, the one it had reached by the time of the first editions." To recur to my own analogy, the conventional critical edition is an episode, not a history.

In the absence of enabling technologies, this problem forces an editor to choose between an edition stressing product and one stressing process. As Shillingsburg discovered, neither solution is wholly satisfactory. Reid's digital edition would address the problem by presenting "reliable transcriptions" of states of a work produced during the author's lifetime; other documents pertinent to the work's history; and "supporting collateral information" such as editorial commentary and notes, conventional in themselves but now "linked to readings requiring comment." Additionally, the reader would have access to introductory essays and other scholarly commentary "for browsing and searching." Audio capabilities now commonplace in personal computers would enable readers to hear "the music and other sounds that Conrad's audience could have recognized from allusions in the texts." The Rossetti archive is the obvious example.

Reid resists the giddiness that such possibilities sometimes inspire. He proposes the digital edition as "a partner, not a replacement, for the printed critical edition and reliable paperback reading editions derived from it." His caution is warranted. Reid notes that the Internet may yet become "fully commercialized" and thus more limited than it once promised to be, and he adds that a great many readers in a great many parts of the world don't have access to computers or don't care to use them if they do. If only three of ten American adults use computers, as Reid reports anecdotally, it might be too early to abandon ourselves to populist theories of editing based on an unsubstantiated (and perhaps culturally and economically chauvinistic) belief in universal access. The solution is to continue to offer sound editorial guidance, using a variety of media to reach a variety of readers.

The problems that inform Reid's proposal are characteristic of the textual status of modern literature, with its profusion of documentary data. Philip Cohen and Charles Robinson confront analogous problems in their essays about Faulkner and Mary Shelley, as does Charles Ross in his argument for hypertexts of D. H. Lawrence. Reid and Ross share the teacherly belief that readers should have easy access to good texts. Ross does not, however, share Reid's belief in the continued utility of critical editing, either as a means to produce print editions or as a model for electronic texts. The democratizing "versioning" that interests him exists at the farthest remove from eclecticism.

Enumerating his frustrations with the standard critical edition of the works of Lawrence, Ross asserts that "print's technology of presence" unavoidably results in editions that "fail to liberate the multiple voices of textuality" intrinsic to the halting and, in Lawrence's case, sometimes collaborative process of composition—or intrinsic to the processes that resulted in *Frankenstein* or *Sartoris,* for that matter. Ross wonders what end is served by the Cambridge Lawrence's decision to suppress the fact that Lawrence's fiancée Louie Burrows contributed passages to "Odour of Chrysanthemums" (1911), or by editions that honor Lawrence's perhaps enforced decision to delete from *The Rainbow* (1915) a passage in which Lawrence stresses the biblical resonance of Anna Brangwen's naked dance of rebellion against her husband. In the first instance, a fundamental fact of the compositional process is elided. In the second, a suggestive reading is withheld or at least dumped into an apparatus that Ross, in this respect like Reid, believes will only attract the attention of specialists. James West might say that Ross is objecting to the biographical "portrait" of Lawrence promoted by the Cambridge edition. Certainly the edition presents a "romantic" Lawrence removed from the McGannian social nexus and cleaned up a bit in the process.

The electronic "literary machines" that Ross promotes, by way of contrast, "foreground variation and difference" within a work of literature by allowing Lawrence's readers to sort through various readings, to "version" the work according to criteria that they may confront and articulate, and thus to become "writers who collaborate in the production of the texts they read." Try "Odour of Chrysanthemums" with or without Burrows, but unavoidably, now, with a consciousness of Burrows's role in the writing process. Put Anna's dance into your "Self-Censorship" folder—a mouse-click does it— and examine it in the company of other such passages. What "versions" produce what meanings or, even, what set of assumptions about editing, literature, or sexual taboo? Editing decides; "versioning" presents. One supposes that such an approach might assist Cohen in his analyses of *Flags in the Dust* and *Sartoris.*

Ross agrees with Reid (and Charles Robinson) that texts should represent the complexities of a work's originary status. Like most of the present contributors, he justifies his thesis in terms of pedagogical utility. "His" texts— like Reid's and the Cather editors'—seek to enrich the lives of nonspecialists and specialists alike. But does hypertext therefore represent a level of textual utility unattainable by conventional editing? Ross obviously believes that it docs; Reid at least implies that it might; but Michael Suarez thinks otherwise. Suarez complicates the discussion with a skeptical interrogation of hypertext, a medium that he regards as rife with unacknowledged and not entirely wholesome "theories of textuality and of literary knowledge."[32]

Suarez finds apologists for hypertext disinclined to admit ways in which that medium restricts, rather than expands, a reader's field of choice. Noting that "the markup or encoding of a text always entails a theory of that text," Suarez asserts that hypertexts are often bibliographically shabby states best suited for simple and critically unpromising word searches, "tagged" only to allow the retrieval of "basic structural features" such as imprints and chapter divisions. Or hypertexts may be linked to a myriad of more-or-less related sources that threaten "to drown the once-primary text in so much once-secondary material that we return to the state of literary studies that prompted the New Critics to rescue the text from historical overdeterminism." Suarez hits hard when he links the baggage of hypertext to the historical encumbrances against which the so-called New Critics rebelled in the mid-twentieth century. As D. C. Greetham has observed, the new-critical idea that a work's formal characteristics are its sole producers of meaning is at odds with the idea of a "free play of meaning" championed by much current criticism—and, I would add, by hypertext.[33]

The medium, that is, privileges certain forms of data while implying that others are unworthy of attention. Suarez observes that a scholar tracking a reference to Lovelace as Æneas in Samuel Richardson's immense novel *Clarissa* (1747–48) will welcome the ease of the word-search but will be unable to search systematically for occurrences of classical names in the novel. Such "deep encoding" isn't impossible; it just doesn't happen very often. And in any event it replicates the encoder's own sense of what matters most, critically. Even hypertexts circumscribe meaning.

Suarez has other concerns about the pedagogical value of "encoded" texts. For one thing, he is not convinced that people want to cozy up with monitors the way many of us do with novels. "Most of us read fiction for the pleasures of plot and character," he notes, "but scrutinize screens for data." The disarmingly simple claim enables Suarez to support a far-ranging assertion about hypertext's invitation to mistake information for knowledge and amplitude for freedom. The proliferation of data, Suarez asserts, is something different from the instauration of readerly freedom. He invokes Aristotle in order to argue that "freedom does not mean doing whatever one may feel like" but means rather "the ability to choose wisely." The hypertextualist's job is to provide data; the critical editor's job is to choose and to facilitate further choice by providing a responsible listing and accounting of textual variants. Suarez does not advocate abandoning hypertext but rather proposes a new commitment to the principles of critical editing, enacted electronically as occasion warrants. Hypertexts, he believes, should both choose wisely and encourage other, informed choices. Reid would no doubt agree.

As I have suggested, Shillingsburg's comment about the ability of hypertexts "to incorporate multiple editorial intentions and readerly intentions as well as those of the author and producers of books" brackets nicely the essays by Reid, Ross, and Suarez. The point on which Shillingsburg bases that observation addresses the collection more comprehensively:

> The goals of editing are determined by what readers wish to know about texts and by what they want to be able to do with them. A reader who wishes to know what the author wrote will not be well served by an edition edited to show the work in the heavily edited form the early readers of the work encountered in fact. An archive of documents will not help

the reader who wishes to see the author's final intentions if the documents are of mixed authority. Different readers need different editions.

Here Shillingsburg levels the paradigms that he has carefully explained, implying that in the real world of readership they ought to be cooperative rather than competitive, coincident rather than consecutive. In doing so, he accents the movement toward expansiveness that I have proposed as characteristic of textual studies generally and of this collection specifically: the theories and practices of textual studies now more than ever tend toward the promotion of meaningful collaborations between heterogeneous communities of readers and writers. This is a laudable goal, and I will hope that these essays move us closer to it by making the discipline more susceptible to interrogation and thus better equipped to benefit the culture whose icons it would preserve.

Notes

1. Philip Cohen, "William Faulkner, the Crisis of Masculinity, and Textual Instability," in this collection.

2. Two special issues of *Studies in the Novel* concern editing the novel: Warner Barnes and James T. Cox edited *Textual Studies in the Novel* (7.3 [1975]); and Alexander Pettit edited *Editing Novels and Novelists, Now* (27.3 [1995]). For the interrelated histories of novel-studies, textual theory, and editorial practice, see D. C. Greetham, "If That Was Then, Is This Now?" in the 1995 special issue (427–50).

3. The discussion, late in starting, is gaining momentum; see Marilyn Butler, "Editing Women," *Studies in the Novel* 27 (1995): 273–83; J. Paul Hunter, "Editing for the Classroom: Texts in Contexts," *Studies in the Novel* 27 (1995): 284–94; and Julia Briggs, "Between the Texts: Virginia Woolf's Acts of Revision," *TEXT* 12 (1999): 143–65.

4. William Proctor Williams and Craig S. Abbott, *An Introduction to Bibliographical and Textual Studies*, 2nd ed. (New York: Modern Language Association of America, 1989), 56. For a more detailed introduction, see D. C. Greetham, *Textual Scholarship: An Introduction* (New York: Garland, 1992). Philip Gaskell, *A New Introduction to Bibliography* (1972; reprint, New Castle DE: Oak Knoll Press, 1995) is particularly strong on technical matters; perhaps the most teacherly introduction is Peter L. Shillingsburg, *Scholarly Editing in the Computer Age: Theory and Practice,*

3rd ed. (Ann Arbor: University of Michigan Press, 1996). Fredson Bowers's *Bibliography and Textual Criticism* (Oxford: Clarendon, 1964) remains a learned introduction to earlier twentieth-century orthodoxy. For a brief and broad-minded schematic description of critical editing, see Greetham, *Textual Scholarship*, 352–70.

5. Williams and Abbott, *Introduction*, 57.

6. Williams and Abbott, *Introduction*, 57.

7. Greetham's survey of the recent debate about intentionality complements the current essays: see *Textual Scholarship*, 335–46; see also Shillingsburg, *Scholarly Editing*, 29–39. See Greetham, *Textual Scholarship*, 323–35, for a survey of earlier twentieth-century editorial theory.

8. See W. W. Greg, "The Rationale of Copy-Text," *Studies in Bibliography* 3 (1950–51): 19–36. Greg's concurrence with McKerrow about the desirability of early states should not obscure a broader point: "Greg's basic position in [the "Rationale"] was to call into question a widely held textual assumption that the most authoritative copy-text for a scholarly edition should be the last edition published during the author's lifetime" (Greetham, *Textual Scholarship*, 332).

9. Greg, "Rationale," 21.

10. Greg, "Rationale," 26.

11. See, for example, Bowers, "Textual Criticism," in *The Aims and Methods of Scholarship*, ed. James Thorpe, 2nd ed. (New York: Modern Language Association of America, 1970), 29–54; and Bowers, "Some Principles for Scholarly Editions of Nineteenth-Century American Authors," *Studies in Bibliography* 17 (1976): 223–28.

12. The point concerns not only the ephemerality of documents (particularly unprinted ones) but also the development and commercialization of a cult of authorship.

13. For similarities between Greg/Bowers methodology and classical and biblical editing, see, for example, Jerome McGann, *A Critique of Modern Textual Criticism* (1983; reprint, Charlottesville: University Press of Virginia, 1992), 21; and Greetham, *Textual Scholarship*, 333–34. And see Greg, "Rationale," 19–22. For a succinct introduction to classical and biblical textual criticism, see Greetham, *Textual Scholarship*, 297–305.

14. The 1740 edition is used for T. C. Duncan Eaves and Ben D. Kimpel's edition (Boston: Houghton Mifflin, Riverside, 1971); the 1801 for Peter Sabor's edition (Harmondsworth: Penguin, 1980). These are classroom editions with minimal emendations; a good eclectic edition of *Pamela* is ruled out by the author's enthusiasm for revision. The novels of Henry James, noted above, are analogous to those of Richardson in this respect.

15. Assessments like this, if orthodox in some quarters, have been forcefully opposed in others. Fredson Bowers and G. Thomas Tanselle in particular have argued for the broad applicability of intentionalist editing; see, for example, Bowers, "Greg's Rationale of Copy-text Revisited," *Studies in Bibliography* 31 (1978): 90–161; and Tanselle, "The Editorial Problem of Final Authorial Intention," *Studies in Bibliography* 29 (1976): 167–211; rpt. in Tanselle, *Textual Criticism and Scholarly Editing* (Charlottesville: University Press of Virginia, 1990), 27–71.

16. See Gaskell, *New Introduction,* 338–43; and James Thorpe, *Principles of Textual Criticism* (San Marino CA: Huntington Library, 1972), 186–92. Both critics, like Greg and Bowers, regard the recuperation of authorial intention as the proper goal of editing.

17. See Thorpe, *Principles,* 144–46; see also Gaskell, *New Introduction,* 339.

18. Gaskell, *New Introduction,* 339.

19. For later work in which McGann intensifies his discussion of practical editorial matters, see, for example, *The Textual Condition* (Princeton: Princeton University Press, 1991).

20. McGann, *Critique,* 8; see also, more expansively, McGann, *Textual Condition,* 48–68.

21. Hans Walter Gabler, afterword to *Ulysses,* by James Joyce, ed. Gabler, with Wolfhard Steppe and Claus Melchior (New York: Random House, Vintage, 1986), 649. The 1986 edition is based on the "reading text" of *Ulysses: A Critical and Synoptic Edition,* ed. Gabler, with Steppe and Melchior, 3 vols. (New York: Garland, 1984).

22. The quotations are from the *Archive's* home page, at <http://jefferson.village. virginia.edu/rossetti/rossetti.html>. The completed archive will be published on the Internet by the University of Michigan Press. See also McGann, "The Rationale of HyperText," TEXT 9 (1996): 11–32, and, in different form, at <http://jefferson. village.virginia.edu/public/jjm2f/rationale.html>.

23. A number of collections examine textual studies and postmodern theory: *Textual Criticism and Literary Interpretation,* ed. Jerome J. McGann (Chicago: University of Chicago Press, 1985); *Devils and Angels: Textual Editing and Literary Theory,* ed. Philip Cohen (Charlottesville: University Press of Virginia, 1991); *Representing Modernist Texts: Editing as Interpretation,* ed. George Bornstein (Ann Arbor: University of Michigan Press, 1991); *Palimpsest: Editorial Theory in the Humanities,* ed. George Bornstein and Ralph Williams (Ann Arbor: University of Michigan Press, 1993); *The Margins of the Text,* ed. D. C. Greetham (Ann Arbor: University of Michigan Press, 1997); and *Texts and Textuality: Textual Instability, Theory, and Interpretation,* ed.

Philip Cohen (New York: Garland, 1997). The annual TEXT regularly publishes work of this sort.

24. See also Butler, "Editing Women"; Briggs, "Between the Texts"; Brenda R. Silver, "Textual Criticism as Feminist Practice: Or, Who's Afraid of Virginia Woolf Part II," in *Representing Modernist Texts,* 193–222; and Janet Todd, "Pursue that way of Fooling, and be damn'd: Editing Aphra Behn," *Studies in the Novel* 27 (1995): 304–19. *The Margins of the Text* is the most aggressive attempt to address problems of balance within textual studies; the entry most pertinent to the present discussion is Brenda R. Silver, "Whose Room of Orlando's Own? The Politics of Adaptation" (57–82). The rise in interest in women writers coincides with the diminishing of funds for critical editing; see Butler, "Editing Women." But see recent editions of Aphra Behn (7 vols., ed. Janet Todd, 1992–96); Frances Burney (2 vols., ed. Peter Sabor, 1995); Maria Edgeworth (12 vols., ed. Marilyn Butler and Mitzi Myers, 1998); Eliza Haywood (6 vols., ed. Alexander Pettit et al., 2000–2001); and Mary Shelley (8 vols., ed. Nora Crook with Pamela Clemit, 1996), all published by Pickering & Chatto, London.

25. See Shillingsburg, "Editing Thackeray: A History," below; and see "The Center for Scholarly Editions: An Introductory Statement," PMLA: *Publications of the Modern Language Association of America* 92 (1977): 583–97. The statement was also printed as a pamphlet (New York: Modern Language Association of America, 1977). McGann's *Critique* is the most sustained assault on CEAA/CSE principles; see also earlier rebuttals cited in *Critique,* 129 n.2 and 130 n.4.

26. The rebuttal of the charge of "artlessness" allies this essay to an important trend in feminist criticism: the attempt to reclaim women writers from male-authored models of criticism constructed without reference to them and therefore likely to find them inadequate.

27. See Michel Foucault, "What Is an Author?" trans. Josué V. Harari, in *The Foucault Reader,* ed. Paul Rabinow (New York: Pantheon, 1984), 101–20; and Steven Greenblatt, *Renaissance Self-Fashioning: From More to Shakespeare* (Chicago: University of Chicago Press, 1980).

28. See Foucault, "What Is an Author?" 103.

29. *The Frankenstein Notebooks: A Facsimile of Mary Shelley's Manuscript Novel,* ed. Charles E. Robinson (New York: Garland, 1996).

30. Conrad, *The Secret Agent,* ed. Bruce Harkness and S. W. Reid (Cambridge: Cambridge University Press, 1990).

31. The point bears amplification: critical editions are often inaccessible to readers without privileges at the library of a research-oriented university, the main pur-

chasers of these expensive volumes. Sales for critical editions are unlikely to exceed one thousand units and may fall far below that figure. Such data argue for good nonspecialist editions as well as for electronic editions; see Butler, "Editing Women."

32. In his essay, Ross distinguishes his work with "substitutional hypertext" from the interests of other scholars concerned with differently tagged forms of hypertext.

33. See Greetham, *Textual Studies,* 341–42.

The Issue of Authority in a Scholarly Edition

Editing Cather

۞ ۞ ۞

Susan J.
Rosowski,
Charles W.
Mignon,
Frederick M.
Link, and Kari A.
Ronning

The challenge of editing Willa Cather has been to take nothing for granted—a lesson for which three decades of discoveries about her have amply prepared us. Fiction once assumed to be transparent and artless is now recognized for its depth and complexity. A canon once assumed to be slim has been nearly doubled by the discovery of early journalistic writings, and we now know Cather to be one of the most prolific of major American writers, with eighteen volumes and over seven hundred periodical pieces to her credit. A writer once dismissed as regional is now included in the Encyclopedia Britannica's "Great Books of the Western World."

Yet until scholarly editing proved otherwise, conventional wisdom about Cather's texts remained largely unexamined. The common wisdom assumed that they sprang into print fully formed and flawless, the result of her own and her publishers' attentiveness. The corollary assumption was that forms revealing their evolution did not exist, an assumption that resulted partly from Cather's request that all her manuscripts be destroyed and partly from her suppression of early versions of the works. But our research has demonstrated that Cather's texts exist in multiple forms, some in typescripts heavily revised and corrected in her own hand, others in a series of printed versions, many revised and corrected by her. Collations also disprove the old belief that Cather received near-perfect editing from her publishers. While many variants result from Cather's revisions, others are corrections of printers' errors, demonstrating the fallibility of even the most conscientious of publishing houses. Printers' errors appear in all the Knopf editions of *A Lost Lady* (1923) and *The Professor's House* (1925) published during Cather's lifetime, and in a personal letter Cather lamented the many errors in both words and punctuation in the original Knopf text of *Death Comes for the Archbishop* (1927).[1]

Cather, in short, attended carefully to both the process and the product of writing. Whereas Faulkner has convinced his editor Noel Polk that certain compositional details were at least sometimes "the stuff that didn't matter" to that author,[2] Cather has convinced us that, where her texts were concerned, pretty much everything *did* matter to her. She habitually sought to exert her authority over the full process governing the preparation and presentation of her novels: from drafting and revising the texts to shaping the physical appearance of the published books.

As Cather's editors, we have chosen to honor Cather's expansive sense of an author's authority over her work. Our commitment to intentionality thus construed animates our presentation of historical introductions, explanatory notes, textual essays and apparatus, and, less conventionally, page format, paper stock, illustrations, and typeface. Other writers, more indifferent to details of editing and production, or less sure of the form they wanted their work to take, demand the different approaches described elsewhere in this volume. Cather's experience as an editor, her clarity of vision as a writer, and her meticulous attention to detail as a reviser demand that her editors respect her intentions and present her as clearly as possible. Such information about her revisions invites textual analyses and interpretations that will bring us closer to understanding her creative process.

Another, related, commitment underlies our efforts as well: a commitment to the "common reader" named in this collection's title. On the face of it, a scholarly edition and Willa Cather seem a contradiction in terms—an academic enterprise foisted onto a writer who explicitly identified *her* reader as someone outside the academy. Acknowledging that to exclude Cather's intended reader from consideration in an edition of her writing would seem perverse, we determined that, along with providing materials of interest to the scholar-critic, we would make these materials accessible to the general reader. Implementing this objective meant adopting policies concerning content, format, design, and style that would make the edition broadly accessible as well as methodologically rigorous. This essay, then, concerns our attempts to realize Cather's unusually precise intentions for her work, including her intention to reach a diverse readership. Here, as in the volumes of the Cather Scholarly Edition, our interest is in the yield to readers of our investigations into Cather and her texts. Our larger claim is that however specialized its methods might be, critical editing is uniquely equipped to facilitate the transmission of meaning from authors to both specialist and nonspecialist communities of readers. It is not always accorded this power, to understate the case.

To understand Cather's involvement in all aspects of her writing, we must remember that for the twenty years, beginning in 1892, her sophomore year at the University of Nebraska, Cather worked in various editorial capacities, including a stint as fiction editor and managing editor at that "supernova in the journalistic firmament," *McClure's Magazine*.[3] Not surprisingly, when she began publishing with Houghton Mifflin shortly after leaving *McClure's* staff in 1910, Cather brought editorial expertise and expectations to her own writing. *Alexander's Bridge* appeared in 1912, followed in short order by *O Pioneers!* (1913), *The Song of the Lark* (1915), and *My Ántonia* (1918)—four novels that provided ample opportunity for Cather to experience firsthand the bureaucracy characteristic of a modern publishing house. As James L. W. West III has demonstrated, in such a house the editor functions as a middleman who transfers manuscripts from their authors to the departments responsible for different tasks concerning them.[4] One of the editor's responsibilities is to maintain good relations with "his" authors and to acquire the best possible manuscripts or properties for the publisher; an equally important responsibility is to ensure that employees in other departments be left alone to do their jobs. A corporate structure of this sort attempts to define tasks and to separate the people performing them.

Cather's correspondence with Ferris Greenslet, her editor at Houghton Mifflin, testifies to the limitations of her publisher's bureaucracy for both writer and editor, at least as Cather perceived matters.[5] Her problem was not with Greenslet, for whom she felt lifelong respect; it was with the changing professional situation facing the serious author in America, in which a writer's involvement with her work was expected to end when she transmitted her manuscript to an editor, who would in turn pass it along—assembly-line fashion—to people in marketing, production, and so on. Behind it all was the publisher, a nameless, faceless corporate entity dictating the commercial terms of each transaction. Accustomed to full participation in the broadest range of editorial activities from her days at *McClure's,* Cather wrote to Greenslet about the binding of *O Pioneers!* (she considered the publisher's clay-mud brown cloth ugly), its typography (which she liked), the fancy figure of its colored frontispiece (hardly her idea of Alexandra), and cheap reissues (which she resisted). Frustrations were probably inevitable, given the contrast between Cather's expectations and Houghton Mifflin's reality. Tensions appeared in muted form during the production and release of *O Pioneers!* By the time of *My Ántonia,* Cather was embroiled in issues concerning illustrations, copyediting, and production, as well as advertising, promotion, and reproduction rights.

While Cather's correspondence concerning *My Ántonia* documents her unhappiness with her publisher, the text of the novel testifies to her determination to maintain considerable editorial involvement in her writing. She inscribed herself as an editor/publisher in an introduction to *My Ántonia,* appearing in the first person to tell how she had acquired the manuscript that she was giving to the reader: during a conversation with a childhood friend, Jim Burden, she became interested in his recollections, encouraged him to write them down, and made an agreement with him to do so; some months later, she received his manuscript, which she now gives to the reader, "substantially as he brought it to me."[6] The effect was an imaginative end-run around Houghton Mifflin. By presenting her manuscript directly to her reader, Cather personalized the published form of *My Ántonia;* by styling herself editor of her own book, she prevented any outside editor from interfering with it; and by giving it to the reader directly, she functioned as its publisher. Most important, by blurring the functions of writer, editor, and publisher, Cather anticipated the move to Knopf that would enable her to reconfigure her life and to reclaim the broad and collaborative role of editing that she would never again surrender.

Holograph and typescript manuscripts of Cather's writing for Knopf testify to that role by demonstrating her attentiveness to both substantives and accidentals. Serving as her own copyeditor, she specified capitalization, spelling, punctuation (including single versus double quotation marks), and hyphenation, all designated with standard marks (for example, em-dashes distinguished from en-dashes, small capitals indicated with two lines and initial full capitals with three, and so on), as well as paragraph divisions, line spaces, and section divisions. Cather extended her involvement in preparing her books for publication to their design and manufacture. For example, she expressed her wishes about typography, page format, wrappers, and advertising copy; she chose W. T. Benda as the illustrator for *My Ántonia*, worked closely with him as he prepared line drawings to accompany her text, then specified paper stock for and placement of those illustrations. Cather included Houghton Mifflin's treatment of Benda and his illustrations among her complaints about that publisher. Later, with Knopf, she worked with Harold von Schmidt on illustrations for the second edition of *Death Comes for the Archbishop* (1929). The result of this collaboration was a magnificently illustrated text, a visual enactment of Cather's intentions as well as a verbal one.

So to an exceptional degree Cather's work provides evidence of the close textual attention that modern editing practices respect, while in other ways Cather challenges her editors to expand the definition of "corrupt" and "authoritative" to include the text's whole format and material existence. She behaved in character when she rejected the anthology format of assembling texts of numerous novels within the covers of one volume with tight margins and condensed print (for example, Library of America and recent Houghton Mifflin editions). When they are enacted, such printing and publishing decisions represent their own form of corruption. Given Cather's explicitly stated intentions for her works, an authoritative edition of them must go beyond the sequence of words and punctuation to include other and more overtly physical matters. With this in mind, we have worked closely with our publisher on the design of volumes, respecting Cather's intentions in these matters as we have reconstructed it from correspondence, publishers' records, interviews, and essays. Our reproduction of Benda's illustrations for *My Ántonia* provides one example of our interest in respecting Cather's own decisions regarding her work. In our prefaces, we explain our work with the physical features of the volumes that we produce, just as we explain the procedures governing our treatment of copy-text, variant readings, and other more narrowly textual matters.

Cather's commitment to the verbal and punctuational components of her work makes an argument for the application of Greg/Bowers methodology, however much its more doctrinaire adherents might raise an eyebrow at our intentionalist engagement with physical bibliography or, for that matter, at our enthusiasm for a populist writer like Cather. With respect to substantives and accidentals, our edition proceeds through stages that reflect the familiar, Greg/Bowers inflected guidelines of the Center for Scholarly Editions (later the Committee for Scholarly Editions).[7] There are at least two "final" versions for each work through Cather's middle period, and in some cases for her later works. Emending to establish an eclectic critical text that presents Cather's intention at the time of original composition, we present in clear text (a text unencumbered by notes) the authoritative version that reflects Cather's most intense involvement with the work, and the one that has had the greatest impact upon readers. In the apparatus, we provide textual information relevant to the development of Cather's writing throughout her career.

Collecting copies of Cather's books and assembling materials concerning their composition, production, publication, and reception begins with Joan Crane's *Willa Cather: A Bibliography.*[8] One of the great contributions of a scholarly edition is that the project serves as a magnet for materials relevant to its author, and ours is no exception. Disproving the convention that Cather and her editors destroyed manuscripts, typescripts, and proofs, research for this edition, as we have already noted in passing, has uncovered previously unreported prepublication forms. Typescripts heavily revised and corrected by Cather exist of *My Mortal Enemy* (1926), *Shadows on the Rock* (1931), "Two Friends" (in multiple versions) and "Old Mrs. Harris" from *Obscure Destinies* (1932), "A Chance Meeting" (1933), and *Lucy Gayheart* (1935), as well as unrevised galley proofs of *Death Comes for the Archbishop*, two sets of revised and corrected page proofs of *Lucy Gayheart,* and revised and corrected galley proofs of *Sapphira and the Slave Girl* (1940). Furthermore, Cather's hand is evident in more than one published version of some novels, and there are far more variants among forms of some novels than has generally been supposed. In addition, for those works that first appeared serially, magazine texts exist, some of which had not previously been reported (for example, that of *My Mortal Enemy*).

Volume editors—often working at universities elsewhere—bring their expertise as Cather scholars to the project. Each historical introduction provides a biography of the individual work, including an account of its genesis and growth, its composition, its publication, and its reception and reputation. Within these broad parameters emphases differ in essays for different volumes, reflecting different stages of Cather's career. In discussing *O Pioneers!* (1913), in which Cather "was remembering her early life as a work of art," David Stouck traces the accretion of incidents and allusions that worked their way into the composition of the novel, then discusses the various literary influences upon it, most particularly the influence of Russian literature.[9] In his essay on *My Ántonia,* a book for which Cather drew still more directly upon firsthand experience, James Woodress sets relevant biographical events against their historical background, then traces the ways in which Cather incorporated her personal memories into her novel.[10]

Research on notes for narratives set outside Nebraska presents somewhat different challenges. After working on *Death Comes for the Archbishop,* volume editor John J. Murphy concluded that Cather's Southwestern narrative is, more than Cather's other texts,

> a product of research, the fusion of an astounding array of sources that would be disparate if not combined within its text. Included in these sources are U.S. military and political history; Roman Catholic church history, tradition, and liturgy; Mexican and Indian myth, legend, and history; biography; Biblical scriptures; Southwestern flora and geography; accounts of Spanish conquest and exploration of the Americas; philosophy and theology; French history and geography; architecture, etc.[11]

Whatever the setting of the text, editing Cather, a writer who drew extensively upon actual experience, means providing fuller explanatory notes than is customary in editions of fiction. Explanatory notes present "information relevant to the meaning of the texts . . . for example, the identification of locations, literary references, persons, historical events, and specialized terminology," we rather blithely wrote in our editorial manual, little realizing that preparing these notes would yield their own revelations about particulars and, more frequently still, about the extent of Cather's use of them.

Identification and translations of quotations and allusions from the classics and the Bible appeared at first to be relatively straightforward, but work on *Death Comes for the Archbishop* especially has shown that Cather's use of allusions became increasingly complex as she matured as a writer. Because scholars have long recognized that Cather drew upon Virgil, Shakespeare, and the Bible, we had a head start. Cather characteristically quoted from memory; thus, giving the passages as they originally appeared helps the reader see how Cather has turned a quotation to her own purposes. The passing of time has made allusions to more ephemeral sources obscure to modern readers: who now has read *The Prince of the House of David* (1855) or seen engravings of "The House of the Tragic Poet"? Notes identify and briefly describe such references as they relate to Cather's text. In these notes we recognize that geographical distance, too, may pose barriers to understanding. Cather's readers may require clarification of regional details, such as the yucca soap and greasewood plains of New Mexico, the eels and apothecary's remedies in Quebec, the flybrushes and batter cakes of antebellum Virginia, and the sod houses and corn shellers of Nebraska. Few readers anywhere realize that sod roots extend at least two and a half feet on an unbroken prairie—information that gives heightened meaning to "breaking sod."

The need to clarify the regional setting is complicated for novels set in Quebec, Virginia, and the American Southwest, where the history is longer and the cultural overlays deeper. Moreover, the editor's role in fashioning approaches to the text dramatizes the issue of authority. After describing the sources upon which Cather drew in writing *Death Comes for the Archbishop,* for example, Murphy acknowledges the issue:

The significant controversy generated by *Death Comes for the Archbishop* relates to the nature of certain of these sources of New Mexican history and historical figures. Some (like Twitchell) reflect Anglo prejudices toward a racially mixed Roman Catholic culture. Others (like Howlett) add Franco disapproval and superiority to an already biased portrait. Still others (like Lummis) romanticize what is construed as a mysterious land of exotic cultures. To compensate for this, works by recent New Mexico historians like Erna Fergusson and Hispanic revisionists like Fray Angelic Chavez inform the notes. Balancing Twitchell with Chavez accesses us to grey areas between negative and positive interpretations.[12]

Sources for the Nebraska books (seven of thirteen) are more immediate, and one great advantage of the Cather edition's central location at the University of Nebraska–Lincoln is our ready access to the places and records essential to the exploration of Webster County and Lincoln as Cather knew them, including the personal and local stories that exist outside history books.[13] Contemporary publications from Red Cloud, Lincoln, and the University of Nebraska help to establish a more precise chronology of Cather's life and the experiences on which she drew. The personal columns of the Red Cloud newspapers kept track of the doings of local people and reflected local concerns, enabling the reader even now to participate imaginatively in the life going on around Cather as she absorbed impressions upon which she would later draw in her fiction. Reading these papers closely over a period of several years means that details sometimes flash out with great clarity. For example, in *My Ántonia* Cather describes Mrs. Wick Cutter as paying calls in "rustling, steel-gray brocades" (205); her prototype, Mrs. Mathew Bentley, wore "a handsome steel gray brocaded satin" dress to a wedding, according to the Red Cloud *Chief* (8 February 1889). Newspaper reports of the inquest on Francis Sadilek confirm details of Cather's version of the suicide (*Chief,* 24 February 1881); the news report that one Bohemian (John Polnicky) was at the inquest suggests a prototype for the novel's Anton Jelinek; and reports of shooting and other rowdiness at the real fireman's dances help explain why Jim Burden's grandparents don't want him to attend such functions. Other newspaper reports suggest how lives from the larger world touch a parish community. About the time that Cather was visiting Red Cloud, the *Argus* (10 May 1912) carried an article saying that the queen of Italy had given up hunting when she had children, just as Jim Burden tells Ántonia that she had (332). It is increasingly apparent that Cather's memory was very accurate.

Long after she left Nebraska, Cather stayed in touch with Webster County by subscribing to its newspapers. One of them sparked the writing of *A Lost Lady.* In a 1945 letter, Cather described reading an account of Mrs. Lyra Garber's death in the Webster County *Argus* that had been forwarded to her in Toronto, where she was staying. Later that day when she arose from a nap, the outline of the story was clear in her mind.[14] We now know that the *Argus* printed a long and detailed description of Mrs. Garber's fortunes after she left Nebraska, written by her second husband and quoting her last words (14 July 1921). Working with the dates in the newspaper account—Mrs. Garber died in Oregon in early March 1921, but the news did not reach Red Cloud until late June 1921—helps to date the genesis of the novel. More broadly, of course, the account further illuminates Cather's use of source material.

Local maps, photograph collections, and census records help to fill in the historical backgrounds. Webster County plat books disclose data about land ownership, revealing that Cather's grandparents were among the largest landholders in the county; that her father owned land adjacent to the Sadileks (prototypes for the Shimerdas of *My Ántonia*); and that the Pavelkas (prototypes of Ántonia and Anton Cuzak), who owned no land in 1900, owned 480 acres several decades later. The atlases for the county show the locations of the rural post offices (often in a farmer's house), schoolhouses, churches, and cemeteries upon which Cather modeled her fictional landscape. Insurance maps show the materials, size, shape, and use of every building in downtown Red Cloud in 1886 and 1892, the period of Cather's deepest involvement in the town.[15] Reconstructing Cather's Red Cloud provides background to its fictional reincarnations as Moonstone, Black Hawk, Sweet Water, Haverford, Skyline, and Singleton.

The photographs held by Love Library at the University of Nebraska–Lincoln, the Nebraska State Historical Society (Lincoln), the Willa Cather Pioneer Educational and Memorial Foundation (Red Cloud), the Cather Center of the Nebraska State Historical Society (Red Cloud), and the Webster County Museum (Red Cloud) have yielded images of the places and people upon which Cather drew. A photograph of the University campus recaptures Alexandra Bergson's point of view when in *O Pioneers!* she gazes through the iron fence at the students, wondering if any had known her brother Emil. A crayon enlargement of Lucille, Annie Pavelka's first daughter, recalls the portrait of Ántonia's baby, Martha, that Jim Burden sees.

Study of the census records for Webster County suggests prototypes when origins, occupations, ages, and family situations match those of Cather's characters. In *My Ántonia*, Black Hawk's Danish laundryman, Mr. Jensen, bears many similarities to a Red Cloud laundryman, the Danish-born Peter Hansen, a finding confirmed by Hansen's obituary, which quoted Cather's description of the fictional Jensen and added, "There is no doubt that the inspiration for this sketch came from her acquaintance with Mr. Hansen" (*Argus,* 21 June 1923). In *A Lost Lady,* the fictional Judge Pommeroy has a number of characteristics in common with Judge George O. Yeiser of Red Cloud, including age, Kentucky birth, and an orphaned nephew who lived with him. Census records, along with directories and the newspapers, also suggest names that Cather borrowed from real people for her minor characters: Crow and Kron(n) are Webster County names that appear in *O Pioneers!* and *My Ántonia* respectively. Albert ("Bert") and Adelbert ("Dell") Templeton, the twin brothers in "Old Mrs. Harris," borrow their names and nicknames from two of Cather's contemporaries, the twins Albert and Adelbert Able; Dell Able is also the name of a character in *One of Ours* (1922). At times, tracing the names results in comic connections. For example, Frank Ellinger is the lover of *A Lost Lady*'s Marian Forrester, and Jim Burden is the narrator of *My Ántonia;* the actual Frank Ellinger (the son of a well-known auctioneer in Webster county) attended the University of Nebraska, married the niece of Jim Burden (a storekeeper in Red Cloud), was divorced, and became a traveling salesman.

Thus our research has expanded what we know about ways in which Cather drew upon actual persons for her major characters; moreover, it has enabled us to realize that references to actual people, places, and events characteristically extend to minor characters and occasional episodes and settings. The result is that it is not only an individual's life but also a community's history that appears in Cather's writing.[16]

That principle is dramatically evident in the Nebraska novels. A community's history includes that of flora and fauna of the region, and research here, too, has yielded its surprises. Cather learned methods of close observation as a student at the University of Nebraska when Charles E. Bessey, Frederic E. Clements, and Roscoe Pound were doing their pioneering work in botany and ecology there. Her fiction describes flora and fauna in sufficient detail to facilitate the identification of plant and animal species. In *My Ántonia,* descriptions of the owls that live in the prairie-dog town, an unlikely sounding species, enable us to identify them as *Athene cuniculana,* the burrowing owl, a Nebraska native species that nests in prairie-dog burrows or badger holes. A description of a ringdove's cry identifies it as *Zenaidura macroura,* the mourning dove that has a blue eye-ring. The scrub oaks growing on the chalk cliffs by the river are the native bur oaks, naturally large trees that become dwarfed when they are grown in the unfavorable environment that Cather describes. And the shaggy, red grass of the prairie is *Andropogon gerardii,* the big bluestem—a native grass with thick, deep roots and seed stalks from three to eight feet high that turns reddish after a frost. In such research the Cather edition has the advantage of ready access to the work of early naturalists in the state, who described conditions as Cather would have known them. It gives the researcher a particular pleasure to see that a plant mentioned by Cather is listed in the University of Nebraska herbarium as being collected in Webster County and that another specimen in that herbarium was collected by Cather herself.[17]

An important resource available to us is more difficult to document— working in Lincoln on the University campus and traveling to Red Cloud and Webster County. Cather's childhood home—the model for the homes of the Kronborgs in *The Song of the Lark,* the Templetons in "Old Mrs. Harris," and the Ferguessons in "The Best Years"—is now a museum that still gives a sense of the crowded life that went on there. The open prairie and the rich farmland still spread themselves under the great dome of the sky, just as they did for Cather. And among the students with whom we now read Cather at the university are descendants of the people whom Cather knew and wrote about. Under such circumstances, preparing a scholarly edition becomes a living and profoundly human enterprise.

Again, Cather's southwestern, European, and Québécois texts provide a more complicated challenge for research, though travel to the settings upon which Cather drew demonstrate that her respect for authenticity of place and culture extends throughout her writing. Maps complement explanatory notes in documenting the accuracy with which Cather's fictional geography corresponds to actual place, and when research includes experiences of the places themselves, patterns become clear. As did Cather before writing of the Southwest, Quebec, and France, so volume editors traveled to the places that figure in her books. "As if by incremental repetition," writes John J. Murphy, "Cather's French and Southwestern experiences formed an alternating pattern in her life and art, each adding to and influencing the other," and both influenced by her early experiences in Nebraska and Virginia.[18]

Thus the historical apparatus offers multiple possibilities for inquiry for specialists as well as for the general reader. It demonstrates the extent to which Cather invites interdisciplinary scholarship and broad humanistic inquiry by filling her fiction with references to flora and fauna, to regional customs and manners, to religion, to the classics, the Bible, and to historical events, popular writing, music, art, and other aspects of culture; it supports such inquiry by providing the first comprehensive identification of these references. At the same time that Cather's writing encourages ongoing consideration of cultural ideas and artistic creativity, it belies the mutually exclusive alternatives by which these matters are too frequently cast: educational standards versus popular taste, social and ethical versus aesthetic values, fiction versus fact.

Writing a historical essay and explanatory notes that satisfy the needs of the scholar-critic while remaining accessible to a general reader is one thing; preparing the textual apparatus in such a manner is another. In the Cather edition the underlying design of the textual essay shows a concern first for the texts themselves inasmuch as we indicate the rationale for choosing the copy-text, provide a record of emendations and variant readings in all texts carrying textual authority, discuss any individual readings that present difficulties, and present lists clarifying end-line hyphenations. Our second principal concern in the textual commentary, however, is to describe these matters with sufficient clarity and extension to meet the needs of the general reader who may not be aware of their importance. Our concern here means that, having presented our findings about the text, we also bring critical attention to their significance.

Textual editors try to recover whatever details of the composition, production, and printing history of the text may be available. Cather's letters are often available, as are the interviews that she gave at various times in her life. For *A Lost Lady,* for example, we have not only the record of correspondence with Alfred and Blanche Knopf about the progress of the novel but also letters to Irene Miner and interviews in which Cather discusses her model for Mrs. Forrester, indicating her awareness of the effect that her portrait of Mrs. Garber had on others who knew that woman and offering insights into her compositional technique for the novel.[19] As is the case with other of Cather's novels, firsthand accounts by contemporaries provide additional details. The schedule for the writing and printing of *A Lost Lady* can be established with some precision from a combination of these sources.

Alfred Knopf's memoirs, miscellaneous correspondence, published advertisements, and imprint data also furnish information about the production of *A Lost Lady* and about the arrangements for the *Century Magazine*'s serial version published in April, May, and June 1923, before the first edition in book form. We have established from the timetable for production and from Cather's letters that there were two typescripts, one sent to *Century* and a second on which Cather made corrections and changes before sending it to Knopf for transmission to the Plimpton Press for production as the first edition in book form. Advertisements by Knopf, the firm's records, and imprint data from various printings allow the editors to trace the history of printings and resolve most of the occasional discrepancies between dates: the Knopf records enter an impression in one month, for example, but the printer's imprint notice in the text indicates a different one. External evidence confirms that the serial *Century* version (1923), the first Knopf edition (1923), and the Houghton Mifflin Autograph Edition (1938) are the authoritative texts.

The process of collation, which includes both individual and team readings and machine collations of copies of the potentially authoritative texts, distinguishes variant states within a given impression and identifies differences between one impression and another and between one edition and another, even when publishers make misleading or inaccurate distinctions.[20] For each novel, initial attention is given to a typescript or serial version (if extant), to the first edition in book form, and to the Autograph Edition text, known to have been produced with Cather's full cooperation. In the case of *A Lost Lady,* no holograph or typescript has been located. Because the novel does exist in a serial version, however, this was collated with the first book printing by Knopf, and a list of the variants between the two texts was prepared and checked. Copies of the first book printing were then compared with each other, establishing variant states within the early impressions and issues. The variant readings obtained were then checked against later issues and impressions. As it happens, there were more than two dozen impressions and three separate issues of this edition between 1923 and 1972, including impressions belonging to the first Vintage paperback "edition" and separate issues sold in Canada and England as well as in the United States.

One can argue that any of the three authoritative editions of *A Lost Lady* (the *Century* serial publication, the Knopf first edition, and the Autograph Edition) might be selected as copy-text. In the absence of holograph or typescript copies, the *Century* serial publication could be selected because it is the first printing of the novel; the Knopf publication because it is the first edition in book form and because there is evidence that Cather regarded the typescript used for the *Century* version as a throwaway late draft while she revised a duplicate typescript for the first book edition; the Autograph Edition (1938) because it is the text that represents what might be called Cather's final intention for the novel. In the absence of manuscripts, the policy of the Cather edition is to choose as copy-text the first edition of a novel in book form; the policy is based on the idea that such a choice will best represent the realized intention of the author, and her latest revising hand, at the time closest to the period of composition. Given the alterations to the *Century* serial text and given the distance in time between the composition of the novel in 1922 and 1923 and the Autograph Edition of 1938, for *A Lost Lady,* theory and practice coincide exceptionally well in the first edition by Knopf.

Thus the textual essay presents a concise explanation of all phases of the establishment of the critical text of the volume. The editor describes the earliest forms of the text, explains his or her choice of copy-text, reconstructs the composition and publishing history of the text, discusses Cather's involvement in that publishing history, indicates patterns of authorial revision, and explains special emendation and editorial problems. The textual apparatus fully presents the substantive variants in historical progression, thus setting out chronologically Cather's development and revision of each work. The lists of emendations record all changes introduced into the copy-text, and notes on the emendations explain the bases for those changes that are not obvious. As a guide for quotations from this edition, tables of word divisions record the established forms of ambiguous end-line hyphenation in the copy-text as well as compounds to be hyphenated in the present newly set edition.

Each novel presents, in its unique character, distinct challenges to the imagination, resourcefulness, and tact of its editors. With *O Pioneers!*, revisions between 1913 and 1937 reveal a heightened restraint as Cather matured. In the novel's opening section, for example, Marie's "lusty admirers" become "her uncle's cronies" (19), and the rather sentimental action of Carl's kissing Alexandra "softly, on her lips and on her eyes" disappears from the conclusion of the later version (273). The result was a more consistent text in 1937, but one lacking the youthful exuberance of 1913. Revisions of *My Ántonia* demonstrate a similar principle, and we describe those revisions in the textual essay included in that volume.[21] In altering her introduction for the 1926 revised edition, Cather condensed or eliminated information about the adult lawyer Jim Burden that might distract from his story of Ántonia and his childhood. In 1918 Jim's "naturally romantic . . . disposition" is detailed in the enterprises for which he had raised capital (xi), whereas in 1926 that enthusiasm is conveyed by general descriptions of his love, faith, and knowledge of the country. In 1918 he arrives "with a bulging legal portfolio sheltered under his fur overcoat"; in the portfolio is a manuscript that he "tapped . . . with some pride" (xiii). In 1926 he arrives without the fur overcoat. Cather also greatly reduced the story of Jim Burden's wife, eliminating personalizing details of her name and her background from the 1926 version. Lastly, Cather reduced her own presence in the introduction, eliminating her statement that she had not written about Ántonia herself, her proposal that both she and Jim "set down on paper" all that they remembered of her (xii), and her admission that "[her] own story was never written" (xiii).

Cather's creative involvement in the text of *Death Comes for the Archbishop* is especially interesting for its longevity through its published versions, from serial to galley to first edition, and then through subsequent printings, special issues, and editions. Collations of the galleys with the first edition, for example, reveal Cather's uncertainty about the sex of Contento, one of the two white mules ridden by Latour and Vaillant. And in the months after the publication of the first edition, Cather and her publishers became aware of certain errors of fact that they corrected for the fourteenth printing: "surplices" became "cassocks," "Sacrament" became "Sacrifice," the locations of some towns and cities were adjusted, and so on. Cather rewrote some passages. In one of her longest revisions, the first edition's description of water running uphill without the use of a pump is changed to downplay this "miraculous" suggestion in the second edition, third printing—a suggestion that is almost eliminated in the Autograph Edition.

The revisions between the serial and book publication of *A Lost Lady* do not reveal ways in which Cather matured—the serial publication preceded the book by only three months. Rather, they reveal ways in which she implemented principles of the unfurnished novel, or "the novel démeublé," that she laid out in an essay of that name written during this period (1922). Sometimes the adjustment of a word or phrase reinforces a verbal motif. "Play" and "playful," for example, connote the innocence of childhood and the possibility of a pioneer spirit; and, from the beginning of the novel, Marian Forrester announces the playfulness that Cather ascribes to her: waving a buttery iron spoon or shaking a cherry-stained finger at a new arrival to the Forrester place, running from the new bull in the pasture where she had gone to pick flowers, laughing and clinging to her crimson parasol, carrying a plate of cookies to the boys picnicking in the grove, telling them that she sometimes wades in the creek. In the scene describing Niel Herbert's encounter with Mrs. Forrester in town, the *Century* version had Mrs. Forrester bowing "gaily" in response to Judge Pommeroy's ponderous acceptance of her invitation to dine with them. By changing the adverb to "playfully" (34), Cather not only draws the scene into a motif running through the book, but also sets up a mirror effect with a later scene, in which an older and exhausted Mrs. Forrester admits that she hasn't time to go into the marsh and warns Niel, "And you haven't time to play any more either, Niel. You must hurry and become a successful man" (108). When in the end Niel wonders "whether . . . fine play-acting" was the secret of her ardor (163), the question serves as a coda to one of the central motifs of the revised narrative.

Revisions frequently demonstrate how subtly Cather crafted a scene in order to reinforce the downward action of the novel. Mrs. Forrester simply "poured a glass" of sherry for Niel in the *Century* version, but when she "poured *out* a glass" in the revised text (36, emphasis added), her action underscores the narrative's concern with loss, depletion, and change. When Captain Forrester explains that the boulder on which his sundial is set comes from the Garden of the Gods, then adds in an aside that "Mr. Dalzell has his summer home *up* there" (103, emphasis added), the addition of the adverb "up" underscores the story's concern with class. And writing that Captain Forrester offered his toast, "Happy Days," in a manner of "high courtesy" rather than of "geniality" (as Cather had it in the *Century* version) reinforces the ritual formality of the dinner party, and indeed of the Forresters' lives (48). These last two examples illustrate yet another pattern revealed by Cather's revisions, many of which concern positioning adjectives, adverbs, and prepositions. Studying the list of variants, we have become newly aware of how filled the novel is with such descriptors—not so much positioning the narrative spatially as defining it in terms of class. Captain Forrester utters his toast with "*high* courtesy," and with it seems to knock at the door of Fate "behind which all days . . . were hidden"; he looks "*down*" the table at his wife; and so on (48, emphases added).

Attention to the meaning of changes made in the text is not normally included in the textual commentary of a critical edition, except perhaps in notes on the emendations. Inclusion of this kind of discussion represents our belief in the importance of variants, even those that do not reach the list of emendations. And, again, we know that Cather took an extraordinary interest in accidentals. Cather's holograph insertions in typescripts of letters, her holograph corrections of typescripts and galley proofs, and our collations of typescript and serial versions of her novels with their appearances in book form demonstrate Cather's detailed attention to all kinds of accidentals. She was not one to leave all this to the publisher, as some of her contemporaries did; indeed, Alfred Knopf told the general editor of the Cather edition that house style was never imposed upon Cather's writing.[22] We agree that accidentals—punctuation and spelling—do have an important bearing on meaning and that Cather's practices in these matters are worth considering. Thus we also include significant accidental variants in the sections devoted to historical collations.

Many accidental changes between texts produce at least as much difference in meaning as some substantive variants. In the case of *A Lost Lady,* deleting the comma from *Century*'s "You see$_{<,>}$ there is nothing for me to do" changes a reflection into a statement (77; 74 in Knopf); and replacing the *Century* version's period with a question mark transforms an assertion into uncertainty: "I wonder if you know how we've looked for you?" (111;

105 in Knopf). Dialect forms in *Obscure Destinies* affect the presentation of character. Italicization of French or Spanish words in *Shadows on the Rock* and *Death Comes for the Archbishop* changes the atmosphere of those texts. Patterns of spelling changes can affect tone, if not meaning: English forms of spelling adopted in the 1937 Autograph Edition of *O Pioneers!* contribute to an overall effect of refinement: for example, "neighbor(s)" becomes "neighbour(s)" and "color(ed)" becomes "colour(ed)."

Our particular concerns about texts and our critical attention to the changes between states of a text mean that our textual essays present a face different from those of other editions. The blending of the crucial textual materials with critical elaboration about their meaning is something distinctive to our edition. Our intention here is commensurate with the extended attention we have given in the Cather edition to the historical introduction, the relevant illustrations, the explanatory notes, and the physical particulars of the completed volume. In each instance we seek readers as Cather did: broadly and with a mind to sharing with them the fruits of our labor.

In sum, authorial intention—including the author's intention to reach a general readership—is the principle guiding us in preparing critical editions of Cather's work. Yet while Cather is both an authoritative author and the authority for our edition, to interpret her intention as definitive or fixed would be stretching the point, for Cather complicated authorship in ways that radically destabilize her own texts. It may now be instructive to revisit the introduction to *My Ántonia,* in which Jim Burden gives his manuscript to the unnamed (but Cather-like) speaker/narrator and asks her, "Now, what about yours?" This prompts the speaker to say, "My own was never written, but the following is Jim's manuscript, substantially as he brought it to me" (xiii). Substantially? Whose story is this, anyway? Cather makes storytelling an ongoing and a repetitive act, but she offers an experience of reading that is ongoing and ever-changing. As one commentator notes, "there can be no final version, no last thought. There is always a new view, a new idea, a reinterpretation." This could be a description of reading Cather, but it isn't: we are quoting hypertext pioneer Ted Nelson—the more pertinently, perhaps, as we have begun to make Cather's work available on-line.[23] The apparatuses of our printed editions and the materials on our electronic *Cather Archive* both demonstrate that Cather's texts, like the sorts of texts that interest Nelson, are richly responsive to readings by different pathways. They move the reader into the real world and into theory; they draw readers into other disciplines and beyond disciplinary boundaries; and, most importantly, they encourage readers to talk with one another—the academic and the lay person; the seasoned scholar and the student; the scholarly editor, the literary critic, and the common reader.

Notes

In writing this essay from the Cather Editorial Center at the University of Nebraska–Lincoln, we represent a project that includes persons located elsewhere: James Woodress, University of California–Davis; David Stouck, Simon Fraser University, and John J. Murphy, Brigham Young University. We wish also to acknowledge that the project is made possible in part by a grant from the National Endowment for the Humanities, an independent federal agency.

1. Cather to Norman H. Pearson, 23 October 1937, Beinecke Library, Yale University.

2. See Noel Polk's essay in the present collection.

3. James Woodress, *Willa Cather: A Literary Life* (Lincoln: University of Nebraska Press, 1987), 185.

4. See James L. W. West III, *American Authors and the Literary Marketplace since 1900* (Philadelphia: University of Pennsylvania Press, 1988), 47–76.

5. See, variously, Cather to Ferris Greenslet, Houghton Mifflin Collection, Houghton Library, Harvard University.

6. Cather, introduction to *My Ántonia*, ed. Charles W. Mignon, with Kari Ronning (Lincoln: University of Nebraska Press, 1994), xiii. All citations are to this edition.

7. See "The Center for Scholarly Editions: An Introductory Statement," PMLA: *Publications of the Modern Language Association of America* 92 (1977): 583–97; reprinted as a pamphlet (New York: Modern Language Association of America, 1977).

8. See Joan Crane, *Willa Cather: A Bibliography* (Lincoln: University of Nebraska Press, 1982). Holdings in such libraries as Love Library, University of Nebraska–Lincoln; Alderman Library, University of Virginia; the Harry Ransom Humanities Research Center at the University of Texas at Austin; and the Willa Cather Pioneer Memorial Foundation, Red Cloud, Nebraska, have been especially helpful. When we called for more copies of Cather's works through the WCPM's *Newsletter*, David Stouck provided us with a copy of the eleventh impression of the first edition of *My Ántonia*,

although Crane's bibliography recorded only nine printings. The Lincoln, Nebraska, public libraries yielded an advance review copy of *A Lost Lady*.

9. David Stouck, "Historical Essay," in Cather, *O Pioneers!*, ed. Charles Mignon (Lincoln: University of Nebraska Press, 1992), 290. All citations are to this edition.

10. See James Woodress, "Historical Essay," in Cather, *My Ántonia*, 369–401.

11. John J. Murphy, "Headnote to Explanatory Notes," in Cather, *Death Comes for the Archbishop*, ed. Charles W. Mignon, with Frederick M. Link and Kari Ronning (Lincoln: University of Nebraska Press, 1999).

12. Murphy, "Headnote to Explanatory Notes," in Cather, *Death Comes for the Archbishop*.

13. When Cather was growing up, as many as five newspapers were published at a time in Red Cloud, with others in the smaller towns of the county. The Red Cloud *Chief*, the Webster County *Argus*, and the *Commercial Advertiser* were the longest running papers, and long runs of these have been preserved. Shorter-lived papers are also valuable. One, the Red Cloud *Republican*, was owned in part by Cather's father, and Cather claimed to have edited it for a time; see L. Brent Bohlke, *Willa Cather in Person: Interviews, Speeches, and Letters* (Lincoln: University of Nebraska Press, 1986), 2.

14. See Cather to Irene Miner Weisz, 6 January 1945, Weisz Papers, Newberry Library.

15. The Sanborn Fire Insurance Company updated its maps periodically; by the 1940s they included the residential portions of town as well. These maps confirm, for example, that a separate building in the rear of the Holland House Hotel (prototype for the Boys' Home, its original name, in *My Ántonia*) was used as a sample room for traveling salesmen, as Cather had said it was.

16. Mildred Bennett's *The World of Willa Cather* (1951; reprint, Lincoln: University of Nebraska Press, 1961), which draws on the memories of those who had known Cather and the Webster County of her youth, remains the indispensable starting point for exploring the relationships between Cather's life and work. Other sources unavailable to Bennett, such as the census records of the 1880s and 1900, enable one to verify the memories of Bennett's sources and to trace new relationships.

17. The specimen identified as *Mentzelia Multiflora* A. Gray and "Collected by Willa Cather" in New Mexico, July 1916, was called to our attention by Margaret R. Bolick, curator of botany, and can be seen in the herbarium division of the State Museum, University of Nebraska–Lincoln.

18. John J. Murphy, "Historical Essay," in Cather, *Death Comes for the Archbishop*.

19. See Susan J. Rosowski, with Kari Ronning, "Historical Essay," in Cather, *A Lost*

Lady, ed. Charles W. Mignon and Frederick M. Link (Lincoln: University of Nebraska Press, 1997), 177–233. All citations are to this edition, unless noted otherwise in parenthetical references.

20. The collations, together with data from the imprint pages and publisher's records, will often show that an "edition" is no more than a different impression or a separate issue.

21. Here we extract our description from that essay; see Charles Mignon, with Kari Ronning, "Textual Commentary," in Cather, *My Ántonia,* 481–521.

22. Alfred Knopf, conversation with Susan Rosowski, Purchase, New York, 16 September 1983.

23. Ted Nelson, qtd. in Michiko Kakutani, "Never-Ending Saga," *The New York Times Magazine,* 28 September 1997, 42. The *Cather Archive* is located at <http://www.unl.edu/Cather>.

The Stuff That Don't Matter

🐾 🐾 🐾

Noel Polk

This won't be pretty, I assure you up front, and it could get very ugly, for I am resolved here to talk about the dark underbelly of editing, about the stuff that makes us weep: the stuff that doesn't solve any of literature's or the world's great problems, doesn't get us promotions or raises, doesn't change or confirm or deny tradition or the cosmos: the stuff that Bob Hirst, in conversation, has called "the great black hole of editorial labor." I want to talk about the stuff that, as Faulkner's V. K. Ratliff might put it, don't matter, but which we spend more editorial time and energy over than anything else.

Maybe I only presume that your experience is the same as mine, but in editing Faulkner I spend an inverse proportion of my time and energy on things that don't matter as compared to things that do. For the most part, the big issues in Faulkner's texts are fairly straightforward and fairly easily resolved—at least now, in this kindergarten stage of the editing of Faulkner, during which I am mostly taking the hugely preliminary steps of simply getting into print more of what he wrote, as he wrote it, than his original editors allowed him. That is, to use James B. Meriwether's phrase, right now the editorial task is primarily to *de-edit* Faulkner rather than to edit him,[1] and I get to be a one-man combination judge and jury, both defense and prosecuting attorney, jailer and executioner too; it has willy-nilly fallen to my lot to decide which of the thousands of variants between his typescripts and his published texts become part of the "New, Corrected Texts" that we will probably use, for better or for worse, for quite some time.

I am a Faulkner editor, scholar, and teacher. I am even occasionally a reader, so that I am also my own reading public, and my own most demanding and critical reviewer. But that's fine, because I am also a puritan and I know from the get-go that in editing Faulkner, almost nothing I do is ever going to be completely right, and so there's always a gracious plenty to fret over and beat myself up about. But though I'm a puritan, I'm also secular enough and *courant* enough to know that a great deal of what editing means to me is that the work has made it nearly possible for me to put two kids through college, and I'm glad that Faulkner wrote as much as he did, because if he runs out of novels before I run out of college loans to repay, I'm going to be in big trouble. It remains for a more dedicated and perhaps more objective team of well-funded folks to do the kind of job that eventually, inevitably, Faulkner must get.

Faulkner once described the novelist as a one-armed carpenter trying to build a chicken coop in a hurricane. In some crucial ways, the editor of Faulkner is like a one-armed apprentice carpenter trying to edit the hurricane itself. Throughout his career, Faulkner was a rampaging phenomenon, almost natural in its energy and near ferocity. On any given page, in any given work, he can be both careful and careless, engaged and disengaged, precise and imprecise, systematic and erratic. Frequently his prose and his sensibilities constitute a direct assault on traditional systems of representation; just as frequently he relies on, or defaults into, those traditional systems.

In each work he juggles an astonishing and various number of balls of usage, image, metaphor, language. Juggling is especially difficult for a one-armed man, and it is even more difficult for the one-armed editor, to extend the metaphor ludicrously, who must not only find and recover Faulkner's balls but also must figure out whether he dropped them accidentally or discarded them, deliberately, before figuring out how to, or if he should, reintegrate them into the perceived patterns of the juggling. Thus the "major" stuff in Faulkner—the cosmos of character, setting, and theme that are clearly invested with *meaning*—are relatively easy to deal with. It's the smaller details, the stuff that I'm convinced Faulkner wasn't overworried about, that keep me looking forward to happy hour: the smallest of those details, I mean, the commas and semicolons and spaces and dashes and variant spellings, the designated macadam over which those larger issues have to travel to reach the reader. The rub, of course, is that with a modernist author like Faulkner, that stuff matters *when it matters,* and it is the editor's job to discover when it matters and when it doesn't; this aspect of our labor also, not incidentally, requires us to be careful readers and keen critics, although we are often the only ones who know that.

So I am going to talk about what we are really talking about when we talk about editing: accidentals or, rather, I should perhaps say, accidentals and accidents. Part of the problem with "accidentals," in the text of an author like Faulkner, lies in the mechanical path his texts followed from inception to publication, even the shorter path from inception to typescript. His handwriting, for example, is both as meticulous as a medieval scribe's and often unreadable, apparently even to himself (he once described his handwriting as looking "like a caterpillar that crawled through a ink well and out on to a piece of paper").[2] His various manual typewriters, like all typewriters prior to the electrics, were utterly unpredictable as to spacing and as to heaviness or lightness of imprint; if the paper bail was not aligned properly, sometimes the tails of commas and semicolons wouldn't print; typewriters would occasionally slip a couple of spaces, would sometimes space anyway if the typist did not hit a key hard enough to impress a letter or if he or she had a heavyish thumb on the space bar. From one perspective, of course, there is astonishingly little inconsistency from one page of Faulkner to another or even from work to work, and so little cause for worry. For those of us who must worry about where the comma goes and try to make sure it gets there, however, there are thousands of little things to worry about, because these things impact on a work's meaning just as surely as those larger issues do, even if in more subtle ways. My question is, Where is the author in this bewildering tangle of typing and handwriting, this swamp of irregularity and inconsistency?

These kinds of things drive me to distraction. In *Go Down, Moses* (1942), Boon Hogganbeck speaks of the wilderness as his "kindergarden." Faulkner's spelling, with a *d,* is a perfectly acceptable representation of Boon's pronunciation that poses no problem for the editor, who should not presume to force Boon to speak proper German. The problem is that Faulkner always misspelled the word, even when a third-person narrator uses it, and that fact poses a considerably different editorial problem. What this inconsistency *means,* quite simply, is that, like Boon, Faulkner didn't know how to spell "kindergarten." I have no problem leaving Boon's pronunciation intact and correcting the third-person narrator's misspelling, because *not* correcting the latter would cause a distracting blip on readers' visual screens that I believe Faulkner did not want, although my policy in this instance *creates* an irregularity and presumes at least a default authorial intention.

A slightly more complicated problem occurs in *Pylon,* a modernist novel of 1935 about barnstorming fliers at an air show. Faulkner sets many of this novel's scenes in a huge "rotundra" at an airport; the word occurs twenty times. The original editors deleted the second *r* and restored the word to a very correct "rotunda." I, however, knew my Eliot and honed in on the novel's self-conscious and deliberate, even structural, exploitation of wasteland imagery. Since Faulkner is a known experimenter with language, a writer numerously convicted of neologism and coinage, and since he was absolutely consistent in his spelling of this word throughout the typescript of *Pylon,* it was hardly even a conscious editorial decision to accept it as a deliberate portmanteau word that combined "rotunda" with "tundra" as a way of extending the wasteland imagery of the vast open spaces at the airport. I was very pleased with this "correction" until, some years later, working through the typescript of *The Mansion,* a 1959 novel, I discovered that Faulkner had typed "rotundra" in a context which did not so clearly allow the portmanteau effect. What does this mean? Again, it almost certainly means that Faulkner didn't know how to spell "rotunda." I belatedly discovered that I had certainly imposed a meaning on *Pylon* that he hadn't intended, even though that meaning is demonstrably contained in the language he had used: even in his ignorance, perhaps, he was better than he knew, maybe better even than his intentions would have allowed him to be. But though I believe that "rotundra" is as much better an image than "rotunda" as "soiled fish" is better than "coiled," I'll take the opportunity, in reprints of *Pylon,* to make the correction.

Such problems are comparatively easy to solve, and they are more directly related to traditional notions of literary meaning. More complicated for the editor, and more problematically related to literary meaning, are certain irregularities in punctuation—his use of dashes and ellipses, for example. He typically used three hyphens, closed up to the words on both sides, to indicate a one-em dash: he was so consistent in this practice throughout the major works that you can bet the farm that somebody else typed any type-script page that uses two hyphens and/or spacing on either side of the dash, and you can almost bet that an accidental thumb on the space bar or some other mechanical or manual inadvertency caused any spaces on one side of the dash but not the other.

In the earlier works, though, including *As I Lay Dying* (1930), *Light in August* (1932), and *Sanctuary* (1931), the one-em dash was the only thing he was regular about. To create an ellipsis he sometimes used as many as twelve or thirteen periods. In editing *Sanctuary: The Original Text* (1981), I decided not to decide, and invoked all kinds of aesthetic and conservative editorial grounds to justify my nondecision. There was no particular aesthetic or stylistic reason I could discover to prevent Faulkner from using as many dots as he seemed to want, or at least as many as he put there, so I resolved the problem by reproducing all the ellipsis points exactly as Faulkner had typed them: twelve, thirteen, it didn't matter to this editor, who had both fervor and fear on his side (*what if thirteen periods are actually more important than twelve?*).

In *Sanctuary*, Faulkner also frequently typed between five and thirteen or fourteen hyphens to indicate a dash longer than one-em. The editorial question, of course, is: how much longer? It's easy enough for a literalist editor to divide by three and determine the length of the dash, but—you can see this coming; you may have been here—I found myself in lengthy debates with the non-idiot part of myself over whether Faulkner actually *intended* a distinction between thirteen and fourteen hyphens! I rounded off, of course, and wound up with some five-em dashes in my text. You may imagine what Albert Erskine, Faulkner's editor at Random House for his last novels, thought about these considerations, but he let me have my way on *Sanctuary: The Original Text* and I was proud to have been so faithful to Faulkner's typescript. Proud, at least, until I saw what the printed page looked like, found my eye, my reading, distracted by the visual intrusion of those long ellipses and dashes, which seemed to me to work against the larger issues in the novel. To be sure, critics may indeed argue that a novelist so concerned with stylistic experimentation, with the problems of the visual representation of language, may well have intended such visual elements to be a part of the texture of his prose. This was precisely my argument in editing that early version of *Sanctuary;* I have argued as much about *The Sound and the Fury* (1929),[3] and I do not take lightly any arguments about Faulkner's concerns with style and with the representation of language. But I doubt that in *Sanctuary* he was making a serious distinction between thirteen and fourteen dots or hyphens.

So, having learned my lesson, when the Library of America asked me to prepare new texts of *Sanctuary, As I Lay Dying, Light in August,* and *Pylon,* I adopted a more rational policy—perhaps not the right one, of course—of regularizing dashes and ellipses. Here's the policy, quoted from the note on the texts: "In the Polk texts, three or four hyphens become a one-em dash, five or more become a two-em dash; up to six dots of ellipsis are regularized to three or four according to traditional usage, seven or more become seven." It's all perfectly rational and perfectly arbitrary, so perfectly rational and arbitrary as to have seemed perfectly loony to readers who didn't have to make such decisions. The policy statement in fact became the basis for a piece of whimsy by Veronica Geng in the *New Yorker* about her own usage:

> Eight dots before dialogue indicate that whatever the character says, he or she really means the exact opposite. . . . More than eight dots before dialogue creates a different feeling, more like doubt or distrust. Or maybe the character is just stalling. We don't know. Instead of having the meaning be cut and dried, it's more like: Wait a minute, is this guy on the level or not? That's the realism I depict with the extra dots.[4]

Alas, it's a bit disquieting to me, even now, to recall how close Geng's musings are to my own debate about *Sanctuary*'s ellipses.

During the years following *The Hamlet* (1940), Faulkner managed to rein in his compulsive dashing and ellipsising, and in fact became almost consistent in distinguishing between dashes with three hyphens and those with four. He almost always used three hyphens within sentences and at the beginning of interrupted speech; but he *very* consistently, though not invariably, typed four hyphens at the *end* of interrupted speech. If this means that he intended a two-em dash at the end of interrupted speech, does it also mean that he intended a two-em dash whenever he typed four hyphens, even at the beginning of interrupted speeches, or intended a one-em dash when he typed only three hyphens at the end of an interrupted speech, even though the patterns of his usage would argue for regularizing to two-em dashes? And what does an editor do when Faulkner occasionally typed five hyphens?

To make it more problematical, Faulkner during the second half of his career sometimes typed a space before or after a dash, a space that becomes yet another abyss into which I regularly fall. I of course can, and occasionally do, make the case that such a space is deliberate, that it has implications for rhythm, for the length or quality of the pause being indicated, for the significance of what is being interrupted. But I know too that these spaces are not all deliberate: on such typewriters as he used, that space may well be mechanical slippage, a heavy thumb, a too-light touch on the hyphen key, or even, God knows, a hole in the typewriter ribbon, which probably won't show up on a Xerox copy, and may not even show up on the original typescript page. It is therefore hobgoblinesque to fetishize consistency in such matters, I think. And yet the alternative is to spend hours of anguish parsing out the differences between four and five hyphens while our colleagues are drinking beer and playing with their grandchildren. It's all the more hobgoblinesque because I'm convinced that this is the kind of thing that for the most part simply didn't matter to Faulkner, and probably didn't matter to many other authors.

In fact, for all his punctuational idiosyncrasies, from beginning to end of his career, Faulkner never complained, probably never even noticed, when any editor anywhere added apostrophes to *dont, wont, cant,* and *oclock,* or periods to *Dr, Mrs,* and *Mr,* which he never used—or at least I thought so until I examined the typescript of *The Mansion* closely enough to see that in one pencil revision he in fact interlined the word *Mrs.,* with a bright, clear period following it.[5] Deliberate? I dream about it: it comes at me at odd hours of the night, like the hand at the end of *Deliverance.* But in any case he *never* corrected this sort of thing when it was presented to him in proof. He seldom complained about much of anything editors did to his texts; the seriousness of the things he did care enough about to complain about— when editors changed the title of *If I Forget Thee, Jerusalem* to *The Wild Palms* (1939) over his strenuous objections, for example—provides a sort of index to how little he cared about the other things.

Another kind of problem, more serious in its implications, occurs in *Go Down, Moses,* in which Faulkner typed the word "diningroom" in three different ways: as one word, as two words, and as a hyphenate. Other such variations occur irregularly throughout—to regularize or not? Again, I know in my critical heart of hearts that Faulkner didn't care one way or the other, that such things simply didn't matter to him: he was in a hurry. But as editor I can't treat the problem that way, and so have pored endlessly and masochistically over it, trying to discover *any* difference of rhythm, intonation, or stress that might work toward whatever meanings this novel may have. Nothing: it simply didn't matter to Faulkner, I believe. But in the act of editing this text, any text, I have acted to impose meaning on it, even if I refuse to regularize, and I must decide which meaning to impose. And choose I must: I cannot avoid a choice. If I decide that these three forms do have some—any—meaning in their variance, I have no choice but to leave them alone. If on the other hand I decide that they do *not* have any meaning, I have two options: the first is, again, to let them alone, although even that invests them with a problematical meaning that calls attention to the words in ways Faulkner almost certainly did not intend, and in leaving them alone I thereby create, like the extra-long dashes and ellipses, a visual distraction that works against larger issues in this passage and in the novel.

My second option, to regularize, may in fact be the best way to diminish my imposition of meaning on the irregularities, and so to operate editorially in the higher interests of the text's more important issues. But if I regularize, I run the risk of doing too much work for the reader. To be sure, we are supposed to do *some* of that kind of work: how much, of course, is the crucial question. The answer varies from text to text, and it is a particularly important question for *Go Down, Moses* as a readable text. That is, the top dead center of meaning in that novel lies precisely in Isaac McCaslin's attempt to read—to discover or to impose meaning on—those decidedly irregular, almost illiterate ledgers that document his family's trafficking in plantation and slave ownership. Thus I can and do argue that *Go Down, Moses* is very much *about* writing and reading and interpreting texts. In which case, why should not the reader of the text of the novel be allowed, forced, to run precisely the same risks that Isaac runs? If you answer, and reasonably, *Why not, indeed?* then we can in effect justify doing no editing at all, but merely publishing it in facsimile—but then I'm back to the old question of how I could afford to pay my children's college loans.

Do I believe that Faulkner intended a distinction among these three forms of "diningroom"? Nope. I am certain that he was typing so fast he simply didn't notice what he was doing and that if I had been able to consult him he would have thought the question ridiculous and instructed me to make up my own mind and not bother him. In fact, in 1941, when he was writing *Go Down, Moses,* he wrote to Warren Beck inveighing against the valorization of neatness and tidiness that the very concept of regularizing assumes, and reveling in the robust incorrectness, the laughing and hearty imprecision, of one of his masters: "I had rather read Shakespeare, bad puns, bad history, taste and all, than Pater, and . . . I had a damn sight rather fail at trying to write Shakespeare than to write all of Pater over again."[6] I think he simply didn't care about such things, they wouldn't have mattered: *except,* of course, when they mattered, and his work, his early work especially, is filled with instances where punctuation, accidentals, matter very much indeed. Determining when they matter and how they matter (or just making reasoned judgments about this) sometimes requires editors to set aside their theories and to remind themselves that editing means creating texts that allow readers to read in a commonsensical sort of way, unimpeded by meaningless concerns about multiple forms of, for example, "diningroom." Editorial common sense, I think, suggests that acknowledging unimportance is the necessary first step toward dealing with it editorially.

🐾 We editors have generally dealt pretty well with the fact that these things matter when they matter, but we have often failed to consider the reverse, that often they simply don't matter. The hard part of our task, obviously, is deciding which is which, since on such decisions depend not so much the larger, cosmic, meanings of literature but the smaller, quotidian, even pedestrian meanings that emerge from a reader's or editor's encounter with the mechanics of production—of haste, carelessness, hangnails, headaches, hangovers, bad typing, typewriters in need of repair. I don't mind wrestling editorially with Universal Significance or even with typing or typographical errors, but I hate like hell the thought that I'm really wrestling with a hole in a typewriter ribbon.

Mistakes that occur more often than once can easily be seen as forming a pattern, and patterns (bless them, for they are our critical lifeblood) are the very stuff of intention and of meaning. But we impose meaning on texts as we do on history—that is, backward. We look at the filled page the author has typed and otherwise marred, not at the blank page he or she originally faced, trying desperately (that agony and sweat Faulkner talked about) to find the one exact word or punctuation mark that will get close to whatever meaning he or she may have in mind. In *Requiem for a Nun* (1951), Faulkner described history as "litter from the celestial experimental Work Bench"[7]— a wonderful phrase that easily brings me back to our henhouse in a hurricane metaphor and probably aptly describes the process of writing fiction, certainly of typing and printing it.

I'll close with a bit of heterodoxy, though it may be more exasperation than anything else, a cri de coeur from the loneliness of my office, or merely a petulant grousing. I think authors have some responsibility in all this, especially modern authors who experiment with language, who play with structures of representation, linguistic and otherwise. I think they have more responsibility to their own texts than we have generally been willing to assign to them, enamored as we rightly are of the creative act, of the helter-skelter uncontainable chaos of creation itself, and willing as we rightly are to be handmaidens and valets to genius. I fear that we have sometimes wrongly sentimentalized our authors, taking genius as somehow other than human and perhaps willfully blinding ourselves to even genius's limitations. We worship the author's manuscript in all its passionate intensity, in all its juggling profligate word-by-sentence-by-paragraph-by-chapter progression toward completion or at least toward a reasonable place to stop. But it is, after all, editors' and valets' *jobs* to impose some kind of order on their bosses' lives, to set creative chaos into some kind of workable relationship with the world it has to exist in if it is going to exist at all except as unimaginable splendor in the author's mind.

I thus think that our authors have some responsibility to let us know what is important and what is not, even if we have to saddle them with that responsibility in retrograde. We must require them to help us discover their intentions. There: I have used the *I* word again; it has been skulking, contemptuously, in the underbrush throughout these comments, and I am now going to flush it out into the open and say what I assume all editors think. I have anguished for years over questions of authorial intention, years before recent critics discovered it as a problem rather than merely as a fallacy. As its editor, I know more about the instability of meaning in *The Sound and the Fury* than all other critics combined because I have tracked that instability from comma to comma in all its textual forms, and I am both bored to tears by and mortally exasperated with critics who discuss intentionality without ever having faced any author's passionately intense manuscripts so as to watch creation's painful and magical process that begins with and moves toward some kind of intention, even if that intention is provisional at best and even if it changes from word to word, as all writing does, has to, in the act of getting put on paper. Good writers know that only the previous word makes the next word possible.

Faulkner bought his own ribbons, typed his own typescripts, submitted them to commercial editors, and then mostly forgot about them. He expected his editors to fix what they thought needed fixing. He hardly ever challenged them on anything, important or not, mostly because he was already too busy on the next novel to have time to think about the previous one. For the most part he gave us pretty good guidance to his sentence-by-sentence "intentions" in most of his novels; I don't mean that he didn't make mistakes but that generally his texts are so consistent that a careful reader can discern what seemed important to him and what didn't. But there were thousands of things that he just didn't care about.

Of course *we* have to care about these things and treat them as though they do matter; we have to treat them as guilty of significance until proven innocent and to wrack our brains over dropped balls. But what we do *not* have to do is pretend that *every* jot and tittle in a text is oracular, even if each one is in fact potentially so. We do *not* have to pretend that *everything* matters equally, or that Faulkner gave one tinker's damn about how to spell diningroom or whether there was a space before or after a dash: if it mattered *that* much, by Fredson, he should have told me, or at least typed with a new ribbon. If *he* didn't care, why should I?

Notes

This is a version of a talk delivered at the 1993 Modern Language Association convention in Toronto, at a session sponsored by the Committee for Scholarly Editions on the relationship between editing and literary meaning. For a variety of reasons, I have hoped here to retain the oral-delivery nature of its original presentation. The nature of the comments seems to call for more informality than is my wont—although there may be some disagreement about that too.

1. In classrooms, correspondence, and extended conversations, many years ago.

2. Quoted in *Faulkner in the University,* ed. Frederick L. Gwynn and Joseph L. Blotner (Charlottesville: University Press of Virginia, 1959), 194.

3. "Where the Comma Goes" and "Trying Not to Say: A Primer on the Language of *The Sound and the Fury,*" in Noel Polk, *Children of the Dark House* (Jackson: University Press of Mississippi, 1996), 3–21, 99–136.

4. Veronica Geng, "Codicil," *New Yorker,* 23 Dec. 1985, 29.

5. William Faulkner, typescript at the Alderman Library, University of Virginia, 352; rpt. in *William Faulkner Manuscripts 22,* vol.3, arranged by Michael Millgate (New York: Garland, 1986).

6. *Selected Letters of William Faulkner,* ed. Joseph Blotner (New York: Random House, 1977), 142.

7. William Faulkner, *Requiem for a Nun,* in *William Faulkner. Novels 1942–1954,* ed. Joseph Blotner and Noel Polk (New York: Library of America, 1994), 540.

William Faulkner, the Crisis of Masculinity, and Textual Instability

❧ ❧ ❧

Philip Cohen

My contribution to this collection argues for the importance of attending to the critical significance of contemporary editorial work. My starting point is the belief that literary scholars and teachers ought to make use of the recently reconceptualized discipline of textual scholarship—the study of the genesis, transmission, and editing of texts—because the entire textual process of a work can be an important body of evidence for critical readers, regardless of their theoretical orientation. Once the foundation of American graduate studies in English and literary studies, textual scholarship has ceded its primacy to formalist interpretive criticism with an emphasis on close reading. The New Critics and their later twentieth-century descendants reinforced the distinction between intrinsic criticism, or the interpretation and evaluation of literary works, and extrinsic scholarship, comprising textual scholarship, literary history and biography, and source and influence study. The rise of literary and critical theory over the past twenty years, moreover, has eroded textual scholarship's disciplinary status as more and more American graduate programs in literature have replaced their required courses in research methods and bibliography—with units on textual criticism, editing, and analytical and descriptive bibliography—with required courses on critical theory.

This is not to suggest that textual scholarship and critical theory have developed in isolation from one another. To the contrary: in the 1980s, the theory-driven reconfiguration of English studies penetrated even the staid precincts of textual scholarship. The methods and rhetoric of earlier Anglo-American textual scholars and editors often sought to constitute texts and editions out of complex textual processes according to single-text and authorial premises; that is, they shared with formalist critics a Romantic-Modernist notion of the literary work as a physical object best represented by a single stabilized text. This conception originates both in the development of print technology, with its ability to produce a series of texts that closely resemble each other, and in the Romantic emphasis on authorial consciousness as the ultimate source of textual authority. But in the past few decades many textualists have augmented older theories about single authorial texts and individuated authorship with fresh considerations of the theoretical and practical legitimacy of collaborative and even non-authorial conceptions of literary works. Textual scholars as diverse as George Bornstein, Jerome McGann, D. F. McKenzie, Peter Shillingsburg, D. C. Greetham, Hershel Parker, and Hans Walter Gabler, for example, have argued that competing theoretical assumptions lead editors to constitute different texts for the same literary work.[1]

Thus a particular editorial orientation is now less likely to be taken as logically superior to others than as a pragmatic or rhetorical product; different critical, disciplinary, institutional, and social constraints produce different editorial assumptions, procedures, and presentations. Textual studies now draws our attention to textual instability, to the fact that many literary works often manifest themselves in several substantially different pre- and post-publication authorial and non-authorial states. The discipline also generates empirical evidence about the production, transmission, and reception of literary works—evidence that many readers might find useful, even as they remember that their theoretical constraints will help determine the uses to which they put it. A complex dialectical relationship exists, as it always has, between literary theory and textual scholarship.

The relationship remains largely unnoticed in some quarters. In English studies today, many critics and scholars overlook the relevance of textual scholarship by combining a postmodern critical orientation with a traditional, if unacknowledged, Romantic-Modernist textual orientation. Despite their use of various cutting-edge critical methodologies that stress multiple interpretive contexts, for example, many of the contributors to David McWhirter's recent collection, *Henry James's New York Edition: The Construction of Authorship*, show little interest in employing textual scholarship for interpretive and theoretical purposes. This is curious, given that the New

York Edition (1907) presented James's often radical revisions of novels published as early as 1876, and seems as such to demand of its readers a lively consciousness of textual processes. Many of the essays interrogate various aspects of the edition's physical format, photographs, and order and omission of selections, but the contributors characteristically treat the edition itself as a stable textual product. Most expatiate on James's comments on composition and revision but avoid exploring in any substantive way what James actually did to his earlier fiction as he prepared the edition.[2]

Why should many contemporary scholars focus on a single stable textual product when their own poststructuralist critical and interpretive theories frequently emphasize decentering, dispersal, and multiple contexts and interpretations? Why should they submit to the ratification of a textual product by the authorial single-text orientation and the textual ontology of capitalism, individualism, and Romantic-Modernist ideology, all critical dispensations now out of favor in the academy? Why should they bring postmodern critical practice to bear on a single text of a work, ignoring the larger textual process of which it is a part? For postmodern critics, a work's meaning typically results from the dialectical relationship between textual production broadly conceived (rather than limited to authorial intention) and textual reception, or the functioning of literary works in larger social contexts. So their criticism might reasonably be expected to relate the process by which different hands participated in different stages of a text's history to the process by which individual texts have been received by the reading public. The web of texts and textual processes suggests a notion of authorial, collaborative, and non-authorial intertextuality that is the material counterpart of postmodernist notions of intertextuality that stress discursive relationships between works by different authors. Unlike the fixed conception of textuality that underlies modernist Anglo-American editing and formalist critical practice, such an understanding of intertextuality assumes that only in the context of particular theoretical frameworks or publishing arrangements may we think of published texts as discrete entities.

My point is that scholars need not confine themselves uncritically to a single text or version of a work, whether produced by a commercial publisher or a scholarly editor. Some critical questions are best accessible through examinations of a work's entire textual process. In what follows, I shall illustrate this proposition by considering some of the interpretive implications of the entire textual history of William Faulkner's third published novel, *Sartoris* (1929), including *Flags in the Dust,* the unpublished work from which it descended. I am particularly concerned with the attenuation in the published work of anxieties about masculinity that are an essential element of *Flags,* which were the result of young Faulkner's acquiescence to the demands of his publisher. By examining the textual process of *Flags/Sartoris*—a process not limited either to the text validated by the act of publication or to the earlier text that Faulkner preferred—we are able better to understand Faulkner's exploration of this crisis at the beginning of a crucial period in his artistic development. For it is the entire textual process of *Flags/Sartoris* that anticipates Faulkner's work to come on the psychological, social, and cultural perils of traditional masculinity. The case, as I say, is exemplary: when the state of evidence allows us to do so, we need to examine multiple editions of evolving works in order to be able to comment on the works more judiciously.

Recently, critics have been quick to note that Faulkner's literary output, especially his early work, is characterized by a deep ambivalence and anxiety about masculine roles, about what it means to be a man in the modern period. Indeed, the fiction that he produced during the first half of his career often depicts the crisis and failure of traditional masculinity in a world where men often act like women and women act like men. Moreover, his male characters are often either active masculine realists or passive masculine idealists, each group represented by different linguistic styles and narrative techniques. Men like young Bayard Sartoris, Jason Compson, Popeye, and Thomas Sutpen often perform traditionally masculine activities such as hunting, making money, bootlegging, and fighting. Unreflective, unimaginative, misogynistic, cynical, and taciturn, they frequently come to naught. Although they usually perceive women as "bitches," they nevertheless remain dependent on them and are often vanquished by them. On the other hand, Faulkner's passive idealists like Elmer, Horace Benbow, and Quentin Compson are often effeminate, sexually repressed Prufrockian failures with artistic leanings and quasi-homosexual characteristics. Introspective and imaginative, these characters idealize women as desexualized madonna figures while harboring unconscious sexual desires for them—desires that manifest themselves as voyeurism, dreams, and an obsessive concern with sexuality. While we may initially be struck by how different these two groups of characters are, Faulkner's habitual juxtaposition of his characters and their actions invites us to contemplate more profound similarities between them. Thus his masculine realists and idealists are usually two sides of the same coin: driven by profound feelings of inadequacy and impotence, both types need women and reject them because they need them. Such divisions remind us that Faulkner is the modern novelist less of consciousness than of conflicted consciousness.

Occasionally, as Deborah Clarke, Doreen Fowler, Noel Polk, and Michael Zeitlin have argued, Faulkner connects his masculine characters and their attitudes toward women to the unresolved pre-Oedipal and Oedipal conflicts within their dysfunctional families.[3] In fiction such as *The Sound and the Fury* (1929), *As I Lay Dying* (1930), *Sanctuary* (1931), "A Rose for Emily" (1930), and "Miss Zilphia Gant" (1932), for example, failed parents victimize children who in turn grow up to become victimizers of others, especially children. Thus Faulkner's early fiction depicts the crisis of traditional masculinity every bit as much as, say, Hemingway's fiction does. This crisis of masculinity in Faulkner's early work is especially prominent in the textual process of *Flags in the Dust,* his first novel set in his fictional Yoknapatawpha County. *Flags* was cut by fifteen percent and published as *Sartoris* by Harcourt Brace in 1929. Faulkner's portrait of the failed idealist Horace Benbow was truncated in *Sartoris,* thus obscuring the novelist's exploration of failed masculinity at a crucial stage of his career. Indeed, *Flags* was rejected after Faulkner had published two earlier novels and just before he entered the period of furious creativity that produced *The Sound and the Fury, As I Lay Dying, Sanctuary,* and *Light in August* (1932).

The origins of Faulkner's crisis of masculinity, his sense that traditional gender roles had been destabilized, are primarily biographical but also social and cultural. Perhaps following the lead of biographical scholarship on Hemingway in the 1980s, Faulkner's critics have pushed the sources of Faulkner's concerns with masculinity and gender back from the psychic wounds caused by his nonparticipation in World War I to his familial constellation of a strong mother and a weak father. Jay Martin, for example,

has related Faulkner's gender difficulties to his early psychosexual development, especially his painful, ambivalent relationships with his parents Maud
and Murry Falkner.[4] Faulkner's troubled extended courtship of Estelle Old-
ham and the disastrous marriage that followed certainly contributed to these
difficulties.

In the speeches of characters like the writer Fairchild and the sculptor Gordon in *Mosquitoes* (1927), moreover, Faulkner often portrays art as the product of a masculine creative desire to rival or substitute for woman's ability to
give birth. But his male artists or artists manqué are usually effete, effeminate,
or even homosexual, as were a number of Faulkner's literary mentors and literary friends, for example Phil Stone, Ben Wasson, and Starke Young. The
title character of *Elmer,* the unpublished novel that Faulkner abandoned in
1925, is a heterosexual artist who increasingly exhibits homosexual tenden-
cies. Faulkner himself seems to have been haunted, as the different versions
of his introductions to *The Sound and the Fury* make clear, by his Southern
culture's notion that art is an unmanly activity. This division of masculine
roles was constantly played out in the various conflicting public personae
that he adopted as a young man: wounded aviator, grungy bohemian, nattily
dressed idler or fop, binge drinker, and noble hunter. He vacillated among
these roles in both his public and private lives. Even his love life was marked
by this division: Faulkner repeatedly fell in love with popular attractive
women who were drawn to "traditional" males more active, more financially
successful, and more "masculine" than he was, a painful triangle that finds
its way into many of his novels.

In their magisterial three-volume work *No Man's Land,* Sandra Gilbert and
Susan Gubar anatomize the consequences the modern period's destabilization of gender had for literature—a phenomenon that men and male writers,
especially during World War I, often perceived as emasculating. Similarly,
Frann Michel has stressed the effect on Faulkner's artistry of the feminiza-
tion caused not only by the author's failure to participate in World War I but
also by the destabilization of gender roles in the 1920s and 1930s.[5] This
shifting of gender roles and the masculine paranoia and fear that it generated
are particularly evident in *Flags in the Dust.*

An early work with numerous problems, *Flags in the Dust* is nevertheless
suffused with Faulkner's obsession with the failure of contemporary mascu-

linity. The novel's finely drawn portraits of different Southern social classes attempting vainly to cope with the onset of the twentieth century also dramatize a wide-ranging crisis of masculinity to which Faulkner would repeatedly return. His confident sense that the book would make his reputation, however, was not shared by his publisher Horace Liveright, who rejected the manuscript. Eventually, another publisher, Alfred Harcourt, accepted the manuscript on the condition that Faulkner's friend Ben Wasson condense it. In need of money and anxious to see the novel in print, Faulkner agreed to the terms.[6]

Wasson streamlined the novel and unified its plot by removing chunks of material that dealt with characters such as Byron Snopes, Narcissa Benbow, and Narcissa's brother, Horace Benbow, an effete, genteel lawyer who can only withdraw from life. The excisions allowed Wasson to focus the narrative on the fate of young Bayard Sartoris, who has been shattered by the loss of his beloved brother John in aerial combat over France during World War I.[7] As with Faulkner's own cutting of the original version of *Sanctuary* in the fall of 1930, much of what was lost dealt with Horace, whose thoughts, words, and actions were originally juxtaposed with those of the more active and aggressive Bayard Sartoris. And as with *Sanctuary,* the excised material is an integral part of Faulkner's representation of the precarious modern masculine self, which actively or passively asserts its identity even as it undergoes a much-feared dissolution.[8] This material also renders a fuller picture of male resentments, fears, desires, and anxieties concerning women and their sexuality. But it is the complete textual process of both *Flags in the Dust,* which Random House finally published in a volume edited by Douglas Day in 1973, and *Sartoris,* as opposed to either novel alone, that reveals the importance to the young Faulkner of the psychological, social, and cultural failure of traditional masculinity.[9] Examining the cuts made for *Sartoris* serves to focus critical attention on the material's original function in *Flags* and on the possible motivations for its removal. Consequently, the entire textual process of *Flags/Sartoris,* some of which editors have made available,[10] better serves as the object of critical study than one or the other version does.

The excisions that Wasson made in *Flags in the Dust* upset its central narrative strategy of juxtaposing different men and their doomed pursuit of strong women. In *Flags,* young Bayard Sartoris, who has inherited his clan's penchant for violence and foolhardiness, is balanced against the more passive and introspective Horace Benbow and the tormented, animal-like Byron Snopes. Broken by the war and the death of his brother, Bayard returns to Jefferson to seek release from his grief and aggressively courts death in a series of reckless stunts. While Bayard courts Horace's sister Narcissa by treating her cruelly, Horace pensively withdraws from life. Thus Bayard's family heritage of aggressive, destructive masculinity and his active quest for self-destruction had originally been counterpointed against Horace's slow, melancholy surrender to the disreputable charms of Harry Mitchell's discontented wife Belle.

In *Flags,* Faulkner also treated the theme of divided sexuality in the parallel relationships of Horace and Narcissa Benbow. Brother and sister share a sublimated incestuous connection and initially refuse to enter into mature sexual relationships. Their repressed sexual urges, however, return and drive them both to partners very different from one another.[11] Perhaps because a number of passages dramatizing these relationships were cut for *Sartoris,* Maxwell Geismar was able to observe that the relationship between Horace and Narcissa contains "the few genuine scenes of feeling in the novel" and that "Horace must return to his sister to gain the few positive affections which after all contain the pleasure of existence."[12] While Narcissa, even though she eventually marries Bayard, saves the anonymous obscene love letters that Byron Snopes sends to her, Horace pursues first Belle and then her sister Joan Heppleton.

By the time Bayard dies in a plane crash in Dayton and Horace arrives with his new wife Belle in a corrupt new town in the Mississippi Delta, however, their parallel relationship in *Flags in the Dust* has become obvious: both men exemplify different versions of failed or paralyzed masculinity. At novel's end, Bayard and Horace are impotent and dependent on women like Narcissa, who acts as their substitute mother to ease their suffering, or Belle, who arouses Horace's repressed desire. Indeed, Horace is reduced to walking regularly to the train station to fetch foul-smelling cartons of shrimp for Belle. If Bayard and Horace represented two of the masculine avenues open for Faulkner, one active and one passive, both also represented dead ends.

A number of the excisions made for *Sartoris* obscure the parallels between, on the one hand, Bayard's successive abandonment of his first wife Caroline, his grandfather's corpse in a wrecked car, and Narcissa and their unborn son, and, on the other hand, Horace's betrayal of his sister and Belle and her husband, Harry. Much of Horace's affair with Belle's sexually dangerous sister Joan, for example, was excised for *Sartoris*. Seeing Joan for the first time with her "calm, lazy contemptuousness" (*FD* 292; not in *S*) on the streets of Jefferson causes Horace to recall a childhood memory later that night as he lies in bed:

> He was five years old and his father had taken him to his first circus, and clinging to the man's hard, reassuring hand in a daze of blaring sounds and sharp cries and scents that tightened his small entrails with a sense of fabulous and unimaginable imminence and left him a little sick, he raised his head and found a tiger watching him with yellow and lazy contemplation; and while his whole small body was a tranced and soundless scream, the animal gaped and flicked its lips with an unbelievably pink tongue. It was an old tiger and toothless, and it had doubtless gazed through these same bars at decades and decades of Horaces, yet in him a thing these many generations politely dormant waked shrieking, and again for a red moment he dangled madly by his hands from the lowermost limb of a tree. (*FD* 291; not in *S*)

Joan is more of a "carnivorous" sexual predator than her sister; her "flecked eyes that should have been warm but were not" remind Horace of "that tiger yawning with bored and lazy contempt while round and static eyes stared down its cavernous pink gullet" (*FD* 292, 294, 293; not in *S*). Her lack of sentimentality leads her to make "but one request of him: that he refrain from talking to her of love" (*FD* 296; not in *S*).

In *Flags in the Dust,* Horace's affair with Belle's sister marks a further stage in his journey away from the sublimated incestuous bliss he had shared for so long with Narcissa. From Belle's corrupt romanticism, Horace progresses to Joan's cold sexuality, betraying Belle as well as Harry. Reminiscent of Quentin Compson in *The Sound and the Fury,* Horace, with his uneasy, even fearful puritanical alternation between attraction to and revulsion from both Belle and Joan, is another variation of the ambivalent feelings about women and sexuality exhibited by Bayard Sartoris and Byron Snopes, the novel's other young male protagonists. The absence in *Sartoris* of almost half the material dealing with Belle and of all the material concerning Horace's affair with Joan renders the surfacing of Horace's long-repressed sexual and self-destructive urges more difficult to discern. Despite his recognition of Joan's amorality, he continues his affair with her; his gradual decline parallels the increasing despair of both Bayard and Byron.

Like these two men, Horace is not merely a victim of women, but his complicity in his fate is obscured in *Sartoris*. And like so many other characters in Faulkner's fiction, Horace in *Flags in the Dust* is both victim and victimizer. In some of the excised passages from *Flags,* he justifies his transparently reprehensible actions by rationalizations and a cynical philosophical determinism. For example, during a brief reconciliation with his estranged sister, most of which does not appear in *Sartoris,* he avoids shouldering any blame for destroying Harry Mitchell's home and happiness. While Narcissa feels sorry for Harry, her brother excuses his own behavior by saying, "He'll have [his daughter]. . . . He cares more for her than he does for Belle, anyway" and "Dont you think he's well off, rid of a woman who doesn't want him, who doesn't even love his child very much?" (*FD* 287; not in *S*). He then defends himself by appealing to a convenient naturalistic philosophy: "Oh, people . . . Barging around through a lifetime, clotting for no reason, breaking apart again for no reason still. Chemicals. No need to pity a chemical" (*FD* 287–88; not in *S*). Once he has married Belle and moved with her daughter Little Belle to the Delta, Horace refuses to accept any responsibility for ruining Harry's life: "Man's life. No apparent explanation for it save as an opportunity for doing things he'd spend the rest of it not being very proud of" (*FD* 345; not in *S*). In another passage excised for *Sartoris,* he reveals the misogyny that seems to drive many of Faulkner's male characters: "It's only his injured vanity. . . . He's hurt in his own estimation because he couldn't keep the female he had chosen in the world's sight" (*FD* 346; not in *S*).

In *Flags in the Dust,* Faulkner also expanded his portrait of masculine futility by counterpointing a third character, the poor white bookkeeper Byron Snopes, against Bayard and Horace. Faulkner's portrayal of Byron's mounting sexual frustration and impotence is diluted by the absence in *Sartoris* of passages that depict the "obscene images and shapes" of his "sleepless desire" for Horace's sister (*FD* 217; not in *S*). Here too, our initial perception of

Byron as substantially different from his social betters Bayard and Horace may change during our reading of the novel. Seemingly different from the other men because of his animal-like nature and his consuming lust for Narcissa, Byron is finally just as impotent and alienated as Bayard and Horace are, but these parallels are much less evident in *Sartoris* because the material about Benbow and Snopes has been truncated. *Flags,* for example, emphasizes the frustrated and tormented existence of all three men by counterpointing their dreams, both waking and sleeping. Bayard has recurrent nightmares which involve scenes from the war and the death of his beloved brother; and Horace lies abed, tormented by his conflicted feelings about Belle and Joan in passages that did not survive in *Sartoris.* Missing also are Byron's dreams of frustrated lust for Narcissa, from which he wakes "sweating" and in which "her image lived and moved and thwarted and mocked him, with the pillow crushed against his mean, half-insane face" (*FD* 217; not in *S*).

By their own actions, all three men banish themselves from Jefferson and, more importantly, from Narcissa. Our last glimpse of each character finds him embarking upon or already in ignominious exile. After Byron robs the Sartoris bank and invades Narcissa's bedroom to leave his last letter, he flees to Frenchman's Bend for a last visit with his fiancée. In a scene excised for *Sartoris,* he tries to rape Minnie Sue in an attempt to alleviate his frustrated lust. After putting up a struggle, the girl thrusts him away, saying, "You come back tomorrer, when you git over this" (*FD* 260; not in *S*). An utterly defeated Byron sits "for a long time, with his half-insane face between his knees and madness and helpless rage and thwarted desire coiling within him" before he drives away, leaving Yoknapatawpha County forever (*FD* 260; not in *S*). The excision of this scene, however, means that our last glimpse of Byron is not one in which yet another male is bested by a woman. His final sexual humiliation originally prefigured Horace's end in the Delta as transporter of Belle's shrimp and Bayard's death in an experimental plane in Ohio. This emphasis on their shared exile disappears in *Sartoris* because Byron's final sexual humiliation is absent, as is much of the material dealing with Horace in his new home. In *Sartoris,* Bayard's, Horace's, and Byron's relationships with Narcissa and other women thus anticipate less clearly than they might the conflicted, incestuous relationship of the Compson brothers to their substitute mother Caddy in Faulkner's next novel, *The Sound and the Fury,* and similar relationships between Addie and her sons in *As I Lay Dying.*

A number of Wasson's cuts may have been motivated by concerns for sexual propriety: Wasson excised chunks of material dealing with Horace and Narcissa's quasi-incestuous relationship, Horace and Belle's adulterous relationship, Horace's affair with Belle's sister Joan, Horace's nympholeptic ogling of a teenaged girl's underwear as the two play tennis, and Byron's attempted rape of Minnie Sue. These cuts, however, undo narrative strategies and explorations of failed masculinity that Faulkner would return to in *The Sound and the Fury* and both versions of *Sanctuary.* They simplify Horace's depiction as a divided protector and would-be ravisher of virginal women, a characterization that anticipates the divided consciousness of Quentin Compson and Horace himself in *Sanctuary.*[13] The deletion of material in which Horace surreptitiously eyes Frankie's underwear, for example, upsets a significant parallel with Byron's covert surveillance of Narcissa. Such multiple acts of voyeurism in Faulkner often expose the hypocritical similarities between the respectable world of Jefferson and the less reputable denizens of the town. Just as *Sanctuary* reveals troubling similarities between Horace's and Popeye's treatment of women—Horace unconsciously wishes to perform the brutal violations that Popeye acts out; both harbor a virulent misogyny; and both experience impotence and failure in their dealings with women—so Horace's relationships with Narcissa, Belle, Frankie, and Joan were originally balanced against Bayard's and Byron's treatment of women.

In *Flags in the Dust* more than *Sartoris,* Horace evidences an incestuous desire for his sister, and desires and is repelled first by Belle and then by her sister, Joan. As in both versions of *Sanctuary,* he is also a perverse but impotent voyeur in a society in which masculine violation of women, innocent and otherwise, seems the norm. It is precisely this oscillation between idealization of and disgust toward women that Faulkner would develop in Horace's relations with Ruby, Temple, and Little Belle in both versions of *Sanctuary.* The cuts made for *Sartoris* obscure these connections as well as Horace's relationship to Quentin, another failed idealist, voyeur, and would-be violator of a sister in *The Sound and the Fury.* Especially notable is the similarity of Horace's divided consciousness in *Flags* to Quentin's conflict between his conscious puritanical idealizations of Caddy as a substitute mother and his more-or-less repressed Oedipal desire for her. Both Horace's and Quentin's veneration of chaste womanhood masks an obsessive misogyny and a violently ambivalent attitude toward female sexuality. These conflicting impulses are symptomatic of the crisis of masculinity in Faulkner's fiction.

Up until now I have been focussing on the differences between *Flags in the Dust* and *Sartoris,* but the process by which those changes were made and the motivations for making them may also shed light on the matter at hand. For example, feminist and new historicist scholars might be interested in exploring how the complex publication processes that produced these novels were, in part, ideologically inflected social and collaborative acts involving Faulkner and other agents (such as friends and publishers) that resulted in obscuring and thus downplaying Faulkner's depictions of this crisis. Were Wasson's excisions of material representing unconventional sexual desire and behavior a form of expurgation in the interests of marketability, and do they represent a conventional masculinist and editorial sense of what was suitable for or desired by readers of fiction, many of them female? More to the point, was the truncation of Horace's narrative motivated by a desire to eliminate an unacceptable representation of masculinity? To address these questions, one would need to document the production and reception of Faulkner's novels with a particular emphasis on his publishers and an eye toward developing a sociology of general readership that would enable us to gauge, however roughly, the efficacy of the cultural and ideological work that his novels perform. This is a daunting task, which we are only beginning to undertake. Such questions also remind us that the textual process of a work may have as much social and historical significance for some scholars as the published version of that work.

With the exception of *Sanctuary,* Faulkner's novels during the first half of his career reached a painfully small audience. Whether or not his representations of the crisis of modern masculinity had any impact on the small band of readers who read each new novel is as yet impossible to determine. But Faulkner's many readers today run the risk of not recognizing the true dimensions of this crisis, at least in its early manifestation, if they decline to consider the entire textual process of *Flags/Sartoris:* the work that the young author wrote, the one that he consented to have released to the public, and the documentary evidence that comments on the development of the one into the other. To investigate these issues, as Jack Stillinger has recently tried to do, is to set aside the myth of individuated authorship.[14] The conceptual power of this myth has occasionally overwhelmed editorial and critical recognition of the fact that most writers collaborate, delegate, and cooperate with friends, lovers, colleagues, editors, and publishers and that they continue to rewrite the texts of literary works for different reasons, for different audiences, and under different circumstances. Consequently, Romantic-Modernist editors and critics often saw these non-authorial agents as sinister figures corrupting a pristine text, a view that cannot peacefully coexist with postmodernist notions of discourse, identity, and texts as social constructions. Indeed, my allegiance to this Romantic-Modernist exaltation of the individual author led me in my earlier work to privilege *Flags in the Dust* over *Sartoris*. This older editorial narrative especially mystifies the socialized production of modern literature by obscuring the role of the publishing industry with its various incentives and constraints.

One advantage of attending to the entire textual process of a work is that authorial variants are, as Hans Walter Gabler puts it, "an essential category of revision," because "we never come closer to an author's willed structuring of design and meaning than through his conscious choices of language, expression, and style."[15] Although authorial revisions are key pieces of evidence for critics, including me, who are interested in authorial intention, analyzing the changes made by various hands over time does not necessarily presuppose a critical practice founded on authorial intention, construed singly or otherwise. Examinations of a work's textual process stand to help both authorial and non-authorial critics confirm, revise, or refute arguments about a particular text or work. Indeed, poststructuralist critics who value discursive social formations over self-sufficiency and autonomy are perhaps particularly well suited to benefit from analyses of intertextuality and textual instability. Remembering that professional authors, like most writers, routinely revise their work, and that many other agents routinely assist them, can only help critics interested in textual contradiction, disruption, and discontinuity. More broadly, when we think of fictions as processes that involve negotiations among an author, other individuals, and institutions, we help ourselves answer more fully the interpretive questions that we habitually pose.

Notes

1. See, for example, essays by some of these scholars in *Devils and Angels: Textual Editing and Literary Theory,* ed. Philip Cohen (Charlottesville: University Press of Virginia, 1991). For recent commentary on the dialectical relationship between texts and textuality, see *Texts and Textuality: Textual Instability, Theory, and Interpretation,* ed. Philip Cohen (New York: Garland, 1997).

2. See *Henry James's New York Edition: The Construction of Authorship,* ed. David McWhirter (Stanford: Stanford University Press, 1995); and see Philip Cohen, "The Lesson of the Master: The New York Edition, James Studies, and Contemporary Textual Scholarship," *Studies in the Novel* 31 (1999): 98–115. For a refreshing contrast to McWhirter's collection, see *Representing Modernist Texts: Editing as Interpretation,* ed. George Bornstein (Ann Arbor: University of Michigan Press, 1991).

3. Polk and Zeitlin draw upon Freudian models to discuss Oedipal conflicts in Faulkner's work, Fowler uses Lacan's revisions of Freud, and Clarke uses French feminist revisions of Lacan to analyze pre-Oedipal conflicts in the fiction. Lacanian and revised Lacanian readings of Faulkner's families may note their dysfunctionality but often argue that the male characters' fear of and degradation of the feminine "other" is the logical consequence of successful negotiation of the Oedipal stage. See Noel Polk, "'The Dungeon Was Mother Herself': William Faulkner: 1927–1931," in *New Directions in Faulkner Studies,* ed. Doreen Fowler and Ann J. Abadie (Jackson: University Press of Mississippi, 1984), 61–93; Michael Zeitlin, "Faulkner and Psychoanalysis: The Elmer Case," in *Faulkner and Psychology,* ed. Donald M. Kartiganer and Ann J. Abadie (Jackson: University Press of Mississippi, 1994), 219–41; Doreen Fowler, "'Little Sister Death': *The Sound and the Fury* and the Denied Unconscious," in *Faulkner and Psychology,* 3–20; Deborah Clarke, "Of Mothers, Robbery, and Language: Faulkner and *The Sound and the Fury,*" in *Faulkner and Psychology,* 56–77; and Clarke, *Robbing the Mother: Women in Faulkner* (Jackson: University Press of Mississippi, 1994). See also Anne Goodwyn Jones, "Male Fantasies? Faulkner's War Stories and the Construction of Gender," in *Faulkner and Psychology,* 21–55.

4. See Jay Martin, "Faulkner's 'Male Commedia': The Triumph of Manly Grief," in *Faulkner and Psychology,* 123–64. Michael Reynolds and Kenneth Lynn have both argued persuasively that Hemingway's family relations rather than his wound on the

Italian front were primarily responsible for the psychic wounds that marked his life and his writing; see Reynolds, *The Young Hemingway* (Oxford: Blackwell, 1986); and Lynn, *Hemingway* (1987; reprint, New York: Ballantine, 1988).

5. Sandra M. Gilbert and Susan Gubar, *No Man's Land: The Place of the Woman Writer in the Twentieth Century,* 3 vols. (New Haven: Yale University Press, 1988–94); Frann Michel, "William Faulkner as Lesbian Author," *The Faulkner Journal* 4 (1988–89): 5–20.

6. For a biographical account of the composition of the novel, Ben Wasson's editorial surgery, and its publication as *Sartoris,* see George Hayhoe, "A Critical and Textual Study of William Faulkner's *Flags in the Dust*" (Ph.D. diss., University of South Carolina, 1979), 1–11; see also Joseph Blotner, *Faulkner: A Biography,* rev. ed. (New York: Random House, 1984), 527–611. For Wasson's account of his role in the publication of *Sartoris,* see *Count No' Count: Flashbacks to Faulkner* (Jackson: University Press of Mississippi, 1983), 84–86, 88–90. In 1987, Garland published the manuscript and typescript of *Flags* in two volumes as *William Faulkner Manuscripts* 5. For a table listing the substantive differences between *Flags* and *Sartoris,* see Melvin Reed Roberts, "Faulkner's *Flags in the Dust* and *Sartoris:* A Comparative Study of the Typescript and the Originally Published Novel" (Ph.D. diss., University of Texas at Austin, 1974), 64–194. The available evidence seems to warrant the assumption that Wasson was responsible for most of the excisions from *Flags.* Despite Wasson's assertions to the contrary (89), evidence indicates that Faulkner continued to prefer *Flags* to *Sartoris;* see, for example, Faulkner's own comments on the cutting of *Flags* in "William Faulkner's Essay on the Composition of *Sartoris,*" ed. Joseph Blotner, *Yale University Library Gazette* 47 (1973): 121–24; rpt. in *Critical Essays on William Faulkner: The Sartoris Family,* ed. Arthur F. Kinney (Boston: G. K. Hall, 1985), 118–20. More importantly, after James B. Meriwether suggested to Faulkner's editor, Saxe Commins, in 1957 that Random House publish an edition of the *Flags* typescript, Commins mentioned the project to Faulkner who gave his approval. Random House obtained the rights to *Sartoris* in 1959, but it did not publish *Flags* until 1973.

7. Michael Millgate and Melvin Reed Roberts argue that Wasson's surgery created many more problems than it was meant to solve; see Millgate, *The Achievement of William Faulkner* (1966; reprint, Lincoln: University of Nebraska Press, 1978), 76–85; and Roberts, "Faulkner's *Flags in the Dust* and *Sartoris,*" 1–64. For fresh examples in support of their claims, see Philip Cohen, "*Flags in the Dust, Sartoris,* and the Unforeseen Consequences of Editorial Surgery," *Faulkner Journal* 5 (1989): 25–43. Elsewhere, I suggest that substantial cuts made in *Flags* to produce *Sartoris* may also explain why initial and subsequent readers of the two books responded so differently to the work's ending, which remains the same in both versions of the novel;

see Philip Cohen, "The Last Sartoris: Benbow Sartoris' Birth in *Flags in the Dust*," *Southern Literary Journal* 18 (1985): 30–39.

8. Faulkner was, however, the primary agent in the peculiar revision in the fall of 1930 that transformed the galleys of the original version of *Sanctuary* into a best seller. In order to save money by minimizing the damage done to the galleys, he reordered chapters, cut whole chapters and beginnings and endings of chapters but did very little rewriting or new writing.

9. Quotations from *Flags in the Dust* are from Day's edition. For a critique of this edition, see George Hayhoe, "William Faulkner's *Flags in the Dust*," *Mississippi Quarterly* 28 (1975): 370–86; rpt. in *Critical Essays on William Faulkner*, 233–45. The reader should remember that when one refers to *Flags*, one is actually speaking of the preserved *Flags* typescript, a document that may represent an intermediate stage of the novel and not necessarily the lost final version which Wasson transformed into *Sartoris*.

10. See note 6, above.

11. Unconsummated brother-sister incest occurs frequently in Faulkner's fiction. Such relationships in *Soldiers' Pay* (1926), *Elmer,* and *Mosquitoes* anticipate Horace and Narcissa's relationship in *Flags*, which itself foreshadows incestuous relationships in *The Sound and the Fury* and *Sanctuary.*

12. Maxwell Geismar, *Writers in Crisis: The American Novel, 1925–1940* (1947; reprint, Boston: Houghton Mifflin, 1961), 152.

13. Elsewhere, I discuss similarities between Horace in *Flags* and Quentin in *The Sound and the Fury;* see Philip Cohen, "Horace Benbow and Faulkner's Other Early Failed Idealists," *South Carolina Review* 18 (1986): 78–92. Previous critics tended to compare Bayard Sartoris with Quentin perhaps because of the reduced role that Horace plays in the published novel. For example, Robert M. Slabey contends that Bayard and Quentin both "desire to escape the complications and responsibilities of the present by retreating into the past," and Myra Jehlen finds Bayard and Quentin "doomed survivors" who attempt to reconstruct the fall of the old South. See Slabey, "The 'Romanticism' of *The Sound and the Fury*," *Mississippi Quarterly* 16 (1963): 149; and Jehlen, *Class and Character in Faulkner's South* (New York: Columbia University Press, 1976), 27–28.

14. See Jack Stillinger, *Multiple Authorship and the Myth of Solitary Genius* (Oxford: Oxford University Press, 1991).

15. Hans Walter Gabler, "The Synchrony and Diachrony of Texts: Practice and Theory of the Critical Edition of James Joyce's *Ulysses*," TEXT 1 (1981): 309.

The Scholarly Editor as Biographer

🜋 🜋 🜋

James L. W. West III

Of the subdisciplines practiced in and around departments of literature, scholarly editing looks to be one of the few with an empirical foundation. To some extent this is true: scholarly editors do gather and analyze physical evidence, and they present it in the form of facsimiles, variant tables, diagrams, and lists of emendations. Much of the theoretical writing published by editors has an empirical cast, often concerning itself with the rules by which textual evidence should be interpreted. And certainly we appear to be empiricists to those outside the humanities—a perception that many of us welcome. It is almost uniformly believed by those who control the budgets of American universities that truth can best be apprehended through empirical methods. Thus scholarly editors, however low their stock might sink at Modern Language Association–style conventions, are at least able to explain to their deans how they marshal and deploy evidence and why their work has utilitarian importance.

In this essay, however, I should like to suggest that scholarly editing is not, at base, an empirical pursuit. Certainly it has empirical features, but fundamentally it relies on intuition and imagination much more heavily than it does on analysis of evidence. At its very center, I believe, scholarly editing is an exercise in *biography*—one of the most famously slippery and difficult-to-define varieties of writing. What scholarly editors do as they analyze their variants is in fact practice biography. They construct in their minds a conception of the author's creative personality that will undergird all that they, as editors, wish to do to the texts.

Scholarly editing, like biography, is an attempt to recapture and describe moments of behavior from the past. The two pursuits employ many of the same techniques and much of the same data, and both can be hobbled by too little (or sometimes too much) information. The biographer and the editor ask essentially the same questions: Why did my subject behave in this way? Did he really do what he appears to have done, or is the evidence incomplete—or misleading? Did her decisions spring naturally from her personality and prejudices, or was she under heavy influence from others? Was he prevented from taking action or speaking out by social or legal constraints? Did she want matters to turn out as they did, or did she acquiesce from inertia or weariness or a sense of helplessness?

Biographers ask these questions about a great range of behaviors involving childhood, upbringing, education, marriage, finances, sexual preference, political allegiance, and public success. Scholarly editors focus more selectively on the composition and publication of literary works, but their investigations still impinge heavily on the areas just mentioned. This is natural: editors must have in their minds fully fleshed-out portraits of their authors as they attempt to reconstruct what the authors did or how they felt about the works that were passing into print.

I would like to suggest further that what scholarly editors do is more *inductive* than *deductive*. Ideally editors begin by examining the evidence dispassionately and developing sets of conclusions about authors' composing methods and their attitudes toward collaboration and interference from others. But in fact few editors begin with a blank slate: most of them already have preconceptions about their authors, notions taken from biographers and critics who have come before. Such notions cause editors to view the evidence, from the beginning, in a slanted way. Or perhaps editors want to strike out in new directions, reassessing their authors' views on the compositional process and the publishing industry. In these cases editors act as revisionist biographers, arguing (from new facts, if available) that their authors were not the people that previous biographers and critics thought them to be.

Sometimes the process is almost entirely inductive because editors decide ahead of time how they wish to edit a given text. That is to say, they know which text (of the several that can be constructed from the surviving evidence) they want to publish as the established or canonical version. Perhaps it will be essentially the version that has been in circulation all along, with only a few adjustments and corrections, or perhaps it will be a radically different text that must be resurrected from early drafts or proofs. In either case the editor must begin biographically, by constructing an author who will approve (posthumously) of the text that is going to be published.

Much of the current discussion in textual editing is about biography. Editors are not talking about technique or logic; they are instead considering authors' personalities and the decisions that they imagine were made at particular moments in the past. Toward that end editors have developed certain pre-cut patterns that are used to describe their authors. An editor usually selects one of these patterns and then proceeds to edit, basing assumptions about past behavior on the pattern. One might, for example, choose to depict an author as a young innocent, ignorant of the ways of the publishing industry, powerless in dealing with its bureaucracy, and anxious to make whatever concessions might be necessary to see a work appear between hard covers. This authorial personality would require an editing style valuing early, untainted intention over later compromise. Alternately one might portray this same young novelist as talented but callow, inclined to produce overwrought and sophomoric writing, grateful (especially in retrospect) for the guiding hand of the older, wiser trade editor, pleased that his excesses were curbed or her writing toned down for public consumption. Such an authorial personality would justify an editing strategy designed to validate the received text and to rid it only of mechanical error. Both of these approaches could quite easily be applied to the same author and work. It is all a matter of language—of choosing a particular set of verbs, adjectives, and adverbs that will create, as a biographer would, the author necessary to justify the editorial approach.

When this created author matches the standard biographical portrait, the edited text is usually received with approval, but when the portrait differs from the accepted picture, one often encounters resistance. With apologies for discussing my own work, I might offer some examples from the texts of Theodore Dreiser to help clarify this point.[1] Without naming names, I think it is fair to say that many early biographers and critics viewed Dreiser as uneducated and crude—both as an artist and a man. He was seen as a writer who could produce prose on demand but who needed help with spelling,

grammar, style, and even content. Dreiser was portrayed as a child who resisted (but still required) chastisement with the blue pencil. Thus the various trade editors and quasi-collaborators who worked on his writings were
seen, in a peculiar way, as morally superior to him. If he did not approve of
what they did to his texts (and often he did not), then he *should* have approved of it. A particular array of adjectives and adverbs was used to create
this portrait. Dreiser was "careless," "inattentive," and "slap-dash"; he worked
"rapidly" and "hastily"; he was "disinclined" to do the difficult labor of revision and was "indifferent" about the accuracy and grammatical correctness
of his writings. His style was "clumsy," "elephantine," and "opaque." Virtually anything done by editors and amanuenses to improve the readability of
his prose—or to remove crudities of thought or expression from it—must
therefore be good. Dreiser's work was said to require a documentary or historical approach. The received text, no matter how much altered by those
through whose hands it had passed, should be validated. Perhaps selected
passages from early drafts might be included in notes and appendixes as
scraps from the work table, or as examples of the gracelessness of Dreiser's
unedited prose, but the text that we should all read and critique was essentially the one that was already in print.

The problem with this view was that it did not always match the extant
evidence, as many biographical portraits do not. Certainly there was data to
support a view of Dreiser as unlettered, feckless, and boorish, but there was
equally good evidence on which to base a different picture—of Dreiser as
unsystematically but broadly read, of his behavior as unpolished and blunt
but egalitarian and honest, and (most importantly) of his composing and
revising habits as disciplined and methodical. Evidence to support both
views survives, sometimes in irritating profusion. Dreiser's manuscripts and
correspondence show that he was sometimes attentive and sometimes careless about his texts, alternately painstaking and casual about their revision,
and both prickly about their alteration by others and indifferent to their fate
once they left his desk. Dreiser's own conception of literary composition
swung between two poles. Sometimes he saw it as a community enterprise
involving himself, his wife, his lovers of the moment, and various other
friends and advisors. At other times he viewed the act of writing much more

dramatically, seeing himself as a solitary, prophet-like seer who was in contact with the muses and whose utterances should not be meddled with.

Thus when I set out to re-edit *Sister Carrie* (1900), Dreiser's famous first novel, and *Jennie Gerhardt* (1911), his undervalued second novel, I had available the makings of almost any biographical portrait that I wished to present. What I needed was a Dreiser who would justify the approach I meant to take—an approach that would put into print earlier and very different texts from the ones that we had been reading. These new texts, I believed, would represent Dreiser's intentions more faithfully than the published texts did. In the introductions and other ancillary matter for the editions of *Carrie* and *Jennie,* I therefore presented the Dreiser I needed—an author more attentive to his texts and more troubled about editorial tampering than earlier biographers and critics had believed. I developed an alternate vocabulary for describing him at work. He was not "plodding"; rather, he was "steady." His style was "blunt" and "unadorned" instead of "clumsy" and "inept." He was "intellectually restless" and had a "wide-ranging curiosity," not a "wandering attention span" and an "unfocused intelligence." He wrote "fluently" and worked with great "self-discipline" and "doggedness," yielding authority over his texts only when faced with rigid deadlines and obdurate publishing houses. Having established this conception of Dreiser and his intentions, I could analyze the evidence and construct the texts I wanted. I was working inductively, not deductively. I knew the text that I wished to produce: the problem was to create a Dreiser who cared enough about his textual virtue for me to defend it.

The issue, in its broadest terms, is not whether the new texts of *Sister Carrie* or *Jennie Gerhardt* that I published were superior to the old ones— more faithful to real life or more complex or moving. Such evaluations are individual and personal: for me the new texts were better than the old ones, but that is all that I (or any editor) can say. Nor is the issue whether my revised biographical portrait of Dreiser was more nearly valid than earlier portraits. I believe that it was, but biography is so nebulous a discipline that such judgments cannot be made reliably. The important thing in this example is, rather, the sequence in which the thinking took place. Were the texts based on pre-existing biographical portraits of Dreiser, or was a revised portrait developed to validate the radically different texts? I believe that the second sequence took place—that I knew ahead of time which texts of *Carrie* and *Jennie* I wanted to present and then worked as a biographer to create an author who also wanted these texts to come to life.

What made it relatively easy to proceed in this fashion was that a great amount was known about Dreiser's life. By the mid-1970s, when I began work on *Sister Carrie,* he had been the subject of two major biographies, and many of his friends and associates had published reminiscences of him. Dreiser was a newsworthy figure for much of his life; one therefore had reportage, interviews, profiles, and book reviews to draw upon. And he was a pack rat who saved virtually everything: manuscripts, proofs, diaries, letters, maps, ticket stubs, menus, photographs—nearly all of it preserved in his papers at the University of Pennsylvania or in collections at other libraries. All of this was grist for a biographer/editor.

What would happen, though, if a scholarly editor had to investigate a figure about whom much less was known and for whom a much smaller body of evidence was extant? As a matter of fact, such situations have arisen fairly frequently for editors of twentieth-century texts that came from collaborations between authors and trade editors. Editors at trade houses were often immensely influential on particular literary works, but little has been known about most of them—about their rearing and education, prejudices and blind spots, tastes and preferences and standards. Sometimes the editor/biographer has been lucky: Maxwell Perkins, the famous figure at Charles Scribner's Sons who handled F. Scott Fitzgerald, Ernest Hemingway, and Thomas Wolfe, left behind hundreds of letters in the Scribner files (housed at Princeton University) and was the subject of a two-part *New Yorker* profile in 1944 and a full-length biography in 1978.[2] Other editor/biographers, however, have not been so fortunate. Saxe Commins, who edited William Faulkner, Gertrude Stein, Eugene O'Neill, and Robinson Jeffers at Random House, is an obscure figure. A substantial amount of material by and about him survives in the Random House papers at Columbia University, and his widow published a volume of laudatory writing about him in 1978, but his personality nonetheless remains something of a mystery.[3] Ripley Hitchcock, who edited Stephen Crane at Appletons and Dreiser at Harpers, is more obscure still, though there is at least a small collection of his papers at Columbia. And almost nothing is known about Tom Smith, who oversaw the cutting and shaping of Dreiser's *An American Tragedy* at Liveright in 1924. Many of the records of that firm were lost when it went belly-up in 1932; a few things survive at the University of Pennsylvania, but they tell us little about Smith.

Knowledge of such spear-carriers as Perkins, Commins, Hitchcock, and Smith is often of crucial importance to the scholarly editor. What role did Perkins play in the composition of certain of Hemingway's books—*Death in the Afternoon,* for example? What combination of personal politics and company rules prompted Commins to cut ten poems from Jeffers's *The Double Axe* in 1947? What conception of woman's place in society caused Hitchcock to oversee an editing job on Dreiser's *Jennie Gerhardt* that gutted the role of the title character? What mixture of literary judgment and marketplace economics guided Smith as he shepherded *An American Tragedy* into print?

In the absence of biographical data, scholarly editors addressing these questions have usually applied pre-cut biographical patterns to trade editors, just as they have to authors. The trade editor has most commonly been depicted as a bland representative of the publishing establishment and, by extension, as a conservative, limiting, cautionary force. Then, according to the scholar's inclinations for the text, the author has either been allowed to rebel against this paternal figure or has been made to knuckle under to him. Proceeding in this way is simplistic; any scholar who has studied carefully the blue-pencilings of a given editor on a particular manuscript or set of proofs can testify that many of the suggestions, revisions, and bowdlerizations seem more personal and idiosyncratic than they do representative of company policy or of the standards of the dominant culture. But one has little choice if the materials are scanty. One is forced to function as a biographer who possesses little evidence, which is to say that one is thrown back on imagination and speculation.

At least the scholarly editor can imagine and speculate with impunity because all these figures—authors, trade editors, lovers, advisors, amanuenses—are now safely in the great beyond. Dreiser, for example, died in 1945; he cannot object if a scholarly editor's portrait of him seems skewed. No one thought to ask him in detail before he died about his attitudes toward the editing of his texts. Indeed no one knew (other than anecdotally) how extensively they had been cut, revised, and bowdlerized until well after his death, when his manuscripts and other papers came to the University of Pennsylvania and began to be studied. Thus in the absence of specific instructions from Dreiser, editor/biographers are free to follow their own instincts.[4]

But what if a living author *is* asked such questions about his or her texts? With apologies for again drawing upon my own experience, I shall tell a second story—this one about William Styron, whose manuscripts and texts I have studied and whose biography I have written. Styron's mature fiction has been bleached and banned from time to time in various countries—most notably in the United Kingdom—but the incident that brings issues of scholarly editing most clearly to light comes from early in his career. It involves the prepublication cutting and revision of his first novel, *Lie Down in Darkness,* issued in 1951 by Bobbs-Merrill.

Styron submitted his manuscript to Bobbs-Merrill in the spring of 1951. The decision was overwhelmingly for acceptance, but with the stipulation that Styron would have to tone down some of the language in Peyton Loftis's interior monologue, a long Molly-Bloomlike section near the end of the narrative that occurs just before she takes her own life. At issue were references to genitalia, menstruation, promiscuous sex, and incestuous feelings. Hiram Haydn, Styron's editor at Bobbs-Merrill, brokered the changes, soothing Styron's ruffled feelings and arguing that the novel was too good to risk its being misapprehended as a "dirty" book, rather as J. D. Salinger's *The Catcher in the Rye* (also published in 1951) would become, or as *Ulysses* had sometimes been viewed in the decade just after its publication in 1922. Styron yielded to this logic and permitted two rounds of cuts.[5]

I had assumed that if the chance ever presented itself for a restoration of this material, Styron would take it. I had instinctively adopted a pre-cut pattern in constructing a portrait of him as young and powerless, willing to let his first novel be compromised a little if it would get him into print and on the book-review pages of major magazines and newspapers. But I was wrong. A few years ago, Random House—Styron's publisher since 1956—acquired the copyright for *Lie Down in Darkness* from Bobbs-Merrill and announced plans to publish a reissue of the text in a uniform edition of Styron's writings. I asked Styron if he would like to have the censored passages restored to Peyton's soliloquy, and at first he said that he would. But once I had disinterred the words and phrases from Styron's manuscripts at the Library of

Congress, he changed his mind. The cuts recommended by Hiram Haydn, he now said, struck him as judicious and proper. The text should stand as originally published. Thus the Random House reissue of *Lie Down in Darkness* appeared without significant change (a few typos were corrected), and the received text was validated.[6] My own disappointment was tempered considerably by the fact that I agreed with Styron. The gritty details that would have been reinserted into Peyton's deranged monologue would have given it an unsavory tone and would have transformed her into a much less sympathetic figure than she had been in the Bobbs-Merrill text. One would not have felt so sorry for her or identified so closely with her.

Many different influences were operating here, of course. Styron was making his decisions as a mature writer in his sixties; probably he could no longer remember exactly how he felt in 1951 when Bobbs-Merrill required him to bowdlerize his text. His intentions now had little to do with his intentions in 1951—and in any case the earlier intentions could only be divined tangentially from Hiram Haydn's letters *to* him because Haydn had not thought to save Styron's side of the correspondence. And my own reaction, though finally unimportant, was surely influenced by Styron's. The authority in this case was altogether his; perhaps that is why I felt immediately that he was right.

The matter is settled for now, but texts remain unstable and liable to change. How will an editor many years from now view the situation, once *Lie Down in Darkness* enters the public domain and can be re-edited by anyone? The answer is that such an editor will be able to view it in almost any way that he or she chooses. Evidence survives to depict Styron, in 1951, as angry and frustrated with the timidity of Bobbs-Merrill. Evidence of equal weight exists to portray him as grateful for Haydn's guidance and judiciousness. The issue, then, for our hypothetical future editor might well come down to his or her interpretation of Peyton's character, as revealed in the monologue. Which Peyton will our editor-of-the-future prefer? The sexually adventurous Peyton of the manuscripts and typescripts, or the more ethereal and abstracted Peyton of the published book? Just as importantly, which William Styron (presented biographically) will approve of the Peyton that the editor wants? How will that Styron be created? How will his imprimatur be placed on the text?

The technology will surely exist by then to allow our editor some flexibility. If we are viewing most texts on screens, and if those texts are sufficiently fluid, then Styron's readers should be able to experience the two texts alternately, or superimposed one on the other, or side-by-side in double columns. Actually we have the technology to make this happen now. Who knows what we will be capable of in the years to come?

One thing is certain, though: editors in that future time will still be proceeding inductively and biographically as much as they will be operating deductively and empirically. Before they take action to validate a received text or present a new one, they will have to establish in their minds some reasonably firm conclusions about their authors' personalities and preferences. As a consequence, they will sometimes find themselves working in reverse order—deciding first what texts they want to bring to life and then creating authors who will approve of what they wish to do.

Notes

1. The two texts in question are from the University of Pennsylvania Dreiser Edition: Theodore Dreiser, *Sister Carrie,* ed. James L. W. West III, et al. (Philadelphia: University of Pennsylvania Press, 1981); and Dreiser, *Jennie Gerhardt,* ed. West (Philadelphia: University of Pennsylvania Press, 1992).

2. Malcolm Cowley, "Unshaken Friend," *New Yorker,* 1 and 8 Apr. 1944; A. Scott Berg, *Max Perkins: Editor of Genius* (New York: E. P. Dutton, 1978).

3. Dorothy Commins, *What Is an Editor? Saxe Commins at Work* (Chicago: University of Chicago Press, 1978); see also *"Love and Admiration and Respect": The O'Neill-Commins Correspondence* (Durham: Duke University Press, 1986).

4. In letters to H. L. Mencken, Dreiser did imply that he hoped his autobiographical volume *Dawn* might one day be published in uncut form. See, for example, Dreiser to Mencken, 24 June 1916, in *Dreiser-Mencken Letters: The Correspondence of Theodore Dreiser and H. L. Mencken, 1907–1945,* ed. Thomas P. Riggio, 2 vols. (Philadelphia: University of Pennsylvania Press, 1986), 1:239.

5. See Arthur D. Casciato, "His Editor's Hand: Hiram Haydn's Changes in *Lie Down in Darkness,"* in *Critical Essays on William Styron,* ed. Arthur D. Casciato and James L. W. West III (Boston: G. K. Hall, 1982), 36–46.

6. This text was published in the Vintage uniform edition of Styron's writings; the *Lie Down in Darkness* volume appeared in January 1992.

Texts in Search of an Editor

Reflections on
The
Frankenstein
Notebooks *and*
on Editorial
Authority
🐾 🐾 🐾
Charles E.
Robinson

Every novel exists in a plurality of texts, and none dramatizes this fact more than Mary Shelley's *Frankenstein,* the Draft and Fair-Copy Notebooks of which I have recently edited for Garland Press.[1] My editorial labors on this famous novel have made me painfully aware of how it developed through its various texts, from its original conception on ?17 June 1816 through its gestation, quickening, lightening, birth, and development into the novel (or novels) that so many of us now read. I here take the liberty of applying a creative metaphor to describe this developmental process because the novel itself concerns creativity and because both Mary Shelley and her persona Robert Walton took nine months to write their narratives: Robert Walton wrote his series of letters and journals over a period of 276 days between 11 December 17[96] and 12 September 17[97]; and, although Mary Shelley took eleven months between conceiving the story and finishing the Fair Copy (?17 June 1816 through 10/13 May 1817), it appears that the first two months were spent in writing the ur-text of the novel and that she therefore devoted the next nine months to expanding, drafting, and fair-copying her novel. What happened in the novel, therefore, can be seen to parallel or "figure" what happened outside of the novel.[2]

It would be fair to say further that Walton's writing *in* the novel and Mary Shelley's writing *of* the novel are also "figured" by the creative work of Victor Frankenstein himself. Victor's assembling of disparate body parts into his monster is not that different from Walton's assembling his discrete notes about Victor into a narrative; and both these creative acts may be compared to Mary Shelley's esemplastic fusing of words and images and symbols and punctuation into the text of her novel. Mary Shelley herself encouraged this kind of comparison when she bade her novel, her "hideous progeny," to "go forth and prosper," suggesting that her monster was a metaphor for her novel and that both creations would be altered by their experiences in the world.[3] Because of these alterations, it would also be fair to say that the monster and the text were not only "authored" but also "edited"—both words in their etymologies denote a bringing forth, a giving birth to something new.

If we pursue the editing metaphor further, we encounter another collaborator who assisted in the development of *Frankenstein,* namely, the midwife Percy Bysshe Shelley who helped bring Mary Shelley's novel to its full term and then helped present it to an audience on publication day, 1 January 1818. This assistance, as evidenced by his no fewer than 4,000 words in this 72,000-word novel, resulted from his correcting and augmenting portions of the Draft and the Fair Copy (and the proofs and the revises) of the novel. The nature of his editorial labors, which are made manifest in my edition of *The Frankenstein Notebooks,* will be briefly discussed below, but for the moment I wish to draw one more parallel between the actions inside and outside the novel: what Percy Shelley did to (or for) the novel is "figured" by both Walton and Victor Frankenstein serving as editors of each other's narratives. Indeed, the more we look at the novel, the more we are led to the conclusion that *Frankenstein* is a series of texts in search of an editor, one who will ultimately give form and shape to the novel.

Frankenstein is a frame tale and, as such, is very much about the question of authorial and editorial control. That is, the device of a frame tale enabled Mary Shelley to write as if she were Robert Walton writing the narrative of Victor Frankenstein, in which was embedded the story of the monster who recounted not only his adventures but also those of the De Laceys and the Arabian Safie. These interlocked narratives seem to make Mary Shelley's the dominant voice until we realize that Walton is her persona, and it is his voice we hear. After explaining to his sister Margaret that Victor "would commence his narrative the next day" on 20 August 17[97], Walton described how he would serve as both amanuensis and editor for Victor's words:

> I have resolved every night, when I am not engaged, to record, as nearly as possible in his own words, what he has related during the day. If

I should be engaged, I will at least make notes. This manuscript will doubtless afford you the greatest pleasure: but to me, who know him, and who hear it from his own lips, with what interest and sympathy shall I read it in some future day! (*1818*, 1:37–38)

We as readers, of course, are the ones who are destined for the "greatest pleasure" if, like Margaret, we read Victor's narration as edited by Walton. But was Walton the editor who brought forth Victor's tale? It is equally valid to argue that Victor Frankenstein edited the "notes" that Walton made about Victor's history of Victor:

> Frankenstein discovered that I made notes concerning his history: he asked to see them, and then himself corrected and augmented them in many places; but principally in giving the life and spirit to the conversations he held with his enemy. "Since you have preserved my narration," said he, "I would not that a mutilated one should go down to posterity." (*1818*, 3:157)

Victor, it seems, expressed greater concern for his text than he did for his monster. And although it appears that Victor had the last word in his own novel about himself, it was Walton who ultimately voiced Victor's concern for editorial authority. If, however, we privilege author over character and claim that Mary Shelley was the ultimate authority here, the manuscript versions of this passage reveal that Mary Shelley miscopied a phrase when she transcribed the Draft into the Fair Copy and that the error required a later correction by a hand that seems different from that of either of the Shelleys.[4]

The question of editorial authority in this novel gets even more complex if we ask in what form we read Victor's story as edited by Walton edited by Victor edited by Walton—because the question of form potentially introduces yet another collaborator in the editorial process. Do we read the manuscript written out by Walton for Margaret's eyes only—or do we read a version of that manuscript that his sister Margaret received and then edited for the press? Mary Shelley provides no answer to this question, but in either case Margaret acts as a surrogate for the reader. But is Margaret Walton Saville a surrogate only for the reader—or do her initials, MWS, force us to read her as a surrogate for Mary Wollstonecraft Shelley? If these initials are purposeful, then we have a novel written by MWS as if she were Walton writing to MWS—and the silent MWS stands in the corner of this narrative, teasing us to see her as both author and reader (and author and editor) of her own work.

If the questions of editorial authority inside the novel tease us out of thought, even more complex and teasing questions await us outside the novel as we encounter no fewer than ten texts that go into the making of *Frankenstein,* texts that have been edited by Mary Shelley herself (more than once), Percy Shelley (more than once), William Godwin, various publishers' readers and printers, and then the long list of nineteenth- and twentieth-century scholars who have printed and edited and otherwise disseminated the novel to millions of readers, each of whom may be said to "edit" the text while assembling and re-assembling the ideas, words, and punctuation that make up the spirit and matter of the thing we call a novel (which exists, as Percy Shelley would have it, only as it is perceived by the reader).[5] When I was invited to join this editorial procession, I anticipated doing little more than creating a useful "diplomatic" edition of *The Frankenstein Notebooks,* one that would faithfully represent the text of the extant Draft and Fair Copy by reproducing photographs of the manuscript pages, each of which would be faced by a type facsimile of the manuscript of that page. I was familiar with Mary Shelley's hand, having published a similar albeit simpler edition of the Fair Copies of her mythological dramas *Proserpine* and *Midas,*[6] I could recognize Percy Shelley's hand in the manuscript, and I planned somehow to distinguish his hand from that of Mary Shelley. In short, I would serve the scholarly community by bringing empirical and hard evidence into the various debates on Mary Shelley's most famous novel. What I did not anticipate was how much the editing of these Notebooks would force me to contextualize the extant manuscripts by reference to other manuscripts, proofs, revises, printed texts, and editions of *Frankenstein.*

My first step down that road of contextualization resulted from three circumstances that determined the character of my edition: a Garland policy (worked out in collaboration with Donald H. Reiman and the Bodleian Library) to reproduce in photofacsimile all extant manuscript pages, each of which would be faced by a type facsimile of the manuscript; a set of *Frankenstein* manuscripts in which Mary Shelley wrote fewer than ten words in each line; and Garland's predetermined nine-by-twelve-inch format that enabled me to print on each recto not only the type facsimile of the manuscript (with different fonts to distinguish Mary Shelley's hand from Percy Shelley's) but also, in tandem with the manuscript, a literal transcript of the 1818 first edition (all glossed by footnotes at the bottom of each page).[7] On one page, the reader could see what Mary Shelley originally wrote, then what she and Percy Shelley corrected, then what was printed a few months later, and finally the footnotes that addressed not only anomalies in the manuscript but also errors in the text of *1818*. These anomalies and errors forced me to extend my study of the transmission of the text in two directions: backward from *1818* through revises and proofs and Fair Copy and Draft to the ur-text that I hypothetically reconstructed; and forward from the first edition of 1818 through to the third and revised edition of 1831 (and also through to some recent critical editions of the novel). New discoveries about the meaning and form of the novel awaited me at every step in this sequence of texts, the interrelations of which I have discussed in the introduction, chronology, and footnotes in *The Frankenstein Notebooks*. Here, however, I will rely on the following outline to indicate how one text leads directly to another between the years of 1816 and 1831. The two exceptions to this direct sequence are *1818 Thomas* and [1826], both of which have been indented to allow the stemma arrows to pass by them.

The Texts of Frankenstein

1816 **Ur-text**: A novella-length narrative written between ?17 June and ?August
      1816 — not extant: certainly in the hand of Mary Shelley, but no evidence one
↓   way or the other of Percy Shelley's direct involvement.

1816–17 **Draft**: A two-volume novel in two hard-cover notebooks written between
      ?August 1816 and 17 April 1817 — most of the now disbound Notebooks A
      and B survive in 152 leaves (with text on 301 pages) together with three insert
      leaves and two insert slips (with text on a total of eight pages), all of which
      are reproduced in *The Frankenstein Notebooks* and account for approximately
      87 percent of the *1818* text: in the hand of Mary Shelley, with alterations in
↓   the hand of Percy Shelley.

1817 **Fair Copy**: A three-volume novel in ?eleven soft-cover notebooks written be-

tween 18 April and 10/13 May 1817—parts of now disbound Notebooks c1
and c2 survive in twenty-nine leaves (with text on fifty-eight pages) together
with one insert leaf (with text on one page) as well as one substitute leaf (with
text on two pages), all of which are reproduced in *The Frankenstein Notebooks*
and contain approximately 12 percent of the *1818* text: in the hand of Mary
Shelley, with the last twelve and three-quarters pages of Notebook c2 in the
hand of Percy Shelley. There is additional evidence that Percy Shelley cor-
↓   rected other parts of the Fair Copy.

Proofs: A three-volume novel issued between ?23 September and ?3 November
1817—not extant, but there is evidence that both Shelleys read and corrected
the proofs and that Mary and/or Percy made three major additions to the text,
↓   one in September and two in October.

Revises: Three or more sheets of revised proofs printed between ?23 September and
?20 November 1817—not extant, but the three major additions to the proofs
would certainly have resulted in revises that Mary and/or Percy Shelley would
↓   have read.

1818: A three-volume novel (1st ed.) published anonymously on 1 January 1818 in
500 copies by Lackington, Hughes, Harding, Mavor, & Jones.

↓   *1818 Thomas:* Copy of first edition (*1818*) corrected by Mary Shelley and
given to a Mrs. Thomas in Genoa by July 1823—survives at the Pierpont
Morgan Library in New York City.

1823: A two-volume novel (2nd ed.) published on 11 August 1823 in an unknown
number of copies by G. and W. B. Whittaker (set from *1818* rather than from
1818 Thomas)—William Godwin rather than Mary Shelley made the arrangements for this edition, the copy-text for which would have been either *1818*
or a proof copy that Godwin may have possessed. Godwin, it appears, was the
one responsible for the 123 substantive variants introduced into this edition,
almost all of which were carried over to *1831,* suggesting that *1823* was used
as the copy-text for *1831* and that Mary Shelley no longer possessed a copy of
1818 to use for this purpose.

↓   [*1826*]: [?**Re-issue of 2nd ed.** (*1823*)] "published" on 4 April 1826 by Henry
Colburn. Because no copy of an *1826* edition has ever been located or described, Colburn appears to have purchased and offered for sale the unsold
sheets of *1823* without printing a new title page, but no collation of multiple
copies of *1823* has been done to determine if there was in fact a distinct *1826*
re-issue of *1823.*

1831: A one-volume novel (3rd or revised ed.) published on 31 October 1831 in

4,020 stereotyped copies by Henry Colburn and Richard Bentley in the "Standard Novels" series: Mary Shelley was responsible for the substantial changes made to the text, and she apparently used *1823* as copy-text.

This brief outline of the texts of *Frankenstein* should suggest that there were at least three major editorial hands (of the two Shelleys and of Godwin) in the versioning of the novel between the time it was "finished" and fair-copied for the publisher and printer in April/May 1817 and the time it was revised in 1831; this of course does not count the publishers and their readers, or the printers and their compositors, who also exercised some influence on the text. A glance at the extant Fair Copy (which was also printer's copy), for example, will show that more than one unidentified hand made small alterations to the text that had been transcribed by Mary and Percy Shelley.

All these interventions should help to dispel the still-persistent myth of the solitary artist who has total control over a text. Granted, Mary Shelley was responsible for the novel's first words ("It was on a dreary night of November . . ."; see *1831*, xi), and she apparently had the last word when she prepared her revised edition of *1831* — or did she? Wherein lies governance of her text? In 1816, she ruled the margins of Notebook A only to allow her husband-to-be to make alterations, and in 1816 and 1817, Percy Shelley did in fact read, edit, and alter the text in both Draft Notebooks. In April and May 1817, Mary Shelley accepted most of his alterations when she transcribed the Draft into the Fair Copy; and in May 1817, Percy Shelley further changed the text when he fair-copied the last few pages of the novel, and Mary shortly thereafter recopied his transcription and retained nearly all his embellishments. In September 1817, she gave Percy "carte blanche" to make alterations to at least one section of the proofs,[8] and in late October 1817, not long before the novel was published on 1 January 1818, he was probably responsible for one of two major additions to the text. Mary Shelley herself was involved in editing her own prose during all this time, and then a year later in December 1818 she began to correct a copy of *1818,* but we are uncertain whether those corrections actually survived. In all likelihood, however, the copy corrected was the one given to Mrs. Thomas in 1823. Although we have the benefit of the editorial changes in *1818 Thomas,* they do not seem to have affected the received text, for Mary Shelley apparently did not keep a copy of these corrections. Then in the summer of 1823, Mary Shelley's father William Godwin introduced new words into the text of *1823*. Finally, in 1831, Mary Shelley redacted *1823* into *1831,* a text that is substantially different from *1818*.

And then came the scores of "professional" editors who looked back and woefully simplified (or willfully ignored) the textual history of the novel by first privileging *1831,* the text that was reprinted in most editions of the novel until James Rieger's groundbreaking edition of *1818* that not only printed the holograph corrections and additions that Mary Shelley made in *1818 Thomas* but also collated *1818* with *1831*.[9] Mary Shelley scholarship was revolutionized by that edition, for it gave evidence of an artist at work: the "Thomas" corrections showed the care that Mary Shelley took with her prose, and the collations with *1831* (all in one fell swoop in an appendix) demonstrated that she was interested in further emphasizing character and theme. Until now, however, the critical debate has focused primarily on the two published texts, *1818* and *1831*. Now, with the evidence and the arguments made available by *The Frankenstein Notebooks,* other aspects of Mary Shelley's artistry can be studied—particularly the ways in which she expanded one text into another.

One of the most important discoveries made during the editing of *The Frankenstein Notebooks* is suggested by the very title of the edition—namely, that Mary Shelley drafted her novel in two bound, hardcover notebooks, a fact that was not known until this edition was undertaken and until Bruce Barker-Benfield of the Bodleian Library (where the manuscripts owned by Lord Abinger are housed) made the initial discovery. It had formerly been assumed that the now loose sheets had some kind of common source. But only upon inspection of the sewing holes, glue residue, torn edges, offset ink blots, and original foliation and pagination of the individual leaves did it became clear that Mary Shelley actually drafted her novel in bound notebooks, providing incontrovertible evidence that most of the text was drafted in the sequence of the narrative as we have it and as it is paginated in the notebooks. (And exceptions could be clearly identified because of distinct insert leaves, some of which had been cannibalized from later quires in the notebooks.) In fact, the entire quiring sequences of the original notebooks could be reconstructed, thereby providing evidence about the number of missing pages resulting from revisions that were made to the Draft (or resulting from the Fair-Copy pages that were apparently lost during the printing of the novel). The very "look" of Notebooks A and B gives further evidence that what Mary Shelley actually wrote was an "intermediate" Draft, one that was in part copied from another source. Some pages are cluttered by Percy Shelley's additions to the text at that point, but most are almost "clean" enough to go to a printer as Fair Copy.

The manuscript evidence suggesting that Mary Shelley in the Draft was in fact copying from (and expanding upon) an earlier text is further supported by mistakes in the Draft that are best explained as copying errors. These mistakes suggest that Mary Shelley miscopied from her ur-text, sometimes jumping ahead of herself, canceling the error, returning to the ur-text at the proper place, and then beginning again so she could correctly copy what she had miscopied and then canceled. The most persuasive evidence for the existence of an ur-text from which Mary Shelley copied is to be found in her twice writing "Myrtella" for Elizabeth in passages drafted well into the narrative after Elizabeth's name had been written numerous times. In fact, there is considerable evidence in the Draft to suggest that in the ur-text Victor Frankenstein grew up not with Elizabeth and Clerval but with Myrtella and Carignan—and that Victor's mother was Caroline Beaumont rather than Caroline Beaufort. (These and other name changes in the Draft will enable more precise study of the artistic functions of names in *Frankenstein* and Mary Shelley's other fictions.)

The existence of an ur-text is also supported by other evidence. We have always known that Mary Shelley began a "short tale" in June 1816, that Percy Shelley encouraged her that summer to "develope the idea at greater length," and that Percy and Mary "talk[ed] about [the] story" on 21 August 1816.[10] But it is only with the publication of *The Frankenstein Notebooks* that we have been able to speculate that Mary Shelley during that summer wrote something more like a novella than a story—and that it probably contained in one form or another all the major incidents of the narrative (for example, Justine's trial and possibly even part of the story of the De Laceys). The two missing sections of the Draft, however, suggest that Mary Shelley's task in copying and expanding the ur-text into the Draft also involved adding two substantial parts to her narrative: Walton's outermost frame and Safie's innermost tale. What eventually became Walton's four introductory letters to his sister Margaret Walton Saville are now missing with the first forty pages of the Draft, suggesting that these notebook pages were in fact more like a rough draft, discarded after they were copied into some kind of intermediate state that is also now lost. A similar lacuna involving part of Safie's story (together with other manuscript evidence and statements in Mary Shelley's letters and journals) strongly indicates that Mary Shelley did not even conceive the Safie story until late November or early December 1816, at the point in the novel when the monster learned language while overhearing the De Laceys teach French to the Arab Safie. The manuscript evidence that yokes these two parts of *Frankenstein* suggests further relations between the two women in these narratives: "Saville" pronounced as a French name is strongly echoed by "Safie," and it is quite possible that Mary Shelley decided on both names as late as March/April 1817, during her final editing and correcting of the Draft. (In the first versioning of the tale in December 1816, Safie had been called Maimouna and then Amina.) If the names were intended to be homophonic, then we would have added reason to read Safie, as we did Margaret Walton Saville, as a "figure" for Mary Shelley (and Safie's dead mother as a "figure" for Mary Wollstonecraft).

As Mary Shelley expanded her ur-text into a novel, she set in motion a very peculiar symmetry in the text as it developed from 1816 through 1831. The *1816* ur-text would have been one volume at most (and in published form would have most likely shared covers with another text); the *1816–17* Draft was a two-volume novel; the *1817* Fair Copy was a three-volume novel; the *1818* first edition was a three-volume novel; the *1823* edition was a two-volume novel; and the *1831* revised edition returns us full circle to a one-volume edition (which *Frankenstein* shared with volume 1 of Schiller's two-volume *The Ghost-Seer*). None of these versions is identical to another (even with regard to the words therein), and in fact there are very striking differences among them. The aesthetic implications of all these differences (indeed, the very differences themselves), especially the differing formats that occasion different arrangements to the chapters, have never been studied, and I propose at least to outline the relations among these texts in the remainder of this essay.

When Mary Shelley expanded her *1816* ur-text into the *1816–17* Draft, she not only added the outermost and innermost narratives, she consciously divided her text (in the very process of drafting it) into two separate volumes. (This two-volume division was completely independent of the two Notebooks A and B that she used; that is, volume 2 of her novel began well before she finished using Notebook A for her draft.) Volume 1 of the Draft novel consists of chapters numbered 1 to 14 (actually fifteen chapters because of two separate chapters that are numbered "7") that are preceded by what appears to have been Walton's four introductory letters to his sister Margaret (the first forty pages of the Draft are missing, but there are four letters in *1818* dated 11 December 17[96], and 28 March, 7 July, and 5 August 17[97], this last letter extending into a journal with additional dates of 13 August and 19 August). Volume 2 consists of chapters numbered 1 to 18, the last containing or eliding into Walton's final remarks to his sister that are dated in Draft as 13 August 17[97] (26 August 17[97] in Fair Copy and in *1818*), 31 August (2 September in *1818*), 6 September (5 September in *1818*), 7 September (7 September in *1818*), and 12 September (12 September in *1818*).

The textual evidence suggests that as Mary Shelley drafted her novel, she clearly had in mind a two-volume novel with a special structure: after Walton's letters, volume 1 (drafted from August or September until late November 1816) consisted of Victor's narrative of his childhood through the creation of the monster, the death of William, and the trial of Justine—all ending with the Frankenstein family journeying to Chamounix and the dramatic moment of Victor meeting his monster for the first time on the Mer de Glace, which he traversed between Montanvert and Mont Blanc. Percy Shelley himself was privileged in this final chapter of volume 1, because it contained two stanzas from his poem "Mutability" that had been recently published in the *Alastor* volume (1816). And volume 2 (drafted from late November or early December until mid-April 1817) opened with an equally dramatic moment, the beginning words of the monster's narrative ("It is with difficulty that I remember the æra of my being" [*1816–17 Robinson,* 1:271]), and it contained the monster's entire narrative (chapters 1 though 8), the monster's demand for a female mate, the remainder of Victor's narrative until he was taken aboard Walton's ship, and finally Walton's "continuation" that recounted the death of Victor and the encounter with the monster on the ship.

By the time that Mary Shelley finished the Draft of her novel in two volumes in early April 1817 and then corrected it between 10 and 17 April, she had decided to transform her two-volume narrative into a three-volume work. Were it not for the Fair Copy that gives evidence of being in three volumes, I might have conjectured that Mary Shelley's original idea for a two-volume novel was compromised by the commercial interests of a publisher who wished to inflate the price by selling a three-volume rather than a two-volume novel.[11] But the Fair-Copy evidence is unequivocal—and there is further evidence in the Draft that both Shelleys helped to transform the two-volume Draft into a three-volume Fair Copy. That evidence, a series of marginal sums, was baffling to me until I realized that the Shelleys were estimating the number of pages that the Draft would occupy in three volumes. The imbalance of a fifteen-chapter volume 1 and an eighteen-chapter volume 2—together with a novel that may have become longer than Mary Shelley initially envisaged—is a possible reason why Mary and/or Percy decided to make the alteration, but an argument could still be made that the dramatically structured two-volume Draft version was sacrificed to the expediency of expectations and finances in the commercial world of publishing that influenced the Shelleys' decision.

When Mary Shelley transformed her novel into a three-volume Fair Copy, the existing thirty-three chapters of the two-volume Draft had to be reconfigured. The net result in the Fair Copy and in *1818* was twenty-three differently arranged chapters: seven each in volumes 1 and 3, and nine in volume 2. This new structure, occasioned in part because of the Walton letters that began and ended the novel, was not quite matched by the pages in each volume in *1818*: volume 1, chapters 1–7, pages 1–181; volume 2, chapters 1–9, pages 1–156; volume 3, chapters 1–7, pages 1–192.[12] And it could be argued that the new chapters in three volumes were in fact arbitrary, not quite fulfilling Mary Shelley's design in the earlier Draft—especially because she cut into existing chapters as she restructured her novel, as is revealed by the following outline:

Draft	*1818*
Volume 1	Volume 1
chapters 1–2	= chapter 1
chapters 3–4	= chapter 2
chapters 5–6	= chapter 3
chapters 7a–part of 7b	= chapter 4
chapters part of 7b–8	= chapter 5
chapters 9–10–part of 11	= chapter 6
chapters part of 11–12	= chapter 7
	Volume 2
chapter 13	= chapter 1
chapter 14	– chapter 2
Volume 2	
chapters 1–part of 2	= chapter 3
chapters part of 2–3 [13]	= chapter 4
chapter [?4]	= chapter 5
"another chapter"	= chapter 6
chapters [6] [14]–part of 7	= chapter 7
chapters part of 7–8	= chapter 8
chapter 9	= chapter 9
	Volume 3
chapter 10	= chapter 1
chapters 11–part of 12	= chapter 2
chapters part of 12–13	= chapter 3
chapters 14–part of 15	= chapter 4
chapters part of 15–16	= chapter 5
chapter 17	= chapter 6
chapter 18	= chapter 7

   That Mary Shelley herself determined at least some if not all these restructurings is suggested by her holograph in the Draft: "Finish Chap. 2 here" (*1816–17 Robinson*, 1:472). The note appears in volume 2 of the Draft, one-third of the way through chapter 12, at the point where in the *1818* text (and therefore in the Fair Copy, which is missing at this point) chapter 2 does in fact end and chapter 3 begins. This particular alteration does not drastically change Mary Shelley's original chapter divisions: her Draft chapter 12 originally consisted of Victor journeying from Edinburgh to the Orkney Islands, starting to create a female for the monster, then deciding to destroy this half-finished creation, and finally confronting the companionless monster who promised to retaliate by being with Victor on his "marriage night." Her *1818* chapter 2 ends with Victor's early work on the female, and chapter 3 begins with Victor deciding to destroy the female creature, proceeds through the monster's threat about the "wedding-night," and then (embracing all of Draft chapter 13) continues through Victor's sinking of the female creature's parts in the sea and his subsequent apprehension by the Irish, who suspected him of having murdered Clerval. There are other places where the new *1818* chapter divisions take greater liberties with the flow of the original narrative, and a study of the aesthetic implications of all of the alterations needs to be undertaken to determine if Mary Shelley herself compromised the original design of a novel in two volumes.

Of course, such changes as a text moves toward publication are not that unusual, especially to those who have studied the relations among drafts, fair copies, and first editions. And if we had the proofs and revises that intervened between the Fair Copy and *1818,* then we might be able to determine if other changes to the text were made by publishers' readers and/or compositors. But even without these proofs and revises, we can deduce in the case of *Frankenstein* that the Shelleys made at least three substantive changes to the text, the most significant occurring in *1818,* volume 3, chapter 1, pages 17–19, where what appears to have been a two-hundred-word description of Holland (which the Shelleys also used in their collaborative *History of a Six Weeks' Tour* [1817]) was replaced by an important and longer passage in which Victor reflected on Clerval's "wild and enthusiastic imagination," "the sensibility of his heart," and the survival of his "mind" and "spirit" after death—together with quotations from Leigh Hunt's *The Story of Rimini* (1816) and William Wordsworth's "Tintern Abbey" (1798). This important passage, added so late to the novel, reveals that the Shelleys continued to refine the text they were both preparing for publication.

Mary Shelley continued her own editorial improvements in December 1818 when she began to "Correct Frankenstein,"[15] possibly in the very copy of *1818* that she eventually gave to Mrs. Thomas in 1823. In *1818 Thomas* she noted that she wanted to "re-write [the] two first chapters [in volume 1]. The incidents are tame and ill arranged—the language sometimes childish—. They are unworthy of the rest of the . . . narration"; she also noted that Elizabeth's letter to Victor in chapter 5 "ought to be re-written."[16] But she did not comment one way or the other about structuring her novel in two or three volumes. The first to introduce that restructuring was her father, William Godwin, who in 1823 arranged for the publisher Whittaker to publish the novel in two volumes, requiring a resetting of the three-volume *1818* (in 529 pages) into the two-volume *1823* (in 529 pages). The twenty-three chapters in *1818* are translated into *1823* as follows: volume 1, chapters 1–11, pages 1–249; and volume 2, chapters 1–12, pages 1–280, the first chapter of volume 2 opening with the monster's continuing narrative of the De Lacey family, thus indicating that the two-volume *1823* is quite unlike the two-volume Draft that opened with the beginning of the monster's narrative. Although Godwin's two-volume edition has no authority, the 123 substantive changes that he also made to (or oversaw in) *1823* do eventually gain a degree of authority, for Mary Shelley appears to have used *1823* as copy-text for the revised *1831* edition. In doing so, she accepted (perhaps unknowingly) the word changes that Godwin had initiated.

Mary Shelley's final editing of her novel resulted from an opportunity to republish *Frankenstein* in the Standard Novels series that was started by the publishers Henry Colburn and Richard Bentley—a series that encouraged authors to make alterations to their texts. The full extent of the revisions that Mary Shelley made in *1831* may be found in *1818 Rieger* and now in *1818 Crook*,[17] and *1818 Butler* offers a convenient summary of the types of changes made in *1831*.[18] Those who have compared the two texts will remember, among the many changes, that Elizabeth was Victor's first cousin in *1818* but a foundling in *1831*, that the doppelgänger theme became more prominent in *1831*, and that Mary Shelley expanded her description of Victor's early life with Elizabeth and Clerval in Geneva, thereby requiring an additional chapter—so the twenty-three chapters of the three-volume *1818* became twenty-four chapters in the one-volume *1831* novel, the last version of *Frankenstein* that Mary Shelley prepared during her lifetime. However, she did attempt to make at least one more alteration: in a letter to Bentley's assistant Charles Ollier, probably written in February 1833, she inquired, "if

there is another <u>real</u> <introd> edition of Frankenstein—that is if it goes
to the press again—will you remember that I have a short passage to add to
the Introduction. Do not fail me with regard to this—it will only be a few
lines—& those not disagreable to C. & B. [the publishers Colburn and
Bentley]—but the contrary."[19] We can only conjecture what Mary Shelley
might have added, but it could have been a quotation from Percy Shelley's
review of *Frankenstein* that had recently been published in the *Athenæum*
(10 Nov. 1832).

In the preceding paragraphs I have attempted to contextualize the editing
of *The Frankenstein Notebooks* and thereby raise serious questions about the
text of the novel that we read. The more I read in and about Mary Shelley's
most famous novel, the more I am humbled by the richness and complexity
of the issues that it raises. The complexity is sometimes daunting, as it was
the first time that I unsuccessfully attempted to explain my new edition at a
talk at the annual meeting of the Modern Language Association (MLA) in
December 1995, at which time I had neither conceived nor written my introduction to the edition. When I did write that introduction in the summer
of 1996, it ultimately grew to 110 printed pages and offered what I judge to
be a series of useful glosses on *Frankenstein:* (1) an annotated list of short
titles that includes an efficient means to name and order the texts of the
novel; (2) an analysis of the physical makeup of the four extant notebooks
together with quiring charts and beta-radiographs of the watermarks—all
this evidence enabling a reconstruction of the sequence in which the novel
was drafted; (3) reflections on "naming" in the novel; (4) hypothetical reconstructions of both the ur-text and the Fair Copy; (5) remarks on the significance of numbers and dates in *The Frankenstein Notebooks;* (6) a discussion
of the collaboration between the two Shelleys; and (7) a thirty-page, single-
spaced chronology that provides in one place the important dates, facts, and
quotations from letters, journals, and contemporary documents that deal
with *Frankenstein*—so that the reader can experience in much greater detail
(with all the proper citations) what went into the making of Mary Shelley's
monster.

Since publishing *The Frankenstein Notebooks* with its introduction and
chronology, I have given a more thoughtful talk at the MLA meeting of
December 1996 as well as other presentations at some of the bicentennial

conferences in such places as Bristol, New York, Calgary, Cambridge, and Bologna, where Mary Shelley's birth in 1797 and her exceptional creative life were being celebrated. What this edition has taught me most is that much work yet remains to be undertaken on *Frankenstein,* and I hope that my editorial labors will provide others the means for more precise and accurate explorations of the novel, especially with regard to the collaboration between the two Shelleys, the differences between *1818* and *1831* and other versions of the novel, and the new discoveries that are made possible by studying the manuscript evidence in the context of a detailed chronology. Consider, for example, that we now know that Mary Shelley was reading her mother's *Vindication of the Rights of Woman* at the same time she was writing the chapters that concerned Safie's education by her mother.[20] Or consider that a portion of Victor's Draft description of his boat trip with Elizabeth on their wedding night was taken word-for-word from Percy Shelley's journal description of his boat trip with Byron on Lake Geneva in June 1816, at a time when Mary Shelley was beginning to write her ur-text of the novel (see *1816–17 Robinson,* 1:lxxix, 2:560–61). Even after Mary Shelley appropriated Percy Shelley's text for her Draft, Percy made an editorial change to the text, thereby drawing attention to the intimate nature of their collaboration and suggesting that the inner- and inter-textuality of this novel is so complex that it would be impossible ever to purge Percy Shelley's prose or voice from this novel—even given the Draft by which we can now identify his specific alterations.

One final reflection: does the manuscript evidence give us the means for a new edition of *Frankenstein* that would somehow conflate all that was judged "best" from the different versions? At least one recent edition has conflated the revised text of *1831* with the three-volume structure of *1818,*[21] creating a new kind of monster that has no validity, in my judgment. It would be much more defensible to reconstruct hypothetically the revises, the proofs, and the entire Fair Copy, all of which could then be used to filter *1818* back to the two-volume structure of the Draft. Or would we all be better served by merely making available for study the edited and corrected versions of the two-volume Draft and the three-volume *1818* (which has up to 100 textual errors) and the one-volume *1831*—and treat them much as we do William Wordsworth's two-part *Prelude* of 1799, his thirteen-book *Prelude* of

1805, and his fourteen-book *Prelude* of 1850? If the study of the transmission of these texts can teach us more about the creative process, do we then have an added obligation in this electronic age to link all these texts hypertextually in formats being developed by such places as the Electronic Text Center at the University of Virginia? If we exploit the latest electrical, electronic, and scientific technologies, then readers of the future will have all the parts of all the extant texts and thereby be able to assemble their own *Frankensteins*! In effect, these future readers will become authors or at least editors of their own texts of Mary Shelley's novel—with, of course, the threat that a web of undisciplined texts about a monster might produce texts more monstrous than we already have as this novel lumbers toward its own two-hundredth birthday in 2016—or should that be that 2017—or 2018—or 2023—or 2026—or 2031?

Notes

1. *The Frankenstein Notebooks: A Facsimile of Mary Shelley's Manuscript Novel, 1816–17 (with alterations in the hand of Percy Bysshe Shelley) as it survives in Draft and Fair Copy deposited by Lord Abinger in the Bodleian Library, Oxford (Dep. c. 477/1 and Dep. c. 534/1–2)*, ed. Charles E. Robinson, parts 1 and 2 (New York: Garland, 1996); hereafter cited as *1816–17 Robinson*.

2. It can even be argued that Walton's dates of writing from 11 December 17[96] to 12 September 17[97] (the years arrived at with the help of a perpetual calendar) are very close to the dates when Mary Shelley was conceived and born; see *1816–17 Robinson*, 1:lxv–lxvi and nn.

3. [Mary W. Shelley], *Frankenstein: or, The Modern Prometheus*, rev. ed. (London: Henry Colburn and Richard Bentley, 1831), xii; hereafter cited as *1831*. Other editions will be similarly cited in this essay: thus, for example, *1818* provides a short-hand for *Frankenstein; or, The Modern Prometheus*, 3 vols. (London: Lackington, Hughes, Harding, Mavor, & Jones, 1818).

4. See *1816–17 Robinson*, 2:606–7, 2:736–37, 2:806.

5. Percy Shelley more than once remarked that "all things exist as they are perceived"; see, for example, "A Defence of Poetry," in *Shelley's Poetry and Prose: Authoritative Texts, Criticism*, ed. Donald H. Reiman and Sharon B. Powers (New York: Norton, 1977), 505; see also "nothing exists but as it is perceived" (Percy Shelley, "On Life," in *Shelley's Poetry and Prose*, 476).

6. Mary Shelley, *Mythological Dramas: Proserpine and Midas, Bodleian* MS. *Shelley d. 2,* ed. Charles E. Robinson (New York: Garland, 1992).

7. The terms "photofacsimile," "type facsimile," and "literal transcript" are adapted from D. C. Greetham, *Textual Scholarship: An Introduction* (New York: Garland, 1994), 350.

8. *The Letters of Mary Wollstonecraft Shelley,* ed. Betty T. Bennett, 3 vols. (Baltimore: Johns Hopkins University Press, 1980–88), 1:42.

9. Mary Shelley, *Frankenstein or The Modern Prometheus: The 1818 Text,* ed. James Rieger (Chicago: University of Chicago Press, 1982), includes variant readings, an introduction, and notes; hereafter cited as *1818 Rieger.* This important edition was first published in 1974 in the Library of Literature (Indianapolis: Bobbs-Merrill), and reprinted in 1976 (with different pagination and lineation) by Pocket Books (New York). The 1982 Chicago reprint, however, is to be preferred because it corrects "minor errors in the introduction and apparatus" and lists "some additional 1818/1831 variants at the end of the volume" (x).

10. See *1831,* xi, and *The Journals of Mary Shelley, 1814–1844,* ed. Paula R. Feldman and Diana Scott-Kilvert, 2 vols. (Oxford: Clarendon, 1987), 1:130; see also *1816–17 Robinson,* 1:xxxi.

11. The really inflated pricing of triple-deckers was perhaps a decade away, when novels sold at a guinea and a half—that is, 31s.6d. Mary Shelley's *1818* novel, one of the shortest triple-deckers on record, sold for 16s.6d. in boards.

12. Because the extant Fair Copy reveals that Mary Shelley's transcriptions were written to rule, producing leaves with fourteen lines on one side and nineteen lines on the other (with an average of 285 words per leaf), and because these pages run in almost exact tandem with *1818* (where there are approximately 285 words per leaf), I have argued that the Fair Copy itself would have had approximately the same number of pages as *1818.* For more on this complicated issue, see *1816–17 Robinson,* 1:lxii–lxv.

13. The concluding Draft pages for chapter 3 are missing, as are the Draft pages for what eventually became chapter 5 in *1818*—the "trauma" in the text at this point concerns the intersections of Notebook A (continental blue paper) and Notebook B (English white paper).

14. Although unnumbered, this "chapter" beginning Notebook B (with the monster's words, "Such was the history of my beloved cottagers") precedes "Chap. 7th."

15. *Journals of Mary Shelley,* 1:245.

16. Qtd. in *1818 Rieger,* 43n., 62n.

17. Mary Shelley, *Frankenstein or The Modern Prometheus,* ed. Nora Crook, in vol.

1 of *The Novels and Selected Works of Mary Shelley,* ed. Crook, introduced by Betty T. Bennett (London: Pickering & Chatto, 1996). Crook provides four valuable "Endnotes": "Textual Variants" (182–227), in which she prints Mary Shelley's autograph corrections in *1818 Thomas* and the substantive variants in *1823* and *1831;* "A Note on Spelling Variants in *1818, 1823* and *1831*" (228); "Unauthorized Variants" (229), in which she indicates that *1831 Joseph* introduced six textual errors and that *1818 Macdonald* incorrectly listed these errors as *1831* variants of the *1818* text; and "Silent Corrections" (230–31). For full bibliographical information on *1831 Joseph, 1818 Macdonald,* and other frequently used editions, see "Short Titles" in *1816–17 Robinson,* 1:xv–xvii.

18. Mary Shelley, *Frankenstein or The Modern Prometheus: The 1818 Text,* ed. Marilyn Butler (London: Pickering, 1993), 199–201. Butler's edition was reprinted in paper as part of Oxford University Press's series The World's Classics (1994). Both the original and the reprint have an appendix in which Butler prints "The Third Edition (1831): Substantive Changes" together with "Collation of the Texts of 1818 and 1831," but the collations are not complete.

19. *The Letters of Mary Wollstonecraft Shelley,* 2:129, where the letter is conjecturally dated [?February–10 March 1831] and where the angle brackets indicate a restored deletion. I have redated this letter because it seems to refer to the already published introduction of *1831* and to anticipate a resetting of the introduction ("if it goes to press again") in another "real" edition rather than the stereotyped reissue of *1831* in 1832. For more on this, see *1816–17 Robinson,* 1:cv.

20. Mary Shelley read *Vindication* in December 1816. I presented papers on the relations between *Frankenstein* and *Vindication* at the MLA Convention in December 1996 and at the Calgary Institute for the Humanities in August 1997. The papers from the meeting at the Calgary Institute on "Mary Wollstonecraft and Mary Shelley: Writing Lives" are scheduled for publication.

21. Mary Shelley, *Frankenstein or The Modern Prometheus,* ed. Maurice Hindle (London: Penguin, 1992).

Editing
Thackeray
A History

🦋 🦋 🦋

Peter

Shillingsburg

When I entered the profession as "a trained scholarly editor," I thought I knew what was the proper, rational, most useful way to produce scholarly editions. Surely a high standard of accuracy and what A. E. Housman called the "application of thought to textual criticism" would lead logically and inevitably to the principles of the Thackeray edition as I wrote them in 1972. Twenty-five years and two major paradigm shifts in editorial theory and practice later, I feel equally certain of two things: that the next paradigm shift in editorial practice is already under way and that each shift generates enthusiasts who do not understand their business very well and who do not realize that they do not. Enthusiasm is a necessary element for any young editor, for without it the young will not commit themselves irrevocably, or perhaps the word is irretrievably, to major editorial projects. But enthusiasm tends to brush past a multitude of uncomfortable encounters. So at this stage of my career I am convinced that it takes about twenty-five years of experience to make a sound editor.

🦋 This collection of essays on editing emphasizes currency. My one current insight is that shifting fashions in editorial practice are accomplished by an indeterminate proportion of valuable new insights and shoddy, half-baked, unfair characterizations of old insights and editorial practices. I'm guilty too. Success for new insights comes at the expense of old; and the quickest way to make room for the new is to exaggerate the weaknesses of the old—particularly as practiced by enthusiastic but inept amateurs who mistake the tools of editorial practice for rules to be followed. And it is amazing how many editors approach editing the way I approached learning to use a new microwave oven—impatient of details.

The history of the Thackeray edition project is, to a large extent, the discovery that the goals of editing as I had been taught them in the 1960s while working on the Centennial Edition of the Writings of William Gilmore Simms and reading the works of R. B. McKerrow, W. W. Greg, Fredson Bowers, Bruce Harkness, and G. Thomas Tanselle would not do without qualifications and revisions when applied to the works of William Makepeace Thackeray.

In a grant request for the edition, I wrote:

> The Thackeray edition project is the first full-scale edition of Thackeray's works undertaken in over sixty years and the only one ever to be based on an examination of all relevant editions, manuscripts, proofs, and ancillary historical materials. In the last hundred years there have been over a dozen "collected editions" (one of which is in print). But none of these editions is the product of thorough scholarly research nor do any meet the editing standards in the profession today. The multiplicity of printed texts of Thackeray's works is a tribute to their worth and endurance, but the editions themselves are a disgrace to modern literary scholarship.[1]

There's a good deal of truth in all that, but the idea of "meeting the editing standards in the profession today" will itself date pretty rapidly; it won't be long before the Garland Thackeray editions become a disgrace to modern literary scholarship. This, by the way, is not a nostalgic lament. The point is not the lamentable one that our work dates. Rather, because the "standards of today" are different and perhaps currently more exciting than those of yesteryear, the point is that, to be fair, what matters is the fit between the concepts about textual conditions of works of art and the accomplishments of the editorial work produced. What does not count, then or now, is how new or current the theory or practice is. A scholarly edition can meet or fail to meet the standards of any day. If, in a later age, "today's" standards seem inadequate—and there will always come a day when they will seem inadequate—nevertheless, editions that met them once will always meet them.

It is worth observing, I think, that editors have always and probably will always "put" texts in certain lights. There are no objective editions, none that do not ask readers to take the text in a certain way, none in which the editor has managed to avoid all subjective judgment. If the enthusiasm Greg and Bowers felt in the 1950s and 1960s is, to us, misplaced—if our own enthusiasm will in a few years seem quaint to editors in a new day—then the point of enthusiasm is to galvanize action for and to celebrate something new and different, not something right and objective and enduring. If in a few years our objectivity will appear subjective, then it is subjective now.

Editors have always professed two fundamental goals: to be accurate and to be useful. Occasionally they have even claimed their work to be definitive, texts that will never have to be done over; yet, the more objective we try to be, the more dated we end up looking. An old controversy in editorial circles (which will not end with this essay) concerns the extent to which an editor should be an interventionist. If no intervention were necessary, there would be no need for an editor; it follows that editing is interventionist. But which intrusions are necessary, which only desirable or merely allowable? In short, how can the editor be both accurate and useful? Like the pans on a balance scale, as one goes up the other goes down. Unlike the scale, for both pans of which gravity supplies an impartial objective attraction, the concept of balance between accuracy and usefulness changes as our profession develops new notions of what a text is, or how it works, or how it should work.[2]

Another remark in an early grant application for the Thackeray project reads:

> The true significance of this new edition of Thackeray's works lies in its fundamental recognition of the nature of literary art: that works of literary art are seldom if ever rigid, completed perfections but instead are often fluid, changing and indeterminate. The editorial principles of this edition reject the notion of establishing the standard text and provide instead a reading text and guides to each work's development and its alternate authoritative forms.

It is the remark made by an enthusiast. What can be the meaning of the phrases "true significance" and "fundamental recognition" other than to pave the way for a new insight about texts and editing that renders older notions of textual stability nonsense? A view of the shifting fashions of editing here will help establish the "certain light" in which the Thackeray edition tries to "put texts."

I was trained on Greg, Bowers, and Tanselle in the production of definitive editions. The scholarly editor strove to produce a product that would never have to be done again: a product representing the author's final intentions. I will not here try to defend this position or explain its subtleties and complexities or demonstrate the ways in which it was self-conscious about its critical biases. I would only say that recent Bowers bashing has largely failed to understand this paradigm or to judge it by its own notions of the nature of works of art. In particular, Greg's rationale of copy-text has been rendered rigid and ridiculous by critics and editors whose notions of the nature of works of art are quite different from Greg's.[3] The point here is that those notions emphasized, as the goal of editing, production of a single product representing final authorial intentions.

By the 1985 meeting of the Society for Textual Scholarship (STS), a remarkable shift in emphasis and in editorial practice was palpably in motion. Having recently completed the first version of *Scholarly Editing in the Computer Age,*[4] I gave a summary address at the end of the STS convention noting particularly the ways in which the pursuit of single, final texts was giving way to documentation of the process of intentions. Although Jerome McGann's *A Critique of Modern Textual Criticism* was already out,[5] and though McGann gave an interesting explanation of how the textual condition prevented him from summarizing the conference, his views of textuality are best understood as part of a third shift in editorial fashions, not as endemic to the second, the replacement of the single text *product* by the multitexted *process*. The reason for this is important to bear in mind. Process can be seen as the developing changes of intentions which leave a trail of documentary evidence. The first major shift in editorial attention was from "final authorial intention" to "multiple authorial intention." It resulted from the accumulated weight of discontent with the goal of single end-products experienced by editors of modern texts for which a richness of evidence was still extant and whose investigations more and more revealed that authors had changing, developing intentions and sometimes more than one distinct audience. Multiple authorial intentions provided the impetus for the change in emphasis from product to process.

The third shift has yet to be properly named. Its source is quite different from the second. Its primary impetus comes from a recognition of the social implications of production processes. Its emphasis is not on creative processes but on the meaning of production as a social element. McGann is the prime engineer of this movement. It replaces the critical examination of textual evidence to ferret out authorial intentions (with emphasis on their plurality) with the "critical" sequencing of documents in such a way that each new document is seen as a new version of the work. The shift is not always accomplished cleanly. For example, Jack Stillinger distinguished in theory between multiple versions and sequence of documents, but in practice he invariably equates the two. He writes, "I have arbitrarily taken substantive difference—that is, difference in wording—as the principal rule for distinguishing one version from another."[6] But his listing of versions of Coleridge's "Frost at Midnight" notes that version 5 is "substantively identical" to version 3 (55), version 9 is "substantively identical" to version 7, and version 10 is "substantively the same" as version 9 (56). In effect, each production constitutes a new version because the meaning of the edition is defined to include the ways in which it indexes the economics of the marketing and reception of literary works of art.

I believe this third editorial fashion is attractive for three basic reasons: first, it requires no agonizing over indifferent variants (those for which the evidence for intention are equally divided between two or more forms); second, it avoids the charge that emendations made in the text represent nothing more than editorial preference; and third, its ideals can be adequately and elegantly presented in hypertext, multimedia computer forms. The difference between the first and third of these editorial fashions is tremendous: in the first, the editor takes all the responsibility to produce the text the author wanted his public to have; in the third, the editor abjures all responsibilities except that of collecting the evidence and giving a guided tour.

This is not the place to carry out an analysis of these three editorial fashions, though such an analysis has yet to be carried out adequately or persuasively. Suffice it to say that the Thackeray edition, though heavily influenced in its inception by the Greg/Bowers school of single-text editing, in practice tried to adopt the implications of multiple texts. Process, not product, was the word that drove the Thackeray project.[7] And process did not mean the sequence of drafts, manuscripts, proofs, and printed texts; it meant actions taken by specific persons. There was the authorial process that began with conceptions and determination to produce a work, developed through drafts and revisions to one or more stages of completion—in a manuscript, typescript, or publication, which could also contain the work of "helpers" and, therefore, be of "mixed authority." There was the process of production that began with typists or compositors or editorial assistants or typesetters and culminated in a printed or reprinted book—something that can be held in the hand, but which represents the work of many people. And both the authoring and producing processes involved a process that continues with every reader: the process of reading and interpreting signs on the page, making sense of them or making mistakes about them; for, whether it was the author, the compositor, or the reader, no one has had access to the meaning intended by the signmakers save by the indeterminate process of constructing meaning for the signs on the page.

Given this notion of process(es) and given a desire to focus attention on the author's work, the Thackeray edition was edited to demonstrate authorial processes and fulfill authorial intentions for the text. I wince every time I say that. These are formulaic phrases that show up frequently in the pamphlets and editions of the Center for Editions of American Authors (CEAA) and in the writings of Bowers and Tanselle: the goals of the editor are to show what the author did and to produce the text the author wanted. The wince comes from a realization that what the author wanted and what the author did are occasionally demonstrably different things, but more frequently are only probably different things. So there are always fudge phrases, designed to obscure the contradiction in goals thus expressed.

In a grant request, I wrote:

The Thackeray edition provides for the first time:

1. Texts edited according to scholarly standards, i.e. based on thorough investigations of textual history and providing readily usable records of the history of composition, revision and publication.

2. A one-stop reference source for studies of the development of Thackeray's art: We provide the texts, the history of textual variation, and historical accounts of composition, printing, and distribution.

3. A complete collection of Thackeray's works including as yet uncol-
lected material and previously unpublished pieces.

4. Texts combining Thackeray's illustrations with his written words.
No edition has ever been thorough or methodical in the treatment of illustrations. Most editions, in fact, are unillustrated.

It still sounds good to me, but it does not address explicitly the fact that what
the author did and what the author wanted are not always the same thing.

And that brings up another source of controversy in editorial circles. Editorial practice, especially since the publication of Greg's "Rationale of Copy-
Text" in 1950, has depended heavily on notions of "usual practice." Because
crucial evidence is frequently no longer extant, editors have to act without
it. Obviously, they wish to act as if the missing evidence had certain predict-
able characteristics. So it is fundamental to know whether authors usually
submit manuscripts with punctuation, spelling, and capitalization fully indicated; whether compositors are in the habit of changing these matters
or reproducing them accurately; whether authors normally seek help from
the publishing staffs to improve the text of their works; whether publishing
staffs habitually help authors reach the artistic potential of their works or
whether they habitually try to force authors to produce works that fit pre-
conceived patterns. The list of questions goes on and on, and none can be
answered definitively. If they could, there would be no controversy. Every
case is a specific case and can deviate from the norm—if we can even know
what that norm is. Under the influence of Greg's thinking and the experience
of many editors in CEAA projects, it has been thought that normal practice
in the production process was for compositors to "house-style" or otherwise
"improve" accidentals. In the case of authors for whom specific evidence no
longer exists, this assumption is of crucial importance in driving editors to
select copy-texts more likely to preserve authorial practice than to fulfill
compositorial practice.

In editorial theory's current paradigm shift, publishers are being rehabili-
tated as the facilitators of art. It has taken more than a few instances of benign actions by publishers to accomplish this feat, for the instances have
been available to editors for a long time. It has taken a fundamental shift in
notions of the proprietorship of art. The idea that the author was the sole

owner and authority for the work—an idea supported both by Romantic notions of genius and by the developing changes in copyright law and concepts of intellectual property—has given way in some circles to social and materialist ideas in which the author is one of several authorities.[8] To say the idea of authorial preeminence is wrong and a social/materialist view of shared authority is right is to indulge in progressive enthusiasm. Each view has its reasons for appealing to us as useful. By the newest view, an editor without specific evidence on issues requiring a decision, such as the most desirable form of accidentals, is expected to assume that the norm is for publishers' actions to have been benign or necessary. It follows that, in the absence of documentary evidence to the contrary, an editor should choose a printed edition for copy-text, not a manuscript, a mere "way station" toward publication, as Donald Reiman calls it.[9] But if I winced at the juxtaposition of "what the author did" and "what the author wanted," imagine the reaction to the juxtaposition of "what the publisher did" and "what the author wanted." Correcting one apparent oversimplification by substituting another one is a curious sort of progress.

🖘 The Thackeray edition project began as a single-volume edition of *Pendennis* (1848–50) offered to several publishers and finally solicited by Joseph Katz in 1974 to be part of a complete works of Thackeray published by Faust, Inc.[10] On the strength of a contract with Faust, the first funding requests were made to the Mississippi State Research Office in 1974 and to the National Endowment for the Humanities (NEH) in 1975. Faust ceased to exist early in 1978, but work continued until an agreement was struck later in the year with Dawson Publishers in England. Dawson withdrew from the project over a disagreement with the University of Tennessee Press, which had signed on as copublisher in 1979. *Pendennis* was finished and approved by the Modern Language Association's Committee for Scholarly Editions (CSE) in that year, but Tennessee Press postponed publication till a "computerized volume" was ready. *Yellowplush [1837–38] and Gahagan [1838–39]* was approved by CSE in 1982, but it too was "hand made" and Tennessee Press postponed it as well. *Henry Esmond* was delayed by disagreements on editorial policy between the volume editor and the general editor. *Vanity Fair* (1847–48), completed in 1983, was delayed through disagreements between the general editor and the CSE. Tennessee Press withdrew in 1984, ostensibly because their list seemed after all inappropriate for an edition of an English writer. Garland Publishing issued contracts for the first two volumes in 1987 and by 1991 published four volumes.[11] But Garland, whose enthusiasm waned with small sales (as did mine), seemed only too happy to cede all its interests in the edition to the University of Michigan Press, which adopted the Thackeray project in 1994.

By 1977, when I was awarded my first NEH grant, I had had training on a CEAA approved edition, edited *Pendennis,* examined numerous other editions; and I had written an article about textual problems of editing Thackeray's works, an in-house guide to editorial principles, and a general textual introduction.[12] Already, however, I knew that Thackeray's texts involved situations that made the then-standard editorial treatment an uncomfortable one for me. It began with the dawning realization that editions driven by the pursuit of "authorial intentions" had editorial apparatuses designed to show what *editors* did rather than what *authors* did. They did so probably because their format and purpose derived from an editorial tradition concerned with works for which little authorial material was extant or perhaps in reaction against an earlier tradition for which the editorial methods by and large went without saying. I determined, in any case, to remodel the apparatuses to show primarily what Thackeray did and only incidentally to show what the editor had done. To explain the changes, I wrote a paper called "Laying the Cards on the Table: or the Textual Apparatus as Sacred Cow."[13]

Furthermore, I determined to do as little editing as possible beyond restoring what Thackeray had done. Having chosen the earliest extant form as copy-text, I embraced every excuse to leave a passage unchanged. If Thackeray's text was truly ambiguous, I determined to preserve the ambiguity, though traditionally editors tended to rescue their authors from ambiguities. I thought editors exceeded the limits of their responsibilities when they resolved a truly ambiguous text. With Thackeray, there is often no way to know for sure whether he intended to be ambiguous, whether he was careless, or whether he was confident that an editor or compositor would understand and set straight what he had intended—but failed—to write. To explain the inappropriateness of most editorial disambiguation, I wrote a paper called "The Ethics of Scholarly Editing."[14]

Choosing not to impose my will on ambiguous passages entailed opposition for the edition. The first CSE inspector of *Vanity Fair* panned the volume because it was inconsistently edited, preserving authorial forms only
for those parts of the work that still existed in manuscript while adopting
first-edition forms where no manuscript was extant. The inspector proposed
abandoning manuscript forms entirely, preferring consistency throughout
over the preservation of authorial forms incompletely.[15] After much unsatisfactory discussion, the CSE denied its approval to the volume. It is difficult
for me to explain why they did so without sounding partisan. The inspector
clearly disapproved of what I was doing. I was and remain convinced that
he was wrong, that he was imposing a narrow-minded and (I thought) ex-
ploded view of editing, and that he largely misunderstood both the task of
inspection and the principles he thought he was judging. In defense of my
methods I wrote *Scholarly Editing in the Computer Age,* growing in part from
the variety of concerns that occupied me in producing the edition over the
preceding ten years, partly from reaction to McGann's *A Critique of Modern
Textual Criticism,* and partly from my experiences as coordinator, then member, then chairman of the CSE (1976–84), and finally as its rejectee.

In the wake of CSE rejection, I reevaluated my editing of *Vanity Fair,* im-
proved it in ways not suggested by the inspector, altered the apparatus to
conform more to the design of the apparatus of *Henry Esmond,* compromised
on one cherished but unimportant matter with the CSE inspector, and stood
my ground on all other matters. A new inspector was more willing to see the
book in the light I chose to put it, and the CSE awarded approval in 1986.
Esmond was approved in 1987. In his review of the two editions, John Sutherland wrote: "This *Henry Esmond,* with its fluid unencumbered lines, will
be a new and exhilarating experience even for those who know the novel
by heart."[16]

🐾 A problem developed from attempts to adjudicate between authorial
practice and intention for the published works. The manuscript represents,
undoubtedly, what the author did but not clearly what he intended to have
published; the first edition represents, undoubtedly, what the publisher did
but not clearly what the author wanted either. Each document failed to fulfill
the goals of my new edition: to present both what the author did and what

he wanted. Rejecting the use of blanket rules that would adopt either the manuscript or the first edition forms out of hand, it became very difficult and time-consuming to determine what should and what should not be done; every variant, even the most trivial punctuation mark, between manuscript and first edition, became a separate editorial decision to emend or not to emend. There were guidelines, but blanket rules would have been easier. To explain or explore the problems, I wrote three papers: "Authorial Intention(s) and Evidence: Defining the Possible," "The Editorial Problem of Indifferent Variants," and "W. M. Thackeray's Rhetorical Style: Unrecorded Authorial Intentions for Punctuation."[17]

Meanwhile, having finished editing *Pendennis* and *Gahagan and Yellowplush* "by hand," the project developed a comprehensive computer-assisted editorial process that was used with *Esmond* and *Vanity Fair*.[18] But major problems developed in editing the latter two. The computer had made easy the manipulation of enormous amounts of textual data, our editorial principles had made it necessary to regard each variant on its own merits rather than as a member of a class, and *Esmond* and *Vanity Fair* were the first two books to have extensive extant manuscript materials to work from. These factors combined to delay the work: there was more work and it was revised easily enough to make revision tempting.

✿ Under the NEH grants in the 1970s, the project developed in 1976 a computer system called CASE (Computer Assisted Scholarly Editing), a series of programs designed to assist editing from initial investigation of source texts, both printed and manuscript, through collation, emendation, development of apparatuses and data banks, to typesetting final texts and apparatuses. The programs were tested, refined, and used to produce the editions of *Henry Esmond* and *Vanity Fair*, as well as to do the research for *The Newcomes* (1853–55), *Denis Duval* (1864), and *The Four Georges* (1860). In addition CASE was used by Miriam Shillingsburg to produce an edition of Washington Irving's *The Conquest of Granada* in the Twayne Irving edition.

In 1984, the NEH sponsored a computer workshop in CASE programs at Mississippi State University. Each participant took away a copy of the programs to be adapted to his home institution's computers. Adapted versions of CASE are employed in the production of the Strouse Carlyle edition and the

Cambridge Conrad Edition. In addition to continued use by the Thackeray project, CASE programs have been adapted for use on editions of Thomas Hardy, D. H. Lawrence, W. B. Yeats, and the Australian Colonial Texts Series. The programs have been used on UNIVAC, IBM, VAX, PRIME, and DEC mainframes and are currently available for use on PCs and Macintosh computers.

CASE was designed from the beginning to generate computer files of text and apparatus suitable as input to a computer-driven photocomposer to produce camera-ready copy. Proofreading normally done on printers' proofs begins at the very first stages of research. Collation and checking of variants files contribute to the purification of the original transcriptions in ways unavailable to manual research. It was an imperative of the process that the final printed text benefit from this purification process by having the computer-generated texts drive the typesetting equipment. It was not originally the plan actually to produce camera-ready copy ourselves or to pay for that part of the book production. But under the conditions of Garland Publishers' contracts, the need arose to prepare camera-ready copy in-house.

Typesetting is done with Donald Knuth's TEX software (the PC-TEX version). Font and special page-formatting specifications become part of the text during the process of editing, while book-design specifications are added later. Page proofs on laser-printer output are produced in the Thackeray edition project office for proofreading and updating of computer files. Once the books are completed and corrected in laser-print form, the .dvi (device independent files) are sent to a commercial composing house to be run through typesetting machines of high resolution to produce high-quality (1200 dpi) camera-ready copy.

❦ Meditating on the history of the Thackeray edition, I wonder why the second-oldest profession advances polemically. Why is there no training program with apprenticeships devoted to the study of editorial theory and practice? Instead there are scattered schools advocating one or another way of editing as the currently most exciting or up-to-date methods. Of course, professionals in any field are constantly learning new things, which they pass on to their protégés. But it seems to me that in the field of scholarly editing, the disputes among current editors, the rejections of outdated editorial methodologies, and the rancorous reviews of other editions proceed too frequently from ignorance of the enabling insights of the opposition.

The rhetoric of editorial dispute seems too frequently to suggest that our choices are between right and wrong ways to edit. The options are more diverse than that. There are, I am firmly convinced, wrong ways to edit. It is wrong to edit without considering all the relevant textual and contextual information. It is wrong to edit carelessly, making mistakes both in and about texts. It is wrong to edit without indicating what has been done to produce the newly edited text. It is wrong to explain that one has edited in one way, while in fact editing in another. And it is wrong to claim that one has edited the text in the only responsible way available.

But the goals of editing are determined by what readers wish to know about texts and by what they want to be able to do with them. A reader who wishes to know what the author wrote will not be well served by an edition edited to show the work in the heavily edited form the early readers of the work encountered in fact. An archive of documents will not help the reader who wishes to see the author's final intentions if the documents are of mixed authority. Different readers need different editions. Perhaps in the electronic scholarly edition we have a medium with the dexterity, capacity, flexibility, and agility to incorporate multiple editorial intentions and readerly intentions as well as those of the author and producers of books.

Notes

1. The gory details up to 1973 are given in Peter Shillingsburg, "Thackeray Texts: A Guide to Inexpensive Editions," *Costerus* 2 (1974): 287–313. Since then a number of reprints, some accompanied by excellent notes, have appeared without improvement to the texts. The Norton Critical Edition of *Vanity Fair* (1994) is based on the scholarly edition (New York: Garland, 1989).

2. Like most metaphors, this one is unfortunately inaccurate itself, for usefulness is not increased by inaccuracies. But no one can argue that editorial changes improve the accuracy of a reproduction; and no one can argue that a totally accurate reproduction has been "edited" to be more useful than its source.

3. See W. W. Greg, "The Rationale of Copy-Text," *Studies in Bibliography* 3 (1950–51): 19–36.

4. Peter Shillingsburg, *Scholarly Editing in the Computer Age* (Occasional Paper no. 3, University College, Australian Defence Force Academy, 1984; rev. ed., Athens: University of Georgia Press, 1986; rev. ed., Ann Arbor: University of Michigan Press, 1996).

5. See Jerome J. McGann, *A Critique of Modern Textual Criticism* (1983; reprint, Charlottesville: University Press of Virginia, 1992).

6. Jack Stillinger, *Coleridge and Textual Instability* (New York: Oxford University Press, 1994), vii.

7. The greatest single evidence of that influence is the clear reading text and placement of all apparatus at the back of the Garland volumes. With the shift in publishers to the University of Michigan Press, the edition will provide all evidence of authorial revision at the foot of the page. The Norton Critical Edition of *Vanity Fair* also provides textual and explanatory annotation in footnotes. To me, this change signals an important emphasis growing from the insights of multiple intentions: that the products of editorial work are editions of the work, not the work itself.

8. See particularly McGann, *Critique;* Stillinger, *Coleridge,* 118–40; and Donald Reiman, *The Study of Modern Manuscripts: Public, Confidential, and Private* (Baltimore: Johns Hopkins University Press, 1993), 117.

9. Reiman, *Study,* 93.

10. Currently the editorial board consists of Professors Edgar F. Harden and John Sutherland. Former board members included Gordon N. Ray, Percy G. Adams, and Miriam Shillingsburg, who oversaw the initial development of the Computer Assisted Scholarly Editing (CASE) computer programs. Contributors to the edition include Robert Colby, Nicholas Pickwoad, Selma Muresianu, and Rowland McMaster.

11. *Vanity Fair* and *Henry Esmond* in 1989, and *Pendennis* and a collection of short novels in 1991. Edgar Harden edited *Henry Esmond.*

12. Peter Shillingsburg, "The Text of Thackeray's *Pendennis*" (Ph.D. diss., University of South Carolina, 1970); Shillingsburg, "Problems in Editing Thackeray," in *Editing Nineteenth-Century Fiction,* ed. Jane Millgate (New York: Garland, 1978), 41–59. The introduction appears in William Makepeace Thackeray, *The History of Pendennis,* ed. Peter L. Shillingsburg (New York: Garland, 1991), 404–13.

13. Presented at the annual meeting of the South Central Modern Language Association, 1976.

14. Presented to the Society for Textual Scholarship, 1987.

15. The reasons given indicated that the inspector's rationale, like that of turn-of-the-century editors, favored selection of the last text published in the author's lifetime as copy-text in order to insure that his last revisions would be incorporated but ignored completely the question of accidentals. It was not, as with the new propo-

nents of social materialism, a case of believing that production processes take precedence over authorial processes, especially in formal and materialist senses.

16. John Sutherland, "Interfering or Collaborating?" *Times Literary Supplement,* 15–21 June 1990, 652.

17. Presented respectively at the annual meetings of the South Central Modern Language Association (1980); the South Atlantic Modern Language Association (1981; rev. as Peter Shillingsburg, "Key Issues in Editorial Theory," *Analytical and Enumerative Bibliography* 6 [1982]: 3–16); and the South Central Modern Language Association (1983).

18. Susan Follet, initially under the direction of Miriam Shillingsburg, and following the lead of Peggy Gilbert, wrote the prototype for the CASE collation program. Subsequently, with NEH support, Russell Kegley rewrote the program and added eight other programs to assist editorial work.

Conrad in
Print and
on Disk

🪶 🪶 🪶

S. W. Reid

An Oxford doctorate in hand, a scholar has just
taken her first teaching position in a South American
country, where amidst all sorts of conflicting demands she is trying to complete a book on Joseph
Conrad's style. Her chief focus is the inverted word
order sometimes found in the novels and stories, especially that related to the modification of nouns
by adjectives, relative clauses, and prepositional and
participial phrases, which she associates with the
"pragmatic" word order of Conrad's native Polish.
She has compared such usage in four chapters of one
novel with that in four chapters of its immediate predecessor, with which it shares setting, characters,
and subject. She has found marked differences between the two novels, and by checking these results
against a control sample from other works by Conrad
and by other authors, she has identified in the earlier
novel usages that are abnormal for Conrad, though
normal for native speakers. To explain these she has
seized on a remark made by a secondhand witness
to the effect that two of Conrad's friends helped
straighten out his English in this novel during a fort-
night's visit he made to their home in the Midlands
while still writing the manuscript. Her hypothesis is
that these friends made changes in the manuscript
that explain the atypical usage. When, at the urging
of her prospective publisher, she has asked strangers
with access to the manuscript to verify this and has
been told there are no such changes on the face of
the document, she feels forced to postulate a lost
ur-manuscript containing the friends' alterations. So
sure is she of her basic findings that she persists in
seeking such a documentary explanation when also
told that no such earlier manuscript is likely to have
existed for the particular chapters she has examined

and that, anyway, they had already been typed by the time of Conrad's visit—and, furthermore, that the surviving typescript is equally free of inscriptions other than Conrad's.

Unable to examine the documents herself, which are in two North American libraries thousands of miles apart, this scholar feels stymied by their inaccessibility and her consequent inability to get a handle on the details of the novel's composition process. But this feeling pales by comparison with the dismay that follows, when those she has consulted tell her that the edition of the novel she has been using itself contains stylistic alterations made by the proofreaders of Conrad's monumental 1921 collected editions. She finds that before she can complete her book, she needs not only a more reliable edition than the paperback fetched from an Oxford bookseller's shelf, but also some sort of access to the texts of the manuscript and the typescript and an accurate and disinterested account (if such a thing is possible) of the inscriptions in those documents and their place in the history of Conrad's writing of the novel.

Anecdotes have achieved a respected status as evidence in these latter days, but in the spirit of my author I offer this one because it raises some interesting questions about editions of fiction and about the kinds of needs scholars and readers may have for them in the last few years of this century and the first few of the next. My story is, after all, only partly true. A lot of it amounts to what we are pleased to call fact, but some of it I made up, really. Conrad forged a career on the blurred borderline between fiction and history. Nowhere, perhaps, is this more evident than in his "Author's Note" to *The Secret Agent* (1907), a celebrated example of that mixture of veiled revelation, instinctive deception, and poetic truth that characterizes most of the autobiographical prefaces published in the 1921 collected editions of his works. And perhaps no more convenient illustration of the textual muddle of the collected editions as a whole, and hence of the uncertain state of Conradian texts generally,[1] can be found than this preface.

We have three collected-edition texts of this preface, one in Doubleday's 1921 American Sun-Dial Edition (reprinted in 1923 in Dent's Uniform Edition and many times in Britain since then); a second in Heinemann's 1921 English edition (not reprinted); and a third in Doubleday's 1923 Concord Edition, also reprinted as the Kent, Canterbury, Memorial, and other so-called editions in America. In addition to these three texts, a typescript containing Conrad's revisions survives, as do two other 1921 forms that are of little interest for present purposes.[2] Conrad began writing the preface in late February 1920 and revised the typescript text in early March, and from this was made a second typescript (now lost) that he also revised. This typescript then went to America, where it provided copy for the Doubleday typesetting found in the Sun-Dial printing. Two sets of proof were returned to Conrad's agent, J. B. Pinker, who held one for Heinemann and sent the other to Conrad, who made revisions before returning his set to Doubleday in mid-1920. In late 1920 Pinker sent the unaltered proofs to Heinemann for use in typesetting their edition. In 1923 Doubleday imperfectly altered their text by reference to the Heinemann edition before printing their Concord.

Conrad's most interesting revisions occurred in the central paragraphs of the essay, which concern the role played by Sir Robert Anderson's *Sidelights on the Home Rule Movement* (1906) in stimulating his imagination. Here he tells how "a few words uttered by a friend [probably Ford Madox Ford] in a casual conversation about anarchists" and "the already old story of the attempt to blow up the Greenwich Observatory" came together "about a week later" with "a little passage of about seven lines" in a book containing "the rather summary recollections of an Assistant Commissioner of Police" that precipitated "a mental change" in Conrad comparable to "the process of crystallisation in a test tube containing some colourless solution."[3] Though undoubtedly complex, Conrad's motives for his changes in these paragraphs were at least partly traceable to a lurking consciousness that his account of the three-day (or seven- or ten-day) process was a "stretcher."[4] Among the alterations is one of phrasing, where he changed "All this took about three days" to "It was a matter of three days" (page 7, line 6), making the statement regarding the brief creative "process of crystallisation" (6.21) less sweeping and the claim less disingenuous. In the same vein he deleted "absolutely" from his remark regarding the book's failure to make a lasting impression on him (6.4). This alteration carried on revision of a sentence begun earlier: The original typewritten text of the typescript had said that he had "by now forgotten it absolutely," and Conrad had first qualified this statement about Anderson's book by interlining "the bulk of its contents" over the "it." The deletion of "absolutely" in the Doubleday proofs, which softened the statement still further, reveals Conrad's continuing concern with qualifying an account that was less than entirely candid.

These are but two of numerous revisions carried out by Conrad first in the typescript and then in the Sun-Dial proofs and exhibit his considerable care with the wording and even punctuation of this "Author's Note." In a preface occupying only six pages in the Cambridge Edition, Conrad made a dozen revisions on the Doubleday proofs alone—not only substitutions but also additions and deletions—that are present in the American Sun-Dial edition but not in the Heinemann English edition. In addition to making the two alterations just cited, Conrad cut the vague but nonetheless honorific assertion that Anderson had been appointed Assistant Commissioner "on account of his special experience" (6.2) in these central paragraphs, and he made other changes in the interest of precision or style (if not self-defense). Referring to his "propensity" to justify his actions and explain his motives, Conrad had originally written that "It may be called an amiable weakness and dangerous only so far that it exposes one to the risk of becoming a bore"; this he made more precise by substituting "That kind of weakness is dangerous" for the first clause (3.36). There were two slighter substitutions: "outrage" replaced the typescript's "thing" in the statements that "perverse unreason has its own logical processes. But that outrage [the Greenwich incident] could not be laid hold of mentally in any sort of way" (5.11–12); later, "might" became "may" in the clause "some reader may have recognised" (8.19). When introducing the incident involving Ford's remark with the words "while I was yet standing still as it were and certainly not thinking of going out of my way to look for anything ugly, the subject of the Secret Agent . . . came to me," Conrad added "ugly" (4.37), and he inserted "anarchist" before "outrage" in his account of Anderson's "short dialogue held in the Lobby of the House of Commons after some unexpected anarchist outrage, with the Home Secretary" (6.9–10). These additions to produce greater precision through qualification were matched by a deletion of "a man" that avoided a redundancy (5.33). Three substitutions were relatively straightforward corrections of other obvious faults. One, the alteration of "Secretary of State" to "Home Secretary" (6.10) in the passage just quoted, was perhaps a desirable though technically unnecessary change to remove an apparent inconsistency (compare "Home Secretary" a few lines later at 6.15). Another,

Doubleday's "seemed" for "seems" (8.4), corrected an inconsistency of tense which is preserved in the Heinemann edition despite its almost obsessive concern with such matters. The third eliminated a grammatical error, changing the typescript's "Its" to "It's," though characteristically the Heinemann edition has the more formal "It is" (4.4).

With the exception of this last compound variant, these changes of Conrad's were simply omitted in the Heinemann edition, but the Heinemann also contains its own wholly unique readings. The six variants in wording that first appeared in this edition are apparently editorial. Besides the substitution of "It is" at the beginning of the essay, there was similar editorial cleaning-up toward the end, so that Conrad's "arms-length" became "arm's length" (7.20) and his non-idiomatic "for a caricatural presentation" appeared without the article (7.37–38). A fourth alteration—where the typescript's "bore; for the" became "bore. The" (3.36)—had less to do with logic than neatness. The curious substitution of "hopeless" for "sombre" (7.3) produced an inferior if not nonsensical reading that canceled the "sombre" which Conrad had added quite deliberately in the typescript. Lastly, there was Heinemann's change of "seven" to "ten" (6.7) where Conrad talks about having been "arrested by a little passage of about seven lines" of Anderson's, an alteration that is very hard to account for.

What is even more curious, however, is the strange fate that befell this arbitrary Heinemann reading and others. By the middle of 1921, the Doubleday and Heinemann texts of the "Author's Note" to *The Secret Agent* had been published, the former containing not only undetected printer's errors but Conrad's latest revisions, the latter preserving most of the Doubleday errors but lacking those revisions and adding six more changes in wording. That would have been the ambiguous situation for readers thenceforth, had bad enough been left alone. But it was not. In the "Author's Note," as in the novel, Doubleday's second "edition," the Concord Edition of 1923, deliberately adopted variant readings from the Heinemann, apparently in accord not only with Doubleday's but with Conrad's wishes.[5] The conflation of texts, unfortunately, proved to be less straightforward and the textual situation less satisfactory than either Conrad or Doubleday hoped.

As it turned out, only a few of the Heinemann's variant wordings were actually incorporated in the Concord text—less than one-fourth of the total. These included three of the Heinemann editorial alterations just mentioned: the change of syntax, the mysterious "ten" for "seven," and the precisionist "arm's length" (3.36, 6.7, 7.20). But the more consequential "hopeless" for "sombre" (7.3) and the other two unique Heinemann readings—"It is" (4.4) and "caricatural presentation" (7.37–38)—escaped notice. Moreover, in the process of gleaning these few Heinemann alterations, the Concord also adopted several Heinemann readings which had derived indirectly, through the unaltered Doubleday proofs, from the typescript but which had been superseded by Conrad's revisions in his own set of proofs. Among these were two of the longer rejected passages: the Concord (and consequently all subsequent American Doubleday "editions") reverted to the earlier "It may be called an amiable weakness and dangerous" (3.35) and to "All this took about three days" (7.6), despite Conrad's later substitution of "It was a matter of three days" as part of his attempt to soften his disingenuous statements. This is not to mention the restoration of Heinemann's redundant "a man" (5.33), nor the Concord's incorporation of what looks like at least one bit of Heinemann's styling.

Conrad's attempt during the last decade of his career to have the texts of his works published in a uniform edition that would fix and preserve them for posterity proved to be a vain hope. In this preface, as elsewhere, the technology of the printing process and the human agents directly involved in the processes of transmission complicated matters beyond his control and often his knowledge. Although this preface may not be entirely typical of the collected-edition texts—the number of variants is smaller and their significance less than in the novel it introduces or in other novels—it represents the kind of textual muddle that scholars and readers have had to tolerate. The mixed text of the 1923 Concord and subsequent Doubleday impressions—with their inadvertent reversals of Conrad's revisions—became the standard one in America for the next seventy years. But because Dent used unaltered Doubleday plates for their 1923 "Uniform" and subsequent printings, readers of the British issues have had a text that is in one sense closer to what some would call Conrad's "final intentions,"[6] though in another sense is further removed from them. The Dent impressions contain Conrad's own latest revisions, those followed by Doubleday in 1921 for the Sun-Dial issue, yet they are more at variance with the English Heinemann text that

Conrad seems to have approved in his 1923 letter to Doubleday than are the later American printings. In a preface concerned in part with justifying "the ironic method"[7] of the novel, this is itself something of an irony.

Should the scholar of my opening anecdote, or even the general reader, have to put up with this situation? A marketplace that can bear a seemingly endless stream of paperback editions prepared by responsible scholars, but largely limited by the textual tradition of the collected-book editions, ought to be able to accommodate one critical edition with a freshly edited text, introduction and notes for general use, and backmatter for the scholar doing more intensive research. As all transmitted texts are mediated, a definitive text of Conrad's works is a will-o'-the-wisp; as all texts are constructs, that of a critical edition, and especially one with an eclectic text, must be imperfectly constructed. Even so, it's silly to pretend that all editions are equal or that the words of "E.G." (the ubiquitous proofreader-grammarian of the extant Heinemann proofs) are as good as Conrad's for our scholar's purposes. There are different kinds of mediation and different orders of uncertainty. The variants among the six printings of the first English edition of *The Secret Agent* can be understood in mechanical terms and the Conradian forms distinguished from the compositorial;[8] no reader need be uncertain about which of these forms represents Conrad's text. The relations of the extant texts and their textual history make it possible to identify errors created in the missing typescript of the middle chapters of this novel and to restore Conrad's forms, thus providing as certain a text as could be hoped for when dealing with the unpredictabilities of human behavior and especially of the creative human mind. Research on Conrad's style based on these chapters would have a much surer foundation than in the earlier or later chapters, or than in any edition presenting one of the texts published in his lifetime.

But a critical edition not only has the chance of providing a reader of Conrad with a more reliable text than the one he or she would get simply by accepting the dictates of historical circumstance. It can also tell a critic or linguist just how much to rely on the text, or portions of it, as Conrad's, and it can direct attention, for instance, to those middle chapters of *The Secret Agent*. At the cost of some trouble, its apparatus can enable the reader to ascertain the wording of other texts. The English and American editions of *Almayer's Folly* (1895) share some twenty editorial changes made in a first set of English proofs, apparently without Conrad's knowledge, and the English alone has still another twenty made in a second round; a scholarly edition not only can report but can enable a user to find such forms through its apparatus and commentary, while also eliminating them from its text.[9] It can record the loss of a speech as a result of a typist's eyeskip as well as restore the original text, missing from all other editions (which derive from that typescript).[10] The editor of the Oxford World's Classics paperback of this novel might lament the absence of two substantial passages from the Doubleday collected edition, under the mistaken impression that the evidence for Conrad having cut them is much stronger than it is, but he is powerless to restore them because his text is in the main a photographic reprint of that edition. The editors of a critical edition, on the other hand, have the liberty and motive to examine the historical evidence more fully in their textual essay before approving those cuts, because their text will be entirely reset.[11] For most purposes it would be better to have these passages (missing from both the Doubleday and Heinemann collected editions) restored, even if we couldn't be absolutely certain the cuts were editorial. A critical edition can at least present a text that represents a novel at one stage of its development—say, the one it had reached by the time of the first editions, but without many of the compositorial and editorial alterations made in those editions and transmitted to later ones. Whatever choices between readings the editor has made, the reader can at least determine what he's working with in a properly documented critical edition.

This, however, will not solve all our scholar's problems in a wholly satisfactory manner. The apparatus of most critical editions is designed primarily to document the editing, and certain kinds of information a scholar wants are not always as accessible as could be hoped. Some of them are not accessible at all. The text of the manuscript, for instance, can be reconstructed only at the cost of considerable labor, and its precise forms (its "accidentals") are mostly inaccessible. The physical evidence of inscriptions—the character of the hands, the writing medium—may be briefly described in the textual essay but not fully documented. (The same would probably be true in a full-scale descriptive bibliography.) If our scholar is not willing to trust to the judgments of others, she still needs to see the document as well as have access to its text. Expense of spirit, time, and money remain forbidding.

One partial solution, of course, would be to take the time to write away for photocopies, but these are cumbersome, of variable quality, and unreliable for establishing texts, especially if the document contains inscriptions in media of different colors or shades. Another solution would be facsimile editions of the manuscripts and of the typescripts, which would provide most of the physical evidence or virtually all of it, depending on their quality. These books are, however, expensive, and only well-fitted research libraries are likely to have them. Nor will a facsimile provide a text of the document, which must still be reconstructed from the critical edition or transcribed from the facsimile and then checked against the original. A better solution these days would appear to be a digital edition that included reliable transcriptions of the texts from Conrad's lifetime, images of the documents, and supporting collateral information that would enable our scholar to conduct her research even though remote from the documents themselves.

Such a digital edition should exploit the capacity of the medium for audio and visual as well as verbal presentation, for linking various kinds of information, for quick and thorough searching, and for expandability, allowing users to explore Conrad's works in new as well as familiar ways. There are various ways to configure and present such a resource, and a discussion of the technicalities would be inappropriate here; but a broad outline of the project is perhaps pertinent. Basic, of course, is a text that allows the reader a convenient entrée into the various kinds of information for a given title. This home-text should have a uniform source throughout the digital edition (i.e., across titles) to simplify and ease use. Variants in wording in other texts should be linked to the home-text (presumably through hypertext software). Accurate transcriptions of the texts of Conrad's lifetime should be accessible in this way and also capable of being searched and manipulated on their own. Letters for the period of composition and publication of each title should be accessible in a similar manner.

At another level, images of all pages of manuscripts, typescripts, and marked proofs should be retrievable and linked in such a way to their respective texts so the user could call up an image of the document's page that contained the reading in question. Images of such documents would be fundamental for the graphic component of the digital edition, as would sample pages of the serials, first editions, and later book editions, linked in a similar way to the first variant in the given document. Ideally, however, the digital edition should provide graphics of all pages of the printings—putting them on the same basis as the preprinting documents—as well as, for example, study aids like maps (both contemporary and current), pictures of places alluded to in the texts, and the most relevant pages of the basic sources Conrad would have read. An audio component would include recordings of the music and other sounds that Conrad's audience could have recognized from allusions in the texts, like the "Miserere" from act 4 of Verdi's *Il trovatore* in *Almayer's Folly.*

Lastly, some editorial commentary should be supplied. At a minimum, the entire history of textual variation at a given point in the text should be accessible in a form analogous to the entry in a traditional printed apparatus. Notes (both textual and explanatory) should be linked to readings requiring comment. Beyond that, however, there should be general introductions and textual essays, explications of passages (linked to the home-text), and important essays on the work available for browsing and searching, so that the interested scholar or student could find some of the most basic things that have been learned or thought about a question in which he or she is interested.

For some, this edition will offer the opportunity to read the novels and tales in a different way, freed from the limitations of the book form, if not from the textual control of the author—in short, in a manner that emphasizes the reader's role or treats a given text-document as a sociological phenomenon.[12] But many will use the digital edition as a research tool to complement their reading text of Conrad. Both sorts of approaches can be accommodated in a digital edition if it is not too narrowly conceived. Some coding of the texts will be necessary, not only to provide the links between components but to represent some of the different elements almost universally found in paper documents.[13] This, however, should be done to a recognized standard (e.g., a basic level of Text Encoding Initiative [TEI] and Standard Generalized Markup Language [SGML]) and kept to a minimum. Our scholar should be able to take the text of a manuscript, for instance, and install linguistic tags to aid searching and other manipulation of the text for her particular research, without having to remove or otherwise negotiate a thicket of editorial coding that presumes other uses.

On the other hand, those preparing the digital edition should not neglect their responsibility to provide the user access to what they have learned about the texts of the work in question. In this more fluid medium, it's easy to get lost in the plethora of data. Those who wish to be set loose in an editorial vacuum should be free to proceed, but most users will not wish to sort out the textual problems of each work for themselves before getting on with their own projects and will wish to have access to editorial commentary on such matters. Indeed, many will have neither the inclination nor the technical knowledge to identify remnants of Polish and French in Conrad's prose, to make sense of ever-changing combinations of variation and agreement in a complex family tree, to evaluate the sources of changes made in a given text, or to diagnose the nature of variants between impressions of a single edition-typesetting. Perhaps because the typewriter played such a large part in the transmission of texts once it became available, documents containing important texts of Conrad are quite commonly lost. Moreover, the extent and nature of the changes introduced by typists have been underestimated. The task of reconstructing texts in this situation is almost as daunting as that faced by classical scholars, though it is of a different kind, as it often involves technical matters. Users should be free to pursue these questions by looking at the evidence for themselves, but that does not mean they should be abandoned in the wilderness, without readily accessible guidance.

Few users of a digital edition, for instance, would want to bone up on the early Monotype machines and fonts to decide whether the early or later variants within the first edition of *The Secret Agent* represent Conrad's forms. Likewise, few would want to be bothered with reconstructing lost texts, which play a significant role in the history of Conrad's works. The two typescripts of the first two-thirds of *The Secret Agent* and the two manuscripts of the last third have vanished altogether, as has the entire typescript of "The Secret Sharer" (1912). Those manuscripts and typescripts of Conrad's that survive do so in an unpredictable array and are often incomplete. The extant manuscripts for *Nostromo* (1904) and *The Secret Agent,* for instance, lack the last third of each novel, and that for "Heart of Darkness" (1902) lacks the first ten pages, while the typescript lacks approximately the last four-fifths of the tale. In this maze it's difficult to make even a simple word-count that's useful without having, not only the text of the document established, but its place in the textual history explained. No real purpose can be served, it seems to me, by returning to the days when the passages cut by the magazine editors from the serial version of *The Secret Agent* (which is derived from one of the lost typescripts) were regarded as Conrad's additions to the book version, or when the fussy alterations made by "E.G." in the proofs of the Heinemann collected volumes were thought to be Conrad's and to reflect his growing mastery of English idiom.

The digital edition should make available to users the conclusions drawn by editors and other scholars about these and similar matters, as well as the evidence upon which they are based, for theoretically at least space is not the cost constraint in this medium that it is in a printed book. Still, a digital edition like this is obviously going to take up considerable space and require certain kinds of computer hardware and software to be useful. As nothing is so constant as change in the realm of computerdom, it would be foolish to be doctrinaire about such matters; so a digital edition should be designed, as much as possible, to adapt to such changes and especially to be accessible to several kinds of potential users—our scholar in the so-called third world as well as the privileged American student.

Here the issue of the Internet, with its promise of equal and universal access, comes into play. Computer files mounted on a machine at an editorial center should, in theory, be accessible to the world over telephone lines through the Internet and similar services. In practice, however, there is reason to be skeptical about this scenario. A few years ago a large and prestigious university in western Europe was still running on its system-wide mainframe an antiquated operating system that a middling university in the United States would have been ashamed to use. A similar lag in network access and in PC environments is not uncommon—a marked disadvantage given the increased capabilities and sophistication of text, graphics, and audio now standard on new desktop computers in North America. The software required not merely to connect computers around the world but to operate from a remote site the kind of digital edition just described is still being perfected, and though data formats are beginning to stabilize, the software will continue to evolve. Indeed, it remains likely that users not residing in North America will always be behind the times in sophisticated software.

The laudable aim to make documents and texts that have traditionally been inaccessible to many accessible to all runs the decided risk of creating a world where the division between the haves and have-nots is as difficult to bridge as ever.

This is not to mention, of course, those who still have to make do without the Internet at all. Among them we can count the scholar of my opening anecdote. The will is there, but not the means. Furthermore, there are those who simply do not feel at ease with the computer, including some of our colleagues.[14] A digital edition assumes certain resources, financial and personal (e.g., time and know-how). Almost all can buy a book and manipulate it. Some can afford personal computers, which these days include as standard equipment CD-ROM drives that would be sufficient for running the digital edition described here. But fewer can afford to spend their resources (financial and especially personal) acquiring and installing the sophisticated equipment and software needed to provide genuinely working links to the Internet and remote databases.

For a world-renowned author like Conrad, a digital edition alone is not sufficient. We should think of it as a partner, not a replacement, for the printed critical edition and reliable paperback reading editions derived from it. The promise the computer holds of universal and immediate access to data in virtually unlimited ways seems unlikely to be realized in the near future. The hope that the medium will make texts and images of documents now available to few accessible to all is likely to be disappointed;[15] the technology is complex and in continuous flux and unequal development, and there is always the possibility (for instance) that the Internet will become fully commercialized. Conrad, in short, should be on disk, but he should be in print, too, in reliable editions.

Notes

1. Scholars and other readers of Conrad's works have long relied either directly or indirectly on the texts of the collected editions. Apart from Doubleday's own reprints of their texts and Dent's reimpressions of them for their "Collected Edition" in the mid-1940s and then again in the early 1970s (with introductions and notes by Norman Sherry), there have been the recent photographic reprintings by Oxford in

their World's Classics series and less recent ones like Morton Dauwen Zabel's one-volume edition of *The Nigger of the "Narcissus"* (Harpers 1951). The Heinemann has been the basis of three Norton Critical Editions, Thomas Moser's *Lord Jim* (1968) and Robert Kimbrough's *The Nigger of the "Narcissus"* (1979) and "Heart of Darkness" (1963; rev. 1971, 1988), and also of Bruce Harkness's editions of "Heart of Darkness" (Wadsworth 1960) and "The Secret Sharer" (Wadsworth 1962). The new Penguin and Everyman's series seem to have a more mixed ancestry of book editions.

2. The latter forms appear in *Notes on My Books,* issued by Doubleday and Heinemann in 1921, and in the March 1921 number of the *London Mercury.*

3. This account distills six paragraphs that are worth rereading for their oblique artistry. See *The Secret Agent,* ed. Bruce Harkness and S. W. Reid (Cambridge: Cambridge University Press, 1990), 4–7. The present discussion of this preface's textual history summarizes a more detailed one in this edition (311–22)

4. Actually, it was the other way around: Conrad telescoped a three- or four-month process into three (or fourteen) days. See the Cambridge Edition, xxxi–xxxvii, for a discussion of Conrad's composition of the novel, which shows that Conrad read Anderson three months after beginning the novel and only after three or four of the early chapters had already been written, typed, and partly revised. Citations below are to the page and line numbers of this edition, which also identify variants in the apparatus.

5. In a letter to F. N. Doubleday of 4 October 1923, Conrad wrote: "Am I right, my dear Effendi, in my impression that you said that the Concord Edition will follow the text of the Heinemann Limited Edition. That would please me vastly."

6. Commentary on this slippery term has been legion, though the unsatisfactory nature of the term does not prove the concept it stands for is nonsense; the most convenient discussion of the term's various possible meanings may still be G. Thomas Tanselle, "The Editorial Problem of Final Authorial Intention," *Studies in Bibliography* 29 (1976): 167–211; rpt. in Tanselle, *Selected Studies in Bibliography* (Charlottesville: University Press of Virginia, 1979), 309–53.

7. The article is not insignificant. This is the wording of the typescript, though not published until the Cambridge Edition.

8. See *The Secret Agent,* ed. Harkness and Reid, 271–80.

9. See *Almayer's Folly,* ed. Floyd Eugene Eddleman and David Leon Higdon (Cambridge: Cambridge University Press, 1994), 173–74, 176, 189.

10. See *Almayer's Folly,* ed. Eddleman and Higdon, 84, 222.

11. See *Almayer's Folly,* ed. Jacques Berthoud (Oxford: Oxford University Press, 1992), 218, 225; cf. *Almayer's Folly,* ed. Eddleman and Higdon, 18, 34, 181–84, 254.

12. There is already a considerable body of theory not only on such "foreground-

ing" (I believe that's the correct term) but also on digital editions or archives. See, for example, the essays by Charles Ross and Michael Suarez in the present collection.

13. The hypertext and other enabling coding would be embedded and invisible to most users, but there should also be minimal coding to identify the most basic textual-bibliographical units (e.g., title, head-title, chapter title, section number), fonts, and characters that have both a linguistic and bibliographical function (e.g., ligatures/digraphs, accented characters).

14. A recent broadcast report, I believe, said that even in the United States 70 percent of adults simply do not use computers.

15. So is the hope that it will help preserve perishing documents of the late-nineteenth and early-twentieth centuries, because computer media are quite unstable and could decay sooner than the books and other documents that are rightly the object of such concern these days.

> Books to me are incorporate things, voices in the air, that
> do not disturb the haze of autumn, and visions that don't
> blot the sunflowers. What do I care for first or last edi-
> tions? I have never read one of my own published works.
> To me, no book has a date, no book has a binding.
> —D. H. Lawrence

A Future
for Editing

Lawrence in

Hypertext

☙ ☙ ☙

Charles L. Ross

Lawrence may have had little use for textual scholarship, but he raises the key question for editors in a
preface to the first bibliography of his work. His
paradox of "incorporate" books focuses attention on
the relationships between those "voices in the air"
and their embodiments in "first or last editions." For
Lawrence the relationship was usually frustrating,
the "beastly marketable chunk of published volume"
delivering him into the hands of censorious publishers and public officials. After the banning and
burning of *The Rainbow* (1915), he submitted to
the process of publication as to "a necessary evil."
Nevertheless, he concedes, the "husks" of books are
worth collecting as the "trophies" of "man's fight with
inertia."[1]

I shall contend that all print editions of Lawrence
prolong this "fight with inertia" by fixing his texts in
ways that reduce the variety of their voices, and that
our printed critical editions, despite all their scholarship, fail to liberate the multiple voices of textuality. Though the Cambridge Lawrence edition (Cambridge University Press, 1979–) contains materials
for "versioning," the semiosis of its apparatus—variants, annotations, and copyright claim—combines
with the medium of print to frustrate that goal. As
Lawrence feared, the reader of the Cambridge edition is defeated by the "inertia" of the book.

Print's technology of presence resists variety, even

141

in such notably innovative editions as Hans Walter Gabler's "synoptic" *Ulysses* (1984), which Jerome McGann has called the first "postmodern" critical text.[2] Gabler's text actually suggests a printed book yearning for its electronic transformation, as I have argued elsewhere.[3] The monumental Cambridge edition, in contrast to Gabler's Joyce, appears to be the ne plus ultra of the Anglo-American critical edition in the tradition of W. W. Greg, Fredson Bowers, and G. Thomas Tanselle. Like all scholarly productions in the Late Age of Print, moreover, it has an air of anachronism. Each volume includes an unsustainable copyright claim to be a text "correctly established from the original sources"; a defense of the eclectic text in its introduction; interpretive "explanatory" notes; and a textual apparatus, to borrow a phrase from Gabler, "jumbling together bulks of authorial and transmissional variants in unwieldy fragmentation."[4] Copyright claim and introductory special pleading combine with unwieldy apparatus to inhibit reconstruction.[5] Here I shall extend that argument by examining the interplay of apparatus and interpretation in the Cambridge Lawrence; then I shall describe several hypertext prototypes with which readers may liberate the "voices" or versions in Lawrence's copious textuality. Having called for electronically layered texts in 1996. I report herein on my progress in providing readers with the means to create such texts.

❦ Because authors are protean and "authorial intention" is always retrospective, rationales for editing inevitably contradict themselves. Two general editors of the Cambridge Lawrence, for example, have edited "Odour of Chrysanthemums" (1911) according to quite different notions of Lawrence's intentions. When preparing a prepublication version of the story, James T. Boulton accepted scribal changes made "either deliberately or accidentally" by Lawrence's fiancée Louie Burrows because they had "presumably received Lawrence's approval."[6] Although Boulton does not speak of collaboration, he tacitly endorses Burrows's contribution to Lawrence's creativity. Yet his apparatus does not draw attention to them as Burrows's because "they were accepted by the author himself." By declining to identify Burrows's variants, he masks her collaborative role. Then Boulton's commentary treats the story as the product of Lawrence's "relative immaturity," encouraging the reader to see Lawrence's revisions as a stage in his artistic "growth," a process that involves only gain—"a growing alertness to economy, relevance, and signifi-cant emotion" (8). Of those three evaluative terms, the first is misleading, since Austin Harrison asked Lawrence to shorten the first part of the story in order to save space in *The English Review*. Lawrence complied by cutting more than 1,500 words, as he explained to Burrows: "All the playing part—most of the kiddies share—goes out, I think, I intend it to. The story must work quicker to a climax."[7] It seems likely that Lawrence's new intention grew at least partly from his conversation with Harrison. Boulton's teleologi-cal perspective, however, turns all facts to the one goal of showing that the final version is aesthetically superior. Readers are actively discouraged from responding to the new version in its own terms. Here editorial theory nar-rows choice while validating the products of print culture.

For the Cambridge edition of *The Prussian Officer and Other Stories*, John Worthen chooses to restore many words that Burrows had changed or cut and that Boulton preserved.[8] Worthen tacitly assumes that their collabora-tion is not creative and that Lawrence cannot have authorized Burrows's changes. By purging the text of collaboration with Burrows, Worthen saves Lawrence from himself as well as from her. But his rationale promptly un-ravels, for Worthen restores only those changes by Burrows that remain un-touched through all subsequent forms. That is, Worthen reintroduces ma-terial that was absent when Lawrence was revising a particular version. On the other hand, Worthen retains Lawrence's revisions of Burrows's changes, thereby admitting some collaboration. Here Worthen disagrees with another Cambridge editor, L. D. Clark, who resists what he calls such "constrained revisions" in his edition of *The Plumed Serpent*—that is, Lawrence's revisions of mistranscriptions, often made without consulting the earlier document.[9] And like Boulton, Worthen accepts the cuts that Lawrence made follow-ing the advice of Austin Harrison, another form of collaboration. In sum, Boulton and Worthen construct Lawrence's authority differently not only between versions (Boulton vs. Worthen) but within the same version (Wor-then). Lawrence's control over his texts both is and is not reasserted.

My intention is not to lambaste the Cambridge Lawrence but to demon-strate that *any* editorial rationale construes the "author" interpretively and that our print editions inevitably enable certain sorts of versioning while hampering others. The Cambridge edition can take credit for bringing much new Lawrence to light: not only work he left unpublished, like *Mr. Noon,* but drafts of published work, such as early versions of *Sons and Lovers* (1913) and *Women in Love* (1920). Yet what D. C. Greetham identifies as "modernist" notions of perfected text and clear-text display often lead Cambridge's editors to disparage the versions that might theoretically be fashioned from their apparatus.[10] Lawrence is more various, his texts more multiple and less determinant than our editions currently permit him or them to appear.

Take the case of the Cambridge *Lady Chatterley's Lover.*[11] Though its goal of providing a text "as free from non-authorial interference as possible" is laudable, its most important decision is to sacrifice some "non-expurgative" revisions that Lawrence made while preparing an expurgated typescript for the American publisher Knopf. (Calling the changes "non-expurgative" rather than, say, "voluntary" or "aesthetic" prejudices the case.) The editor, Michael Squires, wanted to discriminate between self-censorship and free choice but was overruled by the editorial board. This expurgated typescript, the only surviving one, was judged to be a "cul-de-sac" because it was neither published nor used as setting-copy for the first edition. Though Squires believes that "an author can simultaneously have mixed intentions," he was persuaded that it was better to "reduce editorial risk" by abandoning the attempt to sort out different types of revision.[12]

Mark Kinkead-Weekes also faced mixed authorial motivation in the missing proofs of *The Rainbow,* which Lawrence reluctantly censored to satisfy a prudish publisher. The revisions are so widespread, however, that one assumes that Lawrence seized the opportunity to rewrite voluntarily. What to do? One might print the typescript on which Lawrence labored without interference as a product of the unconstrained authorial will. Kinkead-Weekes rejects that strategy on the grounds that "it would not be the novel to which [Lawrence] gave his imprimatur," an exaggeration that conveniently ignores the predicament of a recently married writer with no other means of earning a living.[13] Indeed, the authority of print proves so strong that Kinkead-Weekes retains the first edition reading in cases of "any doubt," finally restoring far fewer variants than correspondence implies Lawrence made under duress. As a result the Cambridge text is substantively almost identical to those already available and, more likely than not, contains many nonaesthetic changes that mute the candor on sexual themes achieved in years of rewriting.[14]

Thus print always reinforces the teleology implicit in a theory of "final intentions" and "organic" form.[15] The apparatus enables local revision but not versioning, thereby misrepresenting the ways most authors, particularly Lawrence, rewrote with a sense of the whole firmly in view.[16] Despite its expansion of the canon, the Cambridge edition misses opportunities to supply versions because it is focused on producing "the" authoritative text for each work. The volume *The Fox, The Captain's Doll, The Ladybird,* for example, prints only the last quarter of the manuscript version of *The Fox,* and its apparatus does not record deletions in the manuscript—so the reader can neither reconstruct the original version nor follow Lawrence's artistry.[17] Cambridge declines to supply six thousand words in a slim volume of three hundred pages that is already priced beyond the means of all but libraries and relatively affluent scholars. There is simply no interest in preparing an edition from which different texts can be reconstructed.

The Cambridge Lawrence is also divided against itself, declaring its eclectic texts the only "correct" ones while issuing new versions. Having fashioned a splendid edition of *Sons and Lovers,* for example, Helen Baron and Carl Baron insist that the "botched, censored, and butchered text" of the first edition be "interred."[18] Though Helen Baron claims to have proceeded on "purely bibliographical grounds," she inevitably relied on interpretation to rule out Edward Garnett as a collaborator and to choose among variants made by either Lawrence or compositors in the missing proofs.[19] Thus the Barons' decision to restore all the passages cut by Garnett eliminates censorship but also advice that may have stimulated further revision by Lawrence, as in the less brutal portrait of the father that appears in the first edition. In the absence of proof, moreover, decisions to restore readings from the manuscript or to eliminate readings from the first edition must be entirely interpretive.

Consider, for example, the manuscript passage in which the sexually aroused but frustrated Paul Morel dons Clara's stockings under his pajamas and apparently doesn't take them off when he creeps downstairs to embrace his naked lover before the fire. Paul's cross-dressing is missing from the first edition, presumably removed in proof by Garnett. The Barons restore it but not all the cuts in a sequence of scenes that lead up to it. In a passage from "Lad-and-Girl Love" that Garnett cut in manuscript, Paul asks, "Did *you* want to be a man, mother?" Reassured that she does not, he concludes, "I hate it when a woman wants to be a man." Subsequently, in the famous Oedipal scene in "Strife in Love," a clause that gestured toward Paul's "other women," and specifically Clara before the fire, vanished from the proofs: "Without knowing he gently stroked her face, *as, afterwards, he did to other women, his lovers.*" (The italicized phrase later disappeared.) And later Paul in stockings also disappeared from proof. How do the Barons proceed? They restore the conversation cut by Garnett from the manuscript and then decide that Garnett must also have cut Paul's cross-dressing but that Lawrence and not Garnett removed the reference to "other women." My point is that the editors' decision rests on an interpretation and not on evidence. It would be quite possible to infer that the reference to "other women, his lovers," like the stocking details, was censored in proof.

Yet the rhetoric directed by the Barons against the first edition—"censored and butchered"—and their assertion of "bibliographical grounds" for all decisions to emend will surely discourage readers from considering the apparatus as a resource for creating further versions. Dropped from both the Cambridge trade editions and Penguin reprints, the textual apparatus on the shelves of well-endowed libraries serves merely as a testimony to the editors' thoroughness. Indeed, the "Note on the Penguin Lawrence Edition," which appears in all the Penguin Twentieth-Century Classics reprints of the Cambridge texts, assures buyers that they have purchased what "Lawrence would have expected to see printed." In other words, the reader remains a consumer of the editor's version of Lawrence's textuality.

A critical edition, according to Peter Shillingsburg, "changes and enriches the work much more than it preserves or restores it."[20] Thus the "explanatory notes" in the Cambridge edition contain a wealth of information. Facts of biography, history, and literature mix with superseded readings, the rationale of emendation, and even the physical states of manuscripts and typescripts. More problematically, the so-called explanations actually insist on interpretations—a fact that Cambridge editors are at pains to deny. Paul Eggert ends his praise of a representative note with the assurance that "no overtly literary critical opinion or ready-made interpretation is offered."[21]

On the contrary, overt opinion is everywhere and inescapably evident in the Cambridge notes.

Cambridge's *Lady Chatterley's Lover,* for example, lards its notes with technical information as well as readings from the manuscripts. Asterisks divert the reader's attention to the sort of details that only a textual critic will relish. Even the fascinating manuscript readings, which are inserted without explanation, create trouble for readers. How do these superseded variants "explain" the final readings? What is their relationship to other variants that were not selected? These questions can't be answered because the version from which the variants have been plucked cannot be reconstructed. That the editor includes these variants as though their usefulness is self-explanatory, however, demonstrates the teleological imperative of the Cambridge edition and the need for a more flexible, reader-controlled medium of presentation.

Consider, on the other hand, the effect of linked notes that are unnecessary as "explanation" but that warn readers not to take Ursula's impressions in *The Rainbow* at face value. At one point, confused by her feelings for Anton Skrebensky, Ursula discusses love and marriage with her teaching colleague, Maggie Schofield: "She thought she still loved Anton Skrebensky. But she did not forgive him that he had not been strong enough to acknowledge her. He had denied her." The note flatly contradicts Ursula's impression: "This is hardly true of Skrebensky" (529, note to 382:11). In an obvious sense, however, Ursula speaks truthfully. Skrebensky "denied" her during the harvest wedding dance in "First Love" when he sought to limit her female assertiveness and to "net" and possess her under the brilliant moon. Indeed, after annihilating Skrebensky, Ursula treats her other self similarly: "She denied it with all her might" (299). And at the end of the novel, she tries again to disavow the self that has rejected Skrebensky, once again under the moon ("The Bitterness of Ecstasy"); but her deeper nature, in the shape of the moon and wild horses, will not allow this blasphemy against life. By denying the truthfulness of Ursula's feelings, Kinkead-Weekes imposes an interpretation of her sexual nature that ironically resembles Skrebensky's patriarchal attitude toward what Lawrence elsewhere calls her "indomitable gorgeous female self" (282).

The reproving of Ursula continues in a scene with Anthony Schofield.

Ursula has been gratified by Anthony's attention and even attracted by his animal magnetism, but she rejects his offer of marriage with these thoughts: "She . . . turned round from him, and saw the east flushed strangely rose, the moon coming yellow. . . . All this so beautiful, all this so lovely! He did not see it. He was one with it. But she saw it, and was one with it. Her seeing separated them infinitely" (386). Although the passage hardly requires annotation, the editor interjects a reproof of Ursula. The passage, he writes, provides "another exact measure of the distance between the 'new woman' and the Brangwen Men of the Beginning. . . . It is not simply an advance" (529, note to 386:29). The phrase "new woman" does not appear in the novel; it has been imported to enforce an interpretation that seems patriarchal. It puts Ursula in her place.

There are two theoretical points to be made about such commentary. First, it not only contains but enforces interpretation. Second, it raises doubts about Kinkead-Weekes's motives in choosing not to restore original readings in a range of passages in which Lawrence deals with the intertwined themes of woman becoming independent and a sexuality beyond good and evil.[22] Because I have put that case elsewhere, I shall simply argue here that readers need their own spaces for dialogue, for talking back.[23] In print, editors get their way too easily and arbitrarily with texts and readers. Technology and editorial interpretation combine to transform the print critical edition into the agent of *a* notion of the author and, consequently, *a* way of reading.

What to do? Having recognized the radical shortcomings of print— its fixity and univocality—we must switch media. According to Anthony Smith, "A medium of communication is both an industrial technology and an attempt to reconstruct the process of cognition. In part each new technology . . . reorganizes those processes, thereby influencing works of art performed through other, earlier processes."[24]

As a medium of communication the print critical edition has outlived its usefulness. Today we need editions that fulfill D. C. Greetham's characterization of the "postmodernist edition" in Barthean terms as "*scriptible* not *lisible,* open not closed"—editions that set in motion textual "instability" and that give readers displays of information in which to fashion new texts.[25] We need, in short, hypertexts that turn readers into writers who collaborate in the production of the texts they read.

Electronic editions will reframe editorial praxis. They will be "writing spaces," fields of textuality leveled for the play of readers as creators rather than consumers. By putting the results of textualist labor fully at the service of readers, such spaces will fulfill a long-deferred dream of permitting material reconstructions based on informed interpretation. Therefore, their design should be our highest priority. In what follows I shall describe "literary machines" that suggest the possibilities of hypertext editions.[26] At the outset I distinguish my goals from those pursued by scholars using computers to prepare data for print editions, or to link texts extensively to a growing "web" of other texts, or to mark up digitized texts.[27] I have coined the term "substitutional hypertext" to distinguish this goal from the more familiar linking of fixed texts, as in George Landow's webs or the Internet. Scripted in HyperCard and SuperCard, my literary machines foreground variation and difference, presenting textuality as, in Landow's formulation, "a dispersed field of variants and not . . . a falsely unitary entity."[28] These programs are really texts that read and write other texts and that bring into play the riches of editorial scholarship currently languishing in lists at the back of critical editions. Put another way, hypertext programs make possible reader-controlled versioning of digitized textuality. In place of a textual apparatus that remains secondary to the eclectic text in space, time, and authority, a digitized format allows versions to take shape visibly on screen—rising from and returning to the field of variants according to clearly indicated interpretations.

I am emboldened to describe my literary machines because digital text construction presently seems to be focused on linking or networking as opposed to my goal of "substitutive hypertext." At the 1996 meeting of the Modern Language Association, for example, Michael Groden demonstrated a beta version of "A Multimedia *Ulysses*." Although his team has woven a web of textual, visual, and aural annotation, they have tethered it all to the fixed Gabler reading text, ignoring the rich textual history encoded in Gabler's synoptic display. This arrangement implies that texts remain stable in a changing world, whereas the truth is very different: texts proliferate while the world seems to stand still.

Hypertext is the medium in which the variants compiled diachronically in Gabler's edition can be restructured synchronically to produce an almost countless number of versions. This is technically possible because the structure of an electronic text is abstracted from its verbal expression; its elements are "fundamentally unstable."[29] Compare the claim by Stanley Wells and Gary Taylor to have "destabilized" Shakespeare's texts.[30] For all its innovation, their editing of multiple versions has not fully destabilized the act of reading Shakespeare. Only computer programs working with digitized archives can destabilize and restabilize texts through the choices of readers. Indeed, it is this systole and diastole of digitized textuality that should reassure traditional scholars like David Bevington, who asked in a review of the Wells/Taylor Shakespeare, "What is the scholar—or the high school or college teacher—to do when confronted with a supposedly authoritative text that actually promotes textual indeterminacy?"[31] By bringing textual variety under the control of readers, hypertext will advance the cause of teachers and writers.

Consider, for example, how hypertext can reframe the problem of self-censorship in *The Rainbow*. As we have seen, an editor must speculate about which authorial changes were the result of self-censorship and which were aesthetically motivated. A print edition, of course, must present one or more fixed reading texts while relegating change or difference to appended lists of variants.

In all the prototypes I shall describe, the reader chooses a level of engagement with Lawrence's textuality, typically first encountering complete versions in which to read, as it were, the old-fashioned way, and then delving into the text's archaeology at marked "hot spots." The marked text in the first prototype (figure 1) belongs to a scene in *The Rainbow* from the chapter entitled "The Child," in which Will Brangwen tries to seduce Jennie, a warehouse lass, before returning home to Anna and a night of love both "immoral" and liberating. Interpreting the imaginative logic of this heavily revised scene is complicated by the presence of self-censorship to a greater or lesser degree. In the Cambridge edition, as I argue elsewhere, the authority of the print version justifies retaining all variants but a few blatant examples of self-censorship.[32] Hypertext foregrounds variation and leaves the reader to explore and choose; that is, hypertext shifts the grounds of the debate. Upon opening the digitized "book," readers encounter buttons marked "TS" or "1st ed." or "Archive" that offer choices among, respectively, the typescript that Lawrence sent to the printer, the Methuen first edition, or

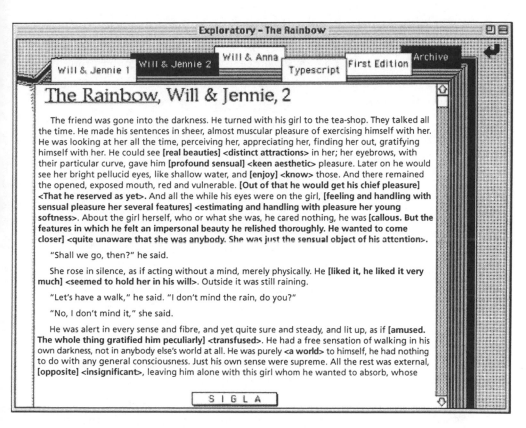

Figure 1. "The Child" chapter in *The Rainbow*, exploratory hypertext. © Donald Buckley and Charles Ross

interactive pages in which not texts but *textuality* can be manipulated. The "Archive" offers a genetic display resembling Gabler's "synoptic" pages in which variants from different documentary states have been diachronically arranged. By clicking on bolded and bracketed hot spots, the reader toggles between typescript (in square brackets) and first edition (in pointed brackets), thereby re-creating the writing scene in the lost proofs. At any time the reader may return to the typescript or the first edition or, indeed, any edition that has been added to the growing hypertext "web." In this prototype, substantive variants in the typescript and first edition remain bolded so as to give readers a notion of how much change is involved, but otherwise those texts have reverted to the fixity of print. In sum, this hypertext edition overcomes some of the static qualities of print, empowering readers to engage in different sorts of interactions with *textuality*.

Yet prototype 1 severely restricts the interactions of readers with an author's textuality. Not only has some editorial authority already marked the texts, itself an interpretive activity, but the format does not provide either the space for annotations or the capacity to edit the text as a whole. In prototype 2 (figure 2), therefore, we include writing spaces in which the reader can inscribe comments and accomplish pre-editing activities such as compiling lists of variants under interpretive categories (e.g., "Free will" or "Self-censorship" or "Corruption"). The scrolling field on the left "page" has bolded and grouped hot spots as in the first prototype. On the right page, buttons indicate the available interpretive categories, which may be augmented or deleted on the fly; the middle field shows the variants that have been visited recently; and the bottom fields serve as repositories of evaluated variants and annotations, depending on which ones the reader chooses to view at a given time. The abbreviation "1 Sc" in the middle field, for example, indicates that the motive for change in the first pairing of variants has been provisionally judged to have been self-censorship. The annotation gives the reader's reasons for his interpretive choice. Clicking on any variant in the growing list of such evaluated variants scrolls the text into view at the proper location. Variants can be de-selected or revalued, and comment fields can be cleared.

The linking of these four fields represents an advance in interactivity and functionality. Now the reader can carry out interpretive operations on the

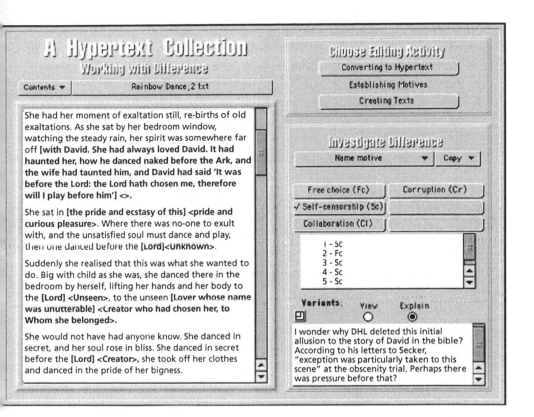

Figure 2. "Anna Victix," *The Rainbow*, constructive hypertext. © Donald Buckley and Charles Ross

text, not only exploring the writing scene but revaluing Lawrence's acts of revision. In this scene from "Anna Victrix," for example, the pregnant Anna Brangwen dances naked in her room as a gesture of freedom from her husband's claims for attention. In the typescript (square brackets) Anna recalls the biblical story of David and then decides to disrobe and dance in imitation of it; but the published text omits that transition. Toggling back and forth between variants, the reader may suspect that the reason for the excision was the reference to Anna's "love" for David and the impropriety of comparing her dance while naked with that of David "naked before the Ark." This suspicion may subsequently be bolstered by Lawrence's own report that at the trial of the novel for obscenity, "exception was *particularly* taken" to this scene.[33] If the tentative conclusion reached is that Lawrence censored himself in this scene, the reader will add these variants to a list under "Self-censorship" and justify her decision in the annotation field. Whatever the decision reached in any particular case, the reader will eventually have explored an archive, recorded interpretations, and compiled lists of variants in various categories—all within the writing space.

Compare the display of information in this hypertext interface and in the Cambridge edition. Whereas the reader of a hypertext interface encounters texts, variants, and interpretation in contiguous space, the reader of Cambridge editions must use memory to struggle against the "relentless sequentiality of print" that stacks information in time.[34] Moreover, different displays set different analytic agendas. Whereas the separation in print of reading text and apparatus tacitly endorses one version, the contiguity of text and variants in hypertext puts textuality into motion.

And what sort of editing will hypertext offer? At the outset I envisaged a hypertext edition on the analogy of an overhead projector and a stack of transparencies. The reader would choose a desired level of detail just as the teacher adds or peels off a transparency from the stack. That analogy, I now realize, works better for the connections between discrete texts, as in the largest hypertext of all—the Internet. Our suite of programs, in contrast, enables students to create new documents from old or, in Landow's phrase, to create new texts from "fields of variants." A collator program enables students to import and mark digitalized texts. The collator searches for the onset of difference, automatically inserts the first or left-hand bracket of a pair, and then waits while the user decides where to insert the right-hand or closing bracket. (Brackets, selected before collation begins, identify originating texts throughout the process of hypertextualization and editing.) The result is a conflated text with bracketed variants arranged side by side (e.g., "[Lord] <Unknown>"). The explorer program, to which this conflated text is exported, turns the bracketed variants into interactive hot spots. This transformation occurs on screen so that readers may see digitized print turning into hypertext.

Then the reader can explore the hypertext variant by variant, making comments and accumulating variants under various and easily changed interpretive categories. Finally, having explored the hypertext locally, variant by variant, the reader edits globally, creating a whole version on the basis of authorial motive or "intention." Figure 3 shows a new text that reflects the interpretive judgment of a reader who has chosen to authorize only "free will" as a motive for change. The button enabling this global change is called "Reconstruct Text" to indicate its structural or synchronic function. Hence all the variants judged to be the result of "self-censorship" have been excluded from the new eclectic text. (For example, the first variant, in which Anna is compared to David, has been retained because the motive for Lawrence's revision was judged to have been self-censorship.) A headnote identifies the motive underlying the new text, which has been cleared of sigla. This newly authorized text, no longer a hypertext, may return to print or remain in electronic format.

Through an interpretive performance enabled by hypertext and foregrounded on screen, the reader has shaped a version of *The Rainbow* from Lawrence's textuality. By revaluing change or revision the reader has reimagined the author who endows the text with coherence or, in Michel Foucault's terms, has reconstituted an "author-function" so as to limit the proliferation of meaning in texts.[35] Different choices by the reader will realize different authors and, therefore, different texts.

Our current suite of programs begins to fulfill the definition of interactivity by Michael Joyce, author of *Afternoon,* in his recent collection, *Of Two Minds.* By enabling readers to explore, evaluate, and rearrange variants, hypertext insures that "initiatives taken by either user or system alter the behavior of the other."[36] If it seems too much to claim with Anthony Smith

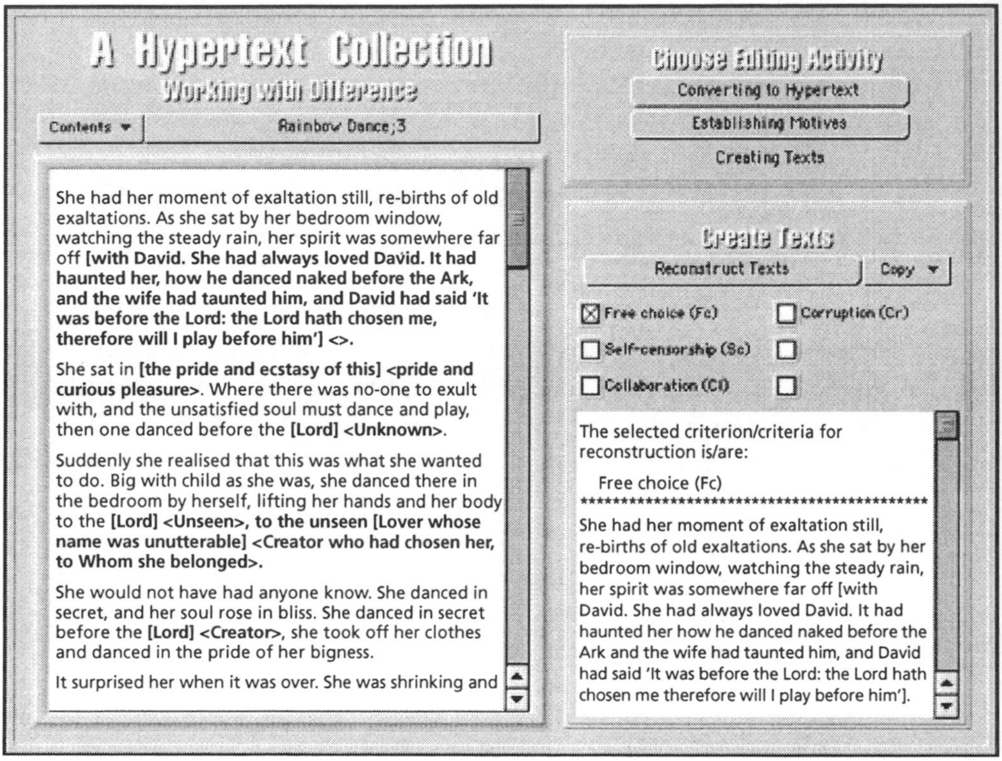

A Hypertext Collection
Working with Difference

Choose Editing Activity
Converting to Hypertext
Establishing Motives
Creating Texts

Contents ▼   Rainbow Dance;3

She had her moment of exaltation still, re-births of old exaltations. As she sat by her bedroom window, watching the steady rain, her spirit was somewhere far off **[with David. She had always loved David. It had haunted her, how he danced naked before the Ark, and the wife had taunted him, and David had said 'It was before the Lord: the Lord hath chosen me, therefore will I play before him']** <>.

She sat in **[the pride and ecstasy of this]** <pride and curious pleasure>. Where there was no-one to exult with, and the unsatisfied soul must dance and play, then one danced before the **[Lord]** <Unknown>.

Suddenly she realised that this was what she wanted to do. Big with child as she was, she danced there in the bedroom by herself, lifting her hands and her body to the **[Lord]** <Unseen>, **to the unseen [Lover whose name was unutterable]** <Creator who had chosen her, to Whom she belonged>.

She would not have had anyone know. She danced in secret, and her soul rose in bliss. She danced in secret before the **[Lord]** <Creator>, she took off her clothes and danced in the pride of her bigness.

It surprised her when it was over. She was shrinking and

Create Texts
Reconstruct Texts   Copy ▼

☒ Free choice (Fc)   ☐ Corruption (Cr)
☐ Self-censorship (Sc)   ☐
☐ Collaboration (Cl)   ☐

The selected criterion/criteria for reconstruction is/are:

Free choice (Fc)
****
She had her moment of exaltation still, re-births of old exaltations. As she sat by her bedroom window, watching the steady rain, her spirit was somewhere far off [with David. She had always loved David. It had haunted her how he danced naked before the Ark and the wife had taunted him, and David had said 'It was before the Lord: the Lord hath chosen me therefore will I play before him'].

Figure 3. "Anna Victix," *The Rainbow,* constructive hypertext. © Donald Buckley and Charles Ross

that hypertext has thereby reconstructed the "process of cognition," perhaps it will be allowed that hypertext changes the process of engagement with literary texts. New structures or ways of reading can materialize in the electronic writing space. The future of editing lies in restructuring textuality on screen. In the near future hypertext will lower the barriers between writers, readers, and editors, turning all into true collaborators in the writing of textuality.

Notes

I thank Dr. Donald Buckley, formerly of the Biology Department at the University of Hartford and presently Director of Instructional Technology for the College of Health Sciences at Quinnipiac University, who scripted the programs and collaborated in designing the interfaces of our literary machines.

1. Edward D. McDonald, ed., "Preface to *A Bibliography of D. H. Lawrence*," in *Phoenix*, ed. McDonald (London: Heinemann, 1936), 232, 235.

2. Jerome J. McGann, "*Ulysses* as a Postmodern Text: The Gabler Edition," *Criticism* 27 (1985): 283–306. See James Joyce, *Ulysses: A Critical and Synoptic Edition*, ed. Hans Walter Gabler, with Wolfhard Steppe and Claus Melchior, 3 vols. (New York: Garland, 1984).

3. See Charles L. Ross, "The Electronic Text and the Death of the Critical Edition," in *The Literary Text in the Digital Age*, ed. Richard J. Finneran (Ann Arbor: University of Michigan Press, 1996), 227.

4. Hans Walter Gabler, "On Textual Criticism and Editing: The Case of Joyce's *Ulysses*," in *Palimpsest: Editorial Theory in the Humanities*, ed. George Bornstein and Ralph G. Williams (Ann Arbor: University of Michigan Press, 1993), 197.

5. See Charles L. Ross, "Editing as Interpretation: Self-Censorship and Collaboration in the Cambridge Edition of *The Rainbow and Women in Love*," in *Editing D. H. Lawrence: New Versions of a Modern Author*, ed. Ross and Dennis Jackson (Ann Arbor: University of Michigan Press, 1995), 79–98; Ross, "A Note on Nomenclature," in *Editing D. H. Lawrence*, 189–92; and Ross, "The Electronic Text," 225–32.

6. James T. Boulton, "D. H. Lawrence's *Odour of Chrysanthemums*: An Early Version," *Renaissance and Modern Studies* 13 (1969): 7.

7. *The Letters of D. H. Lawrence*, ed. James T. Boulton, 7 vols. (Cambridge: Cambridge University Press, 1979), 1:252.

8. D. H. Lawrence, *The Prussian Officer and Other Stories*, ed. John Worthen (Cambridge: Cambridge University Press, 1983).

9. L. D. Clark, "Editing *The Plumed Serpent* for Cambridge: Or, Crossing the Communication Gap," in *Editing D. H. Lawrence,* 110, 115 n.5. The *Plumed Serpent* was first published in 1926; see also Clark's edition (Cambridge: Cambridge University Press, 1987).

10. D. C. Greetham, "Editorial and Critical Theory: From Modernism to Postmodernism," in *Palimpsest,* 9–28.

11. D. H. Lawrence, *Lady Chatterley's Lover; A Propos of Lady Chatterley's Lover,* ed. Michael Squires (Cambridge: Cambridge University Press, 1993). The novel was originally printed, privately, in 1928.

12. See Michael Squires, "Editing the Cambridge *Lady Chatterley's Lover:* Collaboration and Compromise," in *Editing D. H. Lawrence,* 121–22 n.5.

13. Mark Kinkead-Weekes, introduction to *The Rainbow,* by D. H. Lawrence (Cambridge: Cambridge University Press, 1989), ed. Kinkead-Weekes, lxiii.

14. See Ross, "Editing as Interpretation," 80–87.

15. See Charles L. Ross, "The Limits of Idealism in Textual Theory: 'Work' and 'Text' in G. Thomas Tanselle's 'A Rationale of Textual Criticism,'" *Critical Survey* 7 (1995): 358–62; see also Greetham, "Editorial and Critical Theory."

16. See, for example, Mark Kinkead-Weekes, "The Marble and the Statue: The Exploratory Imagination of D. H. Lawrence," in *Imagined Worlds,* ed. Maynard Mack and Ian Gregor (London: Methuen, 1968), 371–418; Charles L. Ross, *The Composition of "The Rainbow" and "Women in Love": A History* (Charlottesville: University Press of Virginia, 1979); Michael Squires, *The Creation of "Lady Chatterley's Lover"* (Baltimore: Johns Hopkins University Press, 1983); and Keith Sagar, *D. H. Lawrence: Life into Art* (Athens: University of Georgia Press, 1985).

17. See D. H. Lawrence, *The Fox, The Captain's Doll, The Ladybird,* ed. Dieter Mehl (Cambridge: Cambridge University Press, 1992). These works were first published in 1923.

18. Helen Baron, "Some Theoretical Issues Raised by Editing *Sons and Lovers,*" in *Editing D. H. Lawrence,* 76. See D. H. Lawrence, *Sons and Lovers,* ed. Helen Baron and Carl Baron (Cambridge: Cambridge University Press, 1992).

19. See Charles L. Ross, review of *Sons and Lovers,* by D. H. Lawrence, ed. Helen Baron and Carl Baron, *D. H. Lawrence Review* 25 (1993–94), 162–64.

20. Peter Shillingsburg, "An Inquiry into the Social Status of Texts and Modes of Textual Criticism," *Studies in Bibliography* 42 (1989): 74.

21. Paul Eggert, "Reading a Critical Edition With the Grain and Against: The Cambridge D. H. Lawrence," in *Editing D. H. Lawrence,* 37.

22. See Charles L. Ross, "Civilization and its Discontents in the Editing of Lawrence," *Documentary Editing* 12 (1990): 40–44.

23. See Charles L. Ross, "Authority in Hypertext: The Analogy of Anthropology," *Convergence: The Journal of Research into New Media Technologies* 1 (1995): 14–15.

24. Anthony Smith, *From Books to Bytes* (London: British Film Institute, 1993), 35.

25. See Greetham, "Editorial and Critical Theory," 9–28.

26. Ted Nelson coined the term "hypertext" to specify "*non-sequential writing*-text that branches and allows choices to the reader, best read at an interactive screen"; see his *Literary Machines* 93.1 (Sausalito CA: Mindful Press, 1992), 0/2.

27. An example of the first is Peter Shillingsburg, *Scholarly Editing in the Computer Age: Theory and Practice,* rev. ed. (Ann Arbor: University of Michigan Press, 1996); of the second, George Landow, *The Dickens Web* (Watertown MA: Eastgate Systems, 1993); and of the third, the Text Encoding Initiative overseen by C. M. Sperburg-McQueen and Louis Burnard.

28. George Landow, *Hypertext 2.0: The Convergence of Contemporary Critical Theory and Technology* (Baltimore: Johns Hopkins University Press, 1997), 56.

29. See Jay David Bolter, *Writing Space, The Computer, Hypertext, and the History of Writing* (Hillsdale NJ: Lawrence Erlbaum, 1991), 21.

30. See Scott Heller, "The New Historicists Put Their Spin on William Shakespeare," *Chronicle of Higher Education,* 3 Jan. 1997, A12; and see Shakespeare, *The Complete Works,* ed. Stanley Wells and Gary Taylor (Oxford: Clarendon, 1986), and Shakespeare, *The Complete Works: Original Spelling Edition,* ed. Wells and Taylor (Oxford: Clarendon, 1988).

31. David Bevington, "Determining the Indeterminate: The Oxford Shakespeare," *Shakespeare Quarterly* 38 (1987): 503.

32. See Ross, "Civilization and its Discontents" and "Editing as Interpretation."

33. See *Letters from D. H. Lawrence to Martin Secker, 1911–1930,* ed. Secker (privately printed, 1970), 21; and see Ross, *Composition,* 44–46.

34. Edward R. Tufte, lecture at St. Joseph College, West Hartford, Connecticut, 10 Feb. 1997. See Tufte's *Visual Explanations: Images and Quantities, Evidence and Narrative* (Cheshire CT: Graphics Press, 1997).

35. "The author is the principle of thrift in the proliferation of meaning"; see Michel Foucault, "What Is an Author?" trans. Josué V. Harari, in *The Foucault Reader,* ed. Paul Rabinow (New York: Pantheon, 1984), 118.

36. Michael Joyce, *Of Two Minds: Hypertext Pedagogy and Poetics* (Ann Arbor: University of Michigan Press, 1995), 135.

In Dreams Begins Responsibility

Novels, Promises, and the Electronic Editor

🐾 🐾 🐾

Michael F. Suarez, S.J.

How do the structures of knowledge that editors embed within electronic editions of print-based texts influence what readers can get out of them? This essay addresses the question in two parts. It begins by considering how readers typically use the computer to ask questions of texts and how the quality of such research may depend upon prior editorial activity. Then, the second part of the essay looks at the impact of hypertext on reading novels and considers how practices adapted from critical editing may help balance the twin goals of comprehensiveness and comprehensibility in the electronic environment.

How Far Can You Go?

In fact, wherever precision is required man flies to the machine at once, as far preferable to himself.—Samuel Butler, *Erewhon* (1872)

Looking back over the work of several decades, scholars engaged in the computer analysis of literary texts have recently acknowledged that "computer-aided literature studies have failed to have a significant effect on the field as a whole." Many critics believe that "after all the programs are finished running, computer analysis of texts does not tell us much we did not know before, and worse, may not prove the important matters any better than a close reading."[1] Proponents of computer-driven literary studies would be hard pressed to refute Thomas Corns's claim that "there is no substantial body of achievement in the field of computer-based literary criticism in English studies"; no wonder then that the director of Brown University's Scholarly Technology Group concedes that "computer-based literary research . . . has failed to be a serious presence in even the narrowest fields of literary studies, let alone a factor in the broader intellectual conversation."[2] Often the conclusions of such investigations are banal or obvious: "*Gulliver* is conceptually different from [*A Tale of a*] *Tub* and its coevals," or "the fictive world of *The Good Soldier* is a mental world which turns inward upon itself . . . whereas the fictive world of *Lord Jim* is a performative world that turns outward."[3] Are these "results" more precise, more reliable, or more objective for having been assisted by computer?

This consistent lack of success in using the computer as an effective critical tool prompts the question: What are computers in the study of literary texts *for*? At present, the answer for most readers is chiefly two-fold: access to texts and the rapid retrieval of words or phrases.[4] Although many electronic texts on the World Wide Web are astonishingly untrustworthy (those associated with the *Gutenberg Project* are perhaps most notorious for poor transcriptions from bibliographically unreliable sources), more and more carefully prepared texts are becoming available, a welcome development for those who might otherwise have difficulty reading these works. Yet we need to ask ourselves how the electronic representation of these texts and the software provided to display and interrogate them embodies theories of textuality and of literary knowledge.

The principal tool that the computer offers the user of electronic texts, whether delivered over the Web or by CD-ROM, is the word search. What kinds of literary knowledge does this form of research make available and therefore privilege? The theory of text underlying the word search as an investigatory tool is that the meaning of the work inheres in its words in such a way that retrieving repeated words or phrases yields essential keys to the themes and significance of the work. So, for example, by retrieving the forty-eight instances of "providence" in *The Spiritual Quixote* (1773) by Richard Graves, I now have the makings of a journal article. Or do I?

Perhaps I ought also to search for such words as "foresight," "care," "God," "divine," "Almighty," "provision," "power," "economy," "guidance," "beneficence," and so on in order to make sure I cover the idea of providence in all its possible manifestations. As if to fulfill the ancient curse, with a word search one gets exactly and only what one asks for. Of course, I could easily be omitting a key word for the retrieval of this concept without ever realizing that I was missing potentially important "hits." One problem of information retrieval is that the user may easily detect the irrelevance of some of the "hits" that result from a search, but most often has no way of knowing what potentially relevant data is missing. In information science this is "the recall problem," where recall is "the proportion of relevant information that was retrieved."[5] The imprecision of a search may be rectified by sorting the results, but there is no remedy for the problem of recall, except to search the database line-by-line with a practiced eye—that is, to undertake the critical task of careful reading.

Having expanded my search and sorted the results, I recall old lessons about the often fugitive and polyvalent nature of literary language learned from William Empson's *The Structure of Complex Words* (1951) and James Boyd White's *When Words Lose Their Meaning* (1984). Considering the evidence, I am reminded that Graves's novel is comic and satirical. Even if I can discriminate among the comic, ironic, and satirical registers in the gobbets dispensed like so many gumballs from the machine, I need to consider each instance of "the providence concept" in light of the main action of the novel: Geoffrey Wildgoose's journey/pilgrimage/crusade in which he encounters and castigates Methodist "enthusiasm." I ought to evaluate each occurrence of the idea of providence, both in its immediate context and in its cumulative effect, and should compare these mentions, or invocations, or discussions of providence with other theological ideas and instances of religious language in the novel to make sure that what I am writing about is really providence and not the misappropriation of traditional religious ideas more generally.

I recall that Mr. Wildgoose himself is a Methodist and that Graves satirizes George Whitefield, his former acquaintance. Are these instances of providence in the novel related to Whitefield's writings, to John Wesley's pamphlets and sermons, or to other Methodist texts? Was Graves reacting in these passages about providence to contemporary critiques of Methodism? Was he responding to current arguments about freethinking and Deism? And how was Graves's treatment of providence in *The Spiritual Quixote* influenced by his own reading of Cervantes? I decide to abandon this methodology and elect instead to read an enjoyable book that I haven't encountered in ten years.

The nature of literary language and the complex structures of artistic works should prompt us to realize that important ideas or themes of the text do not necessarily reside in particular words or phrases that can be located and retrieved. What words would one key in, for example, to make the computer retrieve the concupiscent content of John Cleland's *Fanny Hill* (1748–49)? Where are the verbal loci of the novel's erotic effects? It is said that Cleland, when called before the Privy Council, disingenuously remarked that his book could not possibly be obscene, since it contained not a single obscene word. Lord Granville promptly gave him a government pension.[6]

Cleland's cleverness might make us wonder: to which words or phrases would one attach humor in the novel? What proximity searches (A and B within X words of each other) might one employ to assess the novel's comic effects? Yet *Fanny Hill* is both erotic and funny. How are these qualities— essential to the novel's success—communicated to the reader? Is there a particular lexicon we could isolate? There is not. Figurative language eludes the rudely mechanical. The features that escape such simplistic and superficial methods of inquiry as word searches are often the most significant and aesthetically rich aspects of a text.

If the word search is lacking, then what other tools do we have for asking questions of an electronic text? Most bibliographically reliable electronic texts are not mere transcriptions of printed texts but are encoded with markers or tags in Standard Generalized Markup Language (SGML) according to the protocols of the Text Encoding Initiative (TEI). The most basic function of SGML is to safeguard the structural integrity of electronic texts regardless of how they are "delivered," so that chapter divisions, paragraph breaks, and other structural elements are preserved whenever a text is presented in any electronic format. Encoding the structural elements of a text for electronic presentation is a form of editing because the markup put into the text determines how it appears to all users of that text.[7] In addition, SGML encoding may function as an investigatory tool when the computer assembles tagged elements in order to assist the critic in discerning patterns of meaning. Because the research tools we use shape the way we think, editors and users of electronic texts should understand both the theoretical basis and the practical implications of SGML-TEI. According to Julia Flanders, textbase editor at the Brown University Women Writers Project, "the major insight underlying SGML is that textual structure, not rendition, is the crucial feature of text encoding and storage."[8]

SGML-TEI is the result of much careful thought and collaboration among some gifted academics; it has rightly been hailed as a great breakthrough in humanities computing. SGML is based upon a definition of text as an "ordered hierarchy of content objects" (OHCO) and the belief that the genre of a text determines that hierarchy. The markup of a text is therefore conceived as an objective enterprise based upon the inherent structure of the document, so that each text is "tagged" according to its unique logical hierarchy. It has become increasingly apparent, however, that "perspectives—theories, methodologies, and analytical practices—are at least as important as genre in the identification of text objects" and in determining how these may be viewed as a hierarchy.[9] Thus, the act of encoding a text is not merely a series of mechanical practices but a theoretically based enterprise; the family of text elements used for SGML tagging (e.g., act, scene, speech, soliloquy; poem, verse, stanza, couplet, line, foot; or sentence, noun phrase, verb phrase, determiner, noun) depends upon the encoder's critical decisions, because "there is no unique hierarchy of content objects which is the text" (271).

Nancy Ide and C. M. Sperberg-McQueen, two leading theorists of electronic text markup, rightly hail the "polytheoreticity" of SGML, noting that "the tag-set may pluralistically allow the user [i.e., the encoder] to adopt any of several competing theories. It may eclectically mix the concepts of many theories (thus allowing, at least in principle, encodings reflecting hybrid mixes of theories which might be disowned by purists on either side)."[10] It is, therefore, somewhat misleading when a developer of the TEI writes about "the requirement that the encoding notations be neutral in text-theoretic terms," since the notations might be theoretically neutral, but their use can never be.[11] In other words, "our notion of a text [and hence its markup] is determined in part by the disciplinary or analytic perspective we assume, the methodological communities we are members of, and our purposes and interests," so that a book designer, bibliographer, corpus linguist, historian, or literary critic might each legitimately mark up the same text in a different way.[12] Lamentably, many current encoding applications do not make use of SGML's CONCUR feature, which enables multiple overlapping hierarchies in a single document, and are thus able to accept only one document structure, so that even the most visionary and pluralistic editors/encoders are frequently restricted in the nature and depth of the markup they can apply.

The markup or encoding of a text always entails a theory of that text.[13] The responsibility of the editor is thus at least two-fold: (1) not to relegate the determination of markup to the publisher's staff or to one's assistants but to see markup as an essential aspect of the enterprise of scholarly editing; and (2) to tell the reader/user as clearly and as comprehensively as possible about the editorial principles and analytic perspectives brought to bear on the tagging of the text. In most cases, a further area of responsibility arises. If the word search is an insufficiently sophisticated tool for the scholarly interrogation of electronic texts, and if users are then reliant upon the retrieval of SGML-encoded markers for the conduct of their computer-aided investigations, then how thorough or "rich" should such encoding be?

In a recent article, Ide, the chair of the Steering Committee of the TEI, and her colleague Sperberg-McQueen noted that, "Distinctions among required, recommended, and optional practice are common in standards documents; the TEI Guidelines differ from most such documents in the much smaller relative weight of its requirements, and the much larger weight attached to the definition of purely optional practices."[14] It is therefore easy to imagine two otherwise identical texts of, say, Sarah Fielding's *The Governess* (1749), both of which are SGML-tagged, TEI-conformant documents, but which differ significantly in their markup. Even if the hierarchies were thoroughly unproblematic and the same family of text elements was used, the breadth and depth of the encoding could vary widely.

Within the protocols of SGML-TEI, then, the editor/encoder may devote varying levels of attention and thoroughness to the markup of a text. Most electronic texts, such as the novels made available in Chadwyck-Healey's *Early English Prose Fiction, 1475–1700* and *Eighteenth-Century Fiction,* are minimally encoded. With a few minor exceptions, only the basic structural features of each text—such as imprints, dedications and prefaces, chapter divisions, the introduction of verse, and so on—are tagged. Such encoding is useful for, say, finding which novels have subscription lists, but it is not a significant aid to scholarly research. Not content with minimal encoding, and anticipating the research needs of future users, some editors may add many kinds of descriptive element tags to the electronic text so that it may be said to be "broadly encoded."

Knowing, for example, that Samuel Richardson was a printer, I might want to tag every instance of italics, small capitals, large capitals, and special characters in *Clarissa* (1747–48) to facilitate investigations into typographical form and literary meaning in that novel. I might also want to tag all the proper names in *Clarissa* by adding the <name type='person'> tag to each personal name and the <name type='place'> tag for every place name. Although the undertaking would be very labor intensive, such categories are not ordinarily recoverable for future research unless they are encoded into the text. Part of the theory underlying such a procedure is that minute "truths" about the text are recorded (*this* is italic; *this* is an ornamental type called a digit), so that when they are collectively retrieved, larger truths about the text emerge. Although the editor limits the markup of the text to the denotation of the corresponding element tag (*this* is a personal name), broad encoding may nevertheless require insight, imagination, and foresight if it is to foster genuinely useful scholarly research. Commenting on the *Critique of the* TEI *Guidelines Version 1.1 by the Literature Working Group*, Marcus Walsh rightly finds it remarkable that the document should claim that "literature scholars are not interested in . . . obtaining texts which already contain—explicitly or implicitly—literary interpretations." Textual transmission, he explains, necessarily entails some degree of interpretation; knowing this to be the case, he observes that "informed literary scholarship does not deny or ignore those included interpretations, but seeks to identify and understand them, and to take them into account." [15]

All encoding, whether minimal or broad, that limits markup to the matching of "obvious" textual elements with "obvious" tags (i.e., chapter headings receive chapter-heading tags, names receive name tags) is typically called "shallow encoding." [16] Conversely, in "deep encoding," the editors/encoders do not limit markup to the simple denotations of the tag set, but rather attempt to envision as thoroughly as possible how future researchers might interrogate the text and thus consider each relevant textual phenomenon accordingly. Deep encoding, claims one practitioner of the art, "is an exercise in indexing, in generalizing about the nuances of the remarkable language of primary texts." [17]

The editor/encoder might therefore tag not only all the personal proper names in the novel but also other personal designations such as Belford's calling Lovelace "thy *eagleship*," Clarissa naming herself "The *idiot*," Lovelace labeling Clarissa "a *baby*," and F. J. De La Tour referring to Colonel Morden as "my chevalier." [18] This could be done, for example, by creating a new subset for the "name type" tag: <name type='non-proper personal'> or, depending upon the editor/encoder's critical perspective, by using the interpretation <interp> tag: <interp value='non-proper naming'>. Because this kind of encoding is not as "objective" as tagging all the novel's proper names (though all encoding has an interpretive element), the editor/encoder may indicate personal responsibility by adding "resp" to the <interp> tag: for example, <interp resp=MFS value='non-proper naming'>. This may be especially useful when several editors/encoders—or indeed users/editors/encoders later in the life of the edition—have been collaborating on one text.

It is, alas, unlikely that editors would take the trouble to encode such a phenomenon as non-proper naming, even if they recognized its importance, because of the time and critical attention required to introduce such tags into the text. For most users, encoding is invisible; at this juncture, an editor who might reasonably spend several years deeply encoding *Clarissa* for an electronic edition is unlikely to be sufficiently rewarded by the academy or the publishing industry for producing imaginative, detailed, and nuanced markup that few users will exploit or closely examine. In fact, editors/encoders would be very unlikely to tag all the personal proper names in *Clarissa*— much less other personal designations—because the document would still be TEI-conformant without such tags and most editors would assume that such "textual objects" would be better found by simple word searches. Being accustomed to minimally encoded electronic texts, and developing the habit of asking simplistic questions that rely upon the retrieval of "surface-level" data, most users might never take advantage of what has been so laboriously produced.

Unlike collating the important versions of a work and producing a list of textual variants—a body of evidence that few scholars routinely use but that is essential to producing a critical edition of an acceptable scholarly standard—electronic editors have little incentive to produce editions that are more than minimally encoded because the scholarly community pays so little attention to the quality of markup. A good case in point is the flood of electronic texts published by Chadwyck-Healey in recent years. Though some scholars have rightly criticized the editions used for transcription and even the works chosen for inclusion in various databases, very few have commented that the minimalist encoding of the texts makes them virtually useless for SGML searching. The word search is thus the primary electronic research tool for interrogating these texts.

Again the problem of recall comes into play, since a word search will only produce "hits" for what is requested. This is perfectly serviceable if, for example, a researcher wishes to locate the passage where Lovelace compares himself to Æneas and Clarissa to Dido (1142–43) by typing in "Dido"; the electronic edition is in this instance merely a convenience that will save the scholar the time and frustration of flicking through Richardson's capacious text for half an hour to find what she already knows is there. If, however, the researcher is interested in the distribution of classical and Christian names in *Clarissa,* or wishes to locate every mention of Latin and English authors in the novel, or wants to think further about an inchoate thesis concerning onomastics in Richardson's work, then encoding personal proper names is essential.

It is nevertheless telling that, for a researcher considering the very important question of naming in *Clarissa,* such otherwise hidden instances as *"eagleship," "idiot," "baby,"* and "chevalier" are far more critically significant than the standard proper names retrieved by the <name type='person'> tag. A scholar investigating the issue of naming in Richardson's work via Chadwyck-Healey's *Eighteenth-Century Fiction* on CD-ROM would immediately realize that she was encountering a different kind of "recall problem"; her search for personal names would yield no results because none has been tagged—all the texts are only minimally encoded (and indeed were encoded by the publisher's staff without any detailed advice from the project's editorial board). If she were searching the same database as part of Chadwyck-Healey's Literature Online Service (LION) via the World Wide Web, she would soon discover that, because the Web-delivery software the publisher chose for LION (OpenText) is "relational" rather than "full SGML," there is *no* possibility of searching *any* of the SGML markup in any of the databases LION provides.[19] This loss of searching capability limits the kind of questions a scholar can ask and is an enormous disincentive for editors to enrich their electronic editions with anything more than the minimal encoding to make the document TEI-conformant.

One problem of literary analysis based upon tagged texts is that researchers will quite naturally tend to analyze what is easy to find, to do what the editions make it easy for them to do. Searching minimally encoded texts by their SGML tags is almost invariably little more than a form of rapid navigation. Useful results from broadly and deeply encoded texts depend upon the editor/encoder's scrupulous consistency and meticulous attention to the minute details of the text. The user must be able to trust the quality of the markup, since it is not practicably possible to check the enormous number of tags added to a thoroughly encoded novel. Careful scholars will always collate the most important pericopes for their critical arguments against several editions of the text—"soiled fish" or "coiled fish"?—but a scholar undertaking a study of Dickens's use of dialect could hardly be expected to check the whole markup of his *oeuvre*.

Useful results also depend upon the posing of cogent questions and upon a thorough understanding of the principles and practices according to which the text was encoded. It may be obvious to say that, as with a printed text, the quality of the answer one gets from an electronic text depends upon the intelligence of the question one puts to it. Less generally recognized, however, is the truth that the success and critical acumen of the questions posed to an electronic text depend in no small measure upon the investigator's understanding of the encoding of that text. When searching by SGML tags, one is only retrieving the aggregate of a subset of individual observations that have already been made about the text.

Electronic editors should view encoding not as a merely mechanical operation but as embodying theories of texts and as presenting opportunities for making their editions more useful for scholarly research. Clearly, broad encoding would allow readers to move beyond the word search in using the computer to help ask questions of the text. But how thorough should markup be? Given the interpretive element in all encoding, to what extent will scholars want to depend upon someone else's markup as the basis of their study? We need to think seriously about how this fundamental editorial activity affects the quality and reception of electronic texts. Meanwhile, the novels I study and teach will continue to receive my own "markup," as I read and reread with pen in hand.

Is There a Text in This Hypertext?

Friend. The Tale is indeed good. . . . But shall we never return to our Story again?
    Author. It matters not how far we travel from it, since the Magic of a Wish can bring us back in a twinkling.—Henry Brooke, *The Fool of Quality* (1765)

While few scholars have gushed about SGML-TEI, there has been a great deal of hype about hypertext linking and the revolutionary impact it is bound to have on literary studies.[20] Despite the many inflated claims, it is clear that hypertext is a powerful tool that allows authors and editors to overcome the limitations of the codex's page sequence by creating "webs" of linked documents. Freed by the electronic environment from many of the economic and physical constraints upon the display of texts and images, the hypertext editor can create a seemingly limitless weave of intertextuality, a field of play where text and context are reconfigured in such a way that their hierarchical relations are dispersed.

Kathryn Sutherland, herself a hypertext editor as the director of Project Electra, suggests that, "In the case of a serialized novel by Dickens, the effect [of hypertext] would be to re-embed the literary text within a plenitude of cultural codes and discourses," thus encouraging the reader "to site the fictional narrative within a more varied system of evidences than traditional reading and publishing strategies encourage." Such recontextualizing of the literary work via a hypertext web shifts the reader's focus from linguistic analysis to the social relations of the text and so "promotes an understanding of the infusive operations of cultural models within a particular society and time."[21]

Clearly, intriguing possibilities develop when the editor can embed the text in an apparently unbounded constellation of ideas and information and is no longer confined to the footnote or the appendix for the introduction of context. Moreover, many commentators have been especially excited by the fact that the hypertext environment enables the reader to assume the role of editor, generating new links within the web and even adding new documents to it. Yet what are the effects upon the user of hypertext's nonlinear, nonprioritizing, "connectionist" nebulae of information? In a telling article on the use of George Landow's *The Dickens Web* as a teaching tool, Jonathan Smith writes: "The difficulty [for the students] was with what to *do* with a link once they had followed or constructed it."[22]

Smith found that "the effort that must be devoted to learning the technology [of creating hypertext links] . . . does distract students from the content of the course" (126). This was so even though Smith assigned just *two* novels for "an upper-level English class on the nineteenth-century British novel"

(121) so that his students could read and write hypertexts about these texts. He discovered that "students must be taught to read hypertextually" (128), and that "the [Dickens] Web exposed the students to more contextual material than they are usually interested in reading," offering such "short documents" as "Humor in Dickens" or "Public Schools" (123).

Smith dismisses "the obvious potential dangers of relying on what might be called 'sound-bite scholarship'" (123), though my own encounters with Landow's work have left me less convinced. Was it the undergraduates' woefully ahistorical perspective that led "many of the students to complain that very little of the material on the Web seemed to be connected to the novel at all" (125)? Or was it perhaps their sense that, in directing them down a series of links from "Difficulties in Childbirth" to "Sanitation and Disease in Rich and Poor" to "Queen Victoria," the hypertext was leading them away from the *primary* text, away from Dickens's great art—which needs to be enjoyed and thoughtfully considered—to Landow's Victorian micropædia?

Although he found *The Dickens Web* "worth using and worth continuing to use" (128), Smith discovered that many of the emancipatory claims made by hypertext evangelists—such as Landow's conviction that hypertexts "intrinsically promote a new kind of academic freedom and empowerment" or foster "increasing democratization and decentralization of power"—were groundless (127).[23] "Hypertext authors cede less control to the reader than is usually admitted," he discovered, observing that "the hypertext reader's choices are constrained, though constrained differently," and that "hypertext itself is not inherently or necessarily democratic or anti-hierarchical" (128).

The foregoing example has obvious implications for the editor planning to produce an electronic version of a print-based novel. The criteria of relevance and of connection are value judgments that will powerfully affect the reader/user's experience of the primary text, not least because hypertext links, as Steven J. DeRose and David G. Durand point out, "are often as much a part of the document's meaning as the text itself."[24] Although the electronic environment offers the editor seemingly unbounded room to hyper-contextualize and to hyper-link, is more necessarily better?

What happens to the aesthetic experience of reading a novel when the user of an electronic edition is constantly diverting her narrative progress to follow detours that were never part of the writer's art? How does *lectio inter-*

rupta diminish the creative process? Hypertext links produce discontinuities. Is it not possible in the nonprioritizing virtual world of electronic editions to drown the once-primary text in so much once-secondary material that we return to the state of literary studies that prompted the New Critics to rescue the text from historical overdeterminism?

Hypertext maven Jay David Bolter acknowledges that the new structures of electronic texts have far-reaching consequences: "Any text becomes a temporary structure in the changing web of relations. . . . The original text loses its privileged status. . . . The loss of the great text as a touchstone and of the great author as authority is real and unavoidable."[25] Why is this so? Sutherland goes to the heart of the matter when she remarks: "The identity of the text itself is displaced by its own excess," not least because "the electronic environment . . . promises seemingly endless deferral—of choice, preference, exclusion."[26] What, then, are the choices the electronic editor ought to make when reading becomes navigating across a cultural collage, a diffuse surface activity, rather than an intense, in-depth phenomenon focused upon the work of art?

We can begin to answer this important question by looking at one of the most widely publicized hypertext projects in process today: Jerome McGann's *Complete Writings and Pictures of Dante Gabriel Rossetti: A Hypermedia Research Archive.* This project is an ambitious and praiseworthy experiment in using the electronic environment for literary and art-historical research; its ideal is to make available as a digital image "every textual and pictorial document relevant to the study of Rosetti."[27] McGann's previous scholarship has both enlivened students of literature to the sociology of texts and freed critical editing from many of its pseudo-scientific entailments. My concern, however, is that in designing the Rossetti project as an exercise in documentary editing, he is planning to complete only half of the task that needs to be done. According to McGann, "the Rossetti project is an archive rather than an edition," but it may be thought of as a hyperedition: "An edition is 'hyper,'" McGann tells us, "exactly because its structure is such that it seeks to preserve the authority of all the units that comprise its documentary arrays. In this respect a hyperedition resembles that fabulous circle whose center is everywhere and whose circumference is nowhere."[28]

There is no editorial choice that privileges one form of the text—manu-

script, corrected proof sheets, revised proof, first edition, authorially revised fifth edition, and so on—over any of the others. There is no "rationale
of copy-text" for "the decentered text" because there is no critical editing.
McGann believes that "HyperEditing" does not require any central text, either for the organization of the documents or for the orientation of the users:
"Unlike a traditional edition, a HyperText is not organized to focus attention
on one particular text or set of texts. It is ordered to disperse attention as
broadly as possible. . . . Unlike the book, [it] encourages greater decentralization" (10).[29] We might reasonably say, then, that McGann's concept of the
hyperedition more closely resembles a circle whose circumference is everywhere and whose center is nowhere.

McGann's explanation of the difficulties inherent in producing a critical
edition provides a compelling argument for doing so:

> Rossetti typically worked and reworked his poems and pictures in the
> minutest fashion: dozens of authorized textual states survive for most of
> his works, many carrying complex revisions and alterations; and these
> revised documents often stand in labyrinthine patterns of relation with
> each other. Constructing a codex-based critical edition even of Rossetti's
> poetry alone is therefore a daunting, perhaps an impossible, task.[30]

It is precisely *because* the textual relations are so complex and the interaction
of visual and verbal materials so important that Rossetti requires a critical
edition, though it certainly need not be "codex-based."[31] It is naive to believe
that every user of the database becomes his or her own do-it-yourself editor and is thus "empowered" to make decisions based upon whatever value
judgments seem most personally appropriate. With the exception of Rossetti
specialists who are also competent in critical editing, very few users will be
sufficiently qualified to make the intricate and critical choices necessary to
negotiate their way through such a morass of textual indeterminacy. By ab-
dicating the responsibility for establishing a text through the long and demanding process of critical discernment, of carefully weighing complex evidence and deciding in the midst of difficulty, the electronic editor is not
empowering users but obliging them to arrive at judgments they most often
will have neither the time nor the expertise to make.

This is not freedom, but the illusion of freedom. A principle of the virtue ethics derived from Aristotle is that freedom does not mean doing whatever one may feel like; rather, freedom is the ability to choose wisely, to make the best choice available.[32] Hypertext archives unaccompanied by critical editions do not maximize freedom, because—even with their commentaries on individual documents—they do not equip the reader to choose wisely and well. The open editorial program of many electronic publishing projects ignores the hard truths that information is not knowledge, access is not critical understanding.

If I am presented with a critical edition of William Beckford's *Vathek,* for example, and if I generally accept the editorial principles upon which it is based, then I have one choice to make at any point in my encounter with the text: am I able to accept this reading or shall I search for another? This is very different from beginning by asking oneself: what text shall I choose as my basic text—Lausanne 1786? London 1786? Paris 1787? London 1815? London 1816? (if so, which of the three issues should I prefer?), or London 1823? How shall I decide? What grounds, if any, are there for emending passages? Which ones? How should those passages be emended? But I do not want to be my own editor of *Vathek;* I want to read the novel in the best text available, understand the history of its transmission and reception, and be able to consult its significant textual variants.

In an era when hypertext archives may be comprehensive but not comprehensible, scholarly critical editions would do much to help ensure that literary studies do not become chiefly a matter of information management. Electronic editors need not accept, however, the extreme case of establishing *the* definitive edition that forever fixes the text and must be the standard for all subsequent interpretive work: such positivism has no place in so humanistic a discipline as literary editing.[33] Rather, the electronic format allows editors to explain comprehensively the reasons behind their critical decisions and to display all the available evidence—manuscript facsimiles, transcripts, various stages of proofs, printed editions, the "collateral evidence" of letters, printers' ledgers, and so on—upon which their judgments were based.

Unlike the browser of a "decentralized" archive, the user of an electronic critical edition would be given a particular intellectual vision: a set of editorial principles and judgments derived from them. A significant advantage of the electronic critical edition over the codex-based scholarly text is that users wishing to question individual readings are provided not only with a list of variants but also with the opportunity to view them in their contexts. That should quickly destroy any residual positivistic illusions the editor might have. Yet, if editorial certainty is impossible, it does not follow that we should undertake no critical editing and surrender to a textual skepticism that leaves us forever in a world of radical indeterminacy. Peter L. Shillingsburg strikes the right note when he writes, "the best one can hope for [as an editor] is a *less* unsatisfactory text" (63).

It seems to me most helpful to think about electronic critical editions, not as monuments, but as maps. When I go hiking and climbing in the Lake District, I take a set of highly detailed orienteering maps produced by computer from LANDSAT (EOSAT) photographs, though I almost never use them. Instead, my constant reference is a set of hand-drawn maps by A. Wainwright called *A Pictorial Guide to the Lakeland Fells* (7 vols., 1955–66). The maps—which typically show ways of ascent, ridge routes, views, and various descents for each fell—are scrupulously researched renderings of the landscape, though Wainright urges readers to "use these volumes as basic notebooks and make their own corrections as the need arises" (verso of title page).

What makes these maps so useful is not only their accuracy but also the fact that they are *interpretations*. Unlike the LANDSAT maps, which give me every unmediated feature so that I am overwhelmed by the detail of the landscape, Wainwright's pen sketches are necessarily selective—the product of what anthropologists call "local knowledge," earned, in this instance, one step at a time.

Similarly, the critical editor must interpret and select from the masses of potentially relevant data available; the edition is valuable because the editor has spent far more time on the mountain in more kinds of weather than I have. He possesses local knowledge and has developed skills of discrimination that it would take me years to acquire. Nevertheless, there may well be times when I disagree with his interpretation and need to refer to the highly detailed LANDSAT photos of multiple variant texts to find a new route of ascent. I shall feel free to make corrections as the need arises, but think no less of the editor because we come to a different reading: he may have been mistaken or the landscape may have changed. I am no less grateful for his discerning interpretive intelligence which helps to guide my explorations through a landscape of overwhelming detail and does much to help me enjoy and think about the literary work.

Scholars involved in the production and use of electronic texts need to be resolutely critical, not only in their editorial activities but also in thinking about how these texts will shape the future of literary studies. It would not be difficult to read an entire novel on a high-quality monitor, but will anyone? What is the difference between being a user and being a reader? How does altering the physicality of fiction alter our attitude toward the text and, hence, our response?

Most of us read fiction for the pleasures of plot and character but scrutinize screens for data. Readers of literature may even find themselves encountering what Martha Nussbaum has elegantly called "love's knowledge," whereas users of literature databases may unwittingly settle for generating information.[34] The potential hazard of these excellent tools for scholarship and learning is that the patterns of their use—typically six minutes in the reference section of a university library—tend to emphasize the "puzzle principle" of literature over the pleasure principle of all art worth our time and consideration. Using the latest technology to foster creative engagement with a broad spectrum of texts, we need to work toward understanding— the harvest of thoughtful and critical discernment—if knowledge is not to be lost in information. The speed of electronic texts can belie the reality that human understanding takes time.

Notes

I wish to thank Lesley Higgins and Suzanne Aspden, who kindly read this essay in manuscript.

1. Mark Olsen, "Signs, Symbols and Discourses: A New Direction for Computer-Aided Literature Studies," *Computers and the Humanities* 27 (1993): 309, 312.

2. Thomas Corns, "Computers in the Humanities: Methods and Applications in the Study of English Literature," *Literary and Linguistic Computing* 6 (1991): 128; Allen Renear, "Understanding (hyper)Media: Required Readings," *Computers and the Humanities* 29 (1995): 389.

3. Julius Laffal, "A Concept Analysis of Jonathan Swift's *A Tale of a Tub* and *Gulliver's Travels*," *Computers and the Humanities* 29 (1995): 339; C. Ruth Sabol, "Semantic Analysis and Fictive Worlds in Ford and Conrad," *Literary and Linguistic Computing* 6 (1991): 97.

4. In addition, machine-generated concordances may be useful tools; editors often benefit from several software packages—such as COLLATE, PC-CASE, and MAC-CASE—for computer-assisted scholarly editing. See Peter L. Shillingsburg, *Scholarly Editing in the Computer Age,* rev. ed. (Ann Arbor: University of Michigan Press, 1996), 133–48.

5. C. N. Ball, "Automated Text Analysis: Cautionary Tales," *Literary and Linguistic Computing* 9 (1994): 295. See also D. Blair and E. Maron, "An Evaluation of Retrieval Effectiveness for a Full-text Document Retrieval System," *Communications of the ACM* 28 (1985): 298–99, who note that users expressed confidence in electronic retrieval even when the system retrieved less than 50 percent of the extant relevant information (cited in Ball, 295–96).

6. The story of Cleland's appearance before the Privy Council, though often repeated in various forms from the *Gentleman's Magazine* (Feb. 1789, p.180) to the 1985 Penguin edition of *Fanny Hill,* is probably apocryphal; see David Foxon, *Libertine Literature in England 1660–1745* (New Hyde Park NY: University Books, 1965), 58–59.

7. See John Lavagino, "Completeness and Adequacy in Text Encoding," in *The Literary Text in the Digital Age,* ed. Richard J. Finneran (Ann Arbor: University of Michigan Press, 1996), 63–76.

8. Julia Flanders, review of *The Transcription of Primary Textual Sources Using SGML,* by Peter Robinson, *Computers and the Humanities* 30 (1996): 98.

9. Allen Renear, Eli Mylonas, and David Durand, "Refining our Notion of What Text Really Is: The Problem of Overlapping Hierarchies," in *Research in Humanities Computing* 4 (1996): 277.

10. Nancy Ide and C. M. Sperberg-McQueen, "The TEI: History, Goals, and Future," *Computers and the Humanities* 29 (1995): 10.

11. Robin C. Cover and Peter M. W. Robinson, "Encoding Textual Criticism," *Computers and the Humanities* 29 (1995): 123.

12. Allen Renear, "Representing Text on the Computer: Lessons for and from Philosophy," *Bulletin of the John Rylands University Library of Manchester* 74 (1992): 245.

13. For a fine discussion of this issue, see C. M. Sperberg-McQueen, "Text in the Electronic Age: Textual Study and Text Encoding, with Examples from Medieval Texts," *Literary and Linguistic Computing* 6 (1991): 34–46.

14. Ide and Sperberg-McQueen, "The TEI," 8.

15. Marcus Walsh, "The Fluid Text and the Orientations of Editing," in *The Politics of the Electronic Text,* ed. Warren Chernaik, Caroline Davis, and Marilyn Deegan (Oxford: Office for Humanities Communication, 1993), 36. Many bibliographers would argue that interpretations included in texts by the process of their transmission are important keys to understanding their reception and meaning; see, for example, D. F. McKenzie, *Bibliography and the Sociology of Texts* (London: The British Library, 1986); and Jerome J. McGann, "The Monks and the Giants: Textual and Bibliographical Studies and the Interpretation of Literary Works," in *Textual Criticism and Literary Interpretation,* ed. McGann (Chicago: University of Chicago Press, 1985), 180–99.

16. In one sense this is unfortunate because a shallowly encoded text that has been broadly tagged is of much greater use for research than a minimally encoded text.

17. Michael Neuman, "You Can't Always Get What You Want: Deep Encoding of Manuscripts and the Limits of Retrieval," in *Research in Humanities Computing* 5 (1996): 216. The examples that follow are my own but are indebted to the thinking of Neuman and of Willard L. McCarty, "Peering Through the Skylight: Towards an Electronic Edition of Ovid's *Metamorphoses*," in *Research in Humanities Computing* 4 (1996): 240–62.

18. Samuel Richardson, *Clarissa, or the History of a Young Lady,* ed. Angus Ross (London: Penguin, 1985): 191, 521, 605, 1486.

19. Had Lion employed a different software package (DynaWeb), this problem would, I understand, have been obviated.

20. See, for example, Jay David Bolter, *Writing Space: The Computer, Hypertext, and the History of Writing* (Hillsdale NJ: Lawrence Erlbaum Associates, 1991); George P. Landow, *Hypertext: The Convergence of Contemporary Critical Theory and Technology* (Baltimore: Johns Hopkins University Press, 1992); and Richard A. Lanham, *The Electronic Word: Democracy, Technology, and the Arts* (Chicago: University of Chicago Press, 1993).

21. Kathryn Sutherland, "Waiting for Connections: Hypertexts, Multiplots, and the Engaged Reader," *Research in Humanities Computing* 3 (1994): 52, 56.

22. Jonathan Smith, "What's All This Hype About Hypertext? Teaching Literature with George P. Landow's *The Dickens Web*," *Computers and the Humanities* 30 (1996): 124.

23. Smith's two quotations are from George Landow, *Hypertext: The Convergence of Contemporary Critical Theory and Technology* (Baltimore: Johns Hopkins University Press, 1992), 169, 177.

24. Steven J. DeRose and David G. Durand, "The TEI Hypertext Guidelines," *Computers and the Humanities* 29 (1995): 188.

25. Jay David Bolter, "Literature in the Electronic Writing Space," in *Literacy Online: The Promise (and Peril) of Reading and Writing with Computers,* ed. Myron C. Tuman (Pittsburgh: University Press of Pittsburgh, 1992), 36, 37.

26. Kathryn Sutherland, "Looking and Knowing: Textual Encounters of a Postponed Kind," in *Beyond the Book: Theory, Culture, and the Politics of Cyberspace,* ed. Warren Chernaik, Marilyn Deegan, and Andrew Gibson (Oxford: Office for Humanities Communication, 1996), 12, 13.

27. See the *Archive*'s home page at <http://jefferson.village.virginia.edu/rossetti/rossetti.html>.

28. Jerome J. McGann, "The Rationale of HyperText," <http://jefferson.village.virginia.edu/public/jjm2f/rationale.html>, 13. The essay appears in different form in *TEXT* 9 (1996): 11–32.

29. McGann notes that his "Rationale of HyperText" "has been written in a conscious revisionary relation to W. W. Greg's great essay 'The Rationale of Copy-Text'" (17 n.9). See Greg, *Studies in Bibliography* 3 (1950–51): 19–36.

30. Jerome McGann, "The Rossetti Archive and Image-Based Electronic Editing," in *The Literary Text in the Digital Age,* ed. Richard J. Finneran (Ann Arbor: University of Michigan Press, 1996), 149.

31. The *William Blake Archive* <http://jefferson.village.virginia.edu/blake/>, perhaps the most ambitious and visionary of all such scholarly projects on the World Wide Web, addresses the problem of radical textual indeterminacy while still providing variant texts by posting an electronic version of *The Complete Poetry and Prose of William Blake,* ed. David V. Erdman (New York: Anchor, 1988).

32. This ethical school has its origins in the *Nichomachean Ethics;* on freedom as choosing the good rather than being free from all constraints, see Aristotle's *Politics,* 1310a, 24.

33. Richard A. Lanham, who should know better, claims that "establishing *the* fixed text has been the humanistic *raison d'être* since the Renaissance. To nail it down forever and then finally explain it, has been what literary scholars do"; see "The Electronic Word: Literary Study and the Digital Revolution," *New Literary History* 20 (1988–89): 268, rpt. in Lanham, *The Electronic Word.* A salutary antidote to the positivistic element in some schools of editing is McGann, *A Critique of Modern Textual Criticism* (1983; reprint, Charlottesville: University Press of Virginia, 1992).

34. Martha Nussbaum, *Love's Knowledge: Essays on Philosophy and Literature* (Oxford: Oxford University Press, 1990), 261–85 and passim.

Response

Whose Work Is

It Anyway? Or,

How We Learned

to Stop Worrying

about the Author

and Love the Text

🐾 🐾 🐾

Albert J. Rivero

There was a time when critical editions were fashioned according to authorial intentions. Under ideal circumstances, the editor would use the original manuscript as his or her copy-text, presumably because it embodied authorial intentions in their purest form, before the work became contaminated by the process of publication. Fredson Bowers was the most eloquent advocate of this position. Alas, ideal circumstances seldom obtain, and, when the original manuscript did not survive, the editor would generally choose as copy-text the first printed edition, the earliest and thus purest of the surviving documents in the line of transmission from author to reader. Though for Bowers this was a necessary compromise, for others—most prominently, Philip Gaskell—the first printed edition had better claims to being used as copy-text because, supposedly the product of collaboration between author and publisher, it represented the author's final intentions for the *published* book. Both Bowers and Gaskell believed in the authority of authors, but they located that authority in different documents.[1]

Because of the paucity of original manuscripts for many of the works he edited, Bowers's actual editorial practice turned out at times to follow Gaskell's theory more closely than his own. Unless other editions proved more authoritative, the first printed edition became his copy-text by default. Following W. W. Greg, Bowers fully accepted the accidentals of this edition—emending, of course, what could be identified as obvious compositor's errors—and altered the substantives only as warranted by the author's subsequent revisions. For Bowers, then, the work of the editor was first to sift the historical evidence as objectively as possible in order to ascertain the author's final intentions, and then to use those intentions as touchstones to adjudicate between authoritative readings and corruptions. The resultant eclectic text, though having never existed before Bowers's publication of his critical edition, was nonetheless presented as a historically accurate restoration of the work originally intended by the author.

Whose work did Bowers mean to publish in his critical edition? The author's. Whose text did he actually end up publishing? For observers looking back over a spent century, the question may be too easy, especially for those of us who, while perhaps not entirely believing in the death of the author or the demise of objectivity, nonetheless relish the possibilities for textual proliferation opened up by our current critical condition. Academics now tend to regard authorial intention as one of the many fictions that we have fashioned to prop up our critical work. Perhaps because intellectual history discounts methodological inheritance or perhaps because the academic system of publication and promotion makes it seem to do so, we have had to come up with additional ways of justifying our critical readings and editorial procedures. The individual, historically situated author has been taken down a notch or two—though it is worth noting that the New Critics were arguing against intentionalism long before textualists began doing so. Given our self-consciousness in these matters, we can confidently assert that, whatever his claims to historical objectivity, Bowers published his own version of the author's work, though, with commendable modesty, he chose to pass off his work as the author's.

With the possible exception of G. Thomas Tanselle, textualists these days largely agree that Bowers's rigid espousal of final authorial intention as the sole editorial criterion is reductive, and that publication, as Jerome McGann reminded us in 1983, is a collaborative enterprise involving not only authors and publishers but also editors, readers, and others.[2] A work passes through many hands and institutions before it reaches its readers; it prejudices the case to characterize this process as "contamination." McGann's advocacy of the social text, the result of his judging the principles of the Greg/Bowers school inadequate to deal with the multiple versions and other complexities of Byron's *The Giaour* (1813), ought to remind us that, in the last analysis, an editor must adapt his or her theories and practices to the particularities of the work that he or she is editing. In short, the editor is the hero of our textual adventures; and, like the texts that he or she edits, the editor is protean. The essays gathered here suggest that authorial intention has survived its unmasking as a Romantic illusion and has not entirely lost its explanatory power. But they suggest as well that intention is only one of many factors to be taken into account in fashioning a critical edition. By focusing on specific novels and specific editorial problems, the essays exemplify our post-Bowers and arguably post-McGann view of textual editing as eclectic, pragmatic, and contingent.

In the opening essay, on editing Willa Cather, Susan J. Rosowski and her colleagues exhibit some refreshingly old-fashioned views—though sometimes in the service of unorthodox editorial practices. Authorial intentions are alive and well in Nebraska, primarily because there is so much documentary evidence testifying to those intentions. The coalescence of clear intentions and plenteous documents prompts Rosowski and her colleagues to argue for an unusually high degree of attention to an author's wishes. "An authoritative edition" of Cather's works, they believe, "must go beyond the sequence of words and punctuation to include other and more overtly physical matters," such as page format, paper stock, typeface, and so on. While the physical reproduction of the works as Cather would have liked to see them might strike some as pursuing authorial intentions a bit too far, it makes sense for an edition that is meant to reflect Cather's concern for the "common reader."[3]

Of course "the sequence of words and punctuation" is still the crucial editorial problem. Here the wealth of material presents enormous challenges. For example, which of the three "authoritative" editions—the *Century* serial publication, the Knopf first edition, or the Autograph Edition—does the editor choose as copy-text? After assessing the suitability of each edition, Rosowski and her co-writers state their rationale for copy-text in words that suggest that rumors of the death of the Greg/Bowers school have been greatly exaggerated: "In the absence of manuscripts, the policy of the Cather edition is to choose as copy-text the first edition of a novel in book form; the policy is based on the idea that such a choice will best represent the realized intention of the author, and her latest revising hand, at the time closest to the period of composition." This statement is interesting for another reason as well. The Cather editors believe that, in choosing between an earlier and later reading, the editor ought to choose the former because it represents "Cather's intention at the time of original composition," the period of her "most intense involvement with the work." Implicit here is the idea that, with the passing of time, even the author begins to "contaminate" her own work, a view that Bowers would applaud and McGann would deplore. But if Rosowski and her colleagues sound at times like naive intentionalists, the volumes they have actually produced offer their readers, in addition to a readable and long-familiar text, access to a rich and complex historical archive that not only proves but also transcends any simple theory of intention.

Authorial intention worries Noel Polk as well. What if "the stuff that don't matter"—the accidentals of the text like dashes and ellipses—actually do matter? What if a word full of rich critical possibilities—like "rotundra" in the typescript of William Faulkner's *Pylon* (1935)—turns out, upon further review, not to be Faulkner's modernist fashioning of a portmanteau word but evidence that he did not know how to spell "rotunda"? As Polk humorously shares his editorial obsessions and nightmares, we are reminded that these matters, when they matter (but who can tell?), *really* matter, both in our published work and in our classrooms. I can still recall, with bemused horror, the critical fantasies I once wove for my sophomores around the nonsensical phrase "with gleams of varnished spirits," found in the second paragraph of "Heart of Darkness" (1902) as it appeared in the fifth edition of *The Norton Anthology of English Literature* (1986). By restoring the correct reading, "sprits"—a frustratingly unambiguous nautical term—the subsequent edition excised a good ten minutes of spirited discussion from my introductory class on the work, not to mention one of the crucial pieces of evidence in my theory that virtually every word in Conrad's tale exudes psychological complexity. The follies of editors will be visited on those trusting souls who use their texts, especially when those texts are transmitted in institutionally sanctioned critical editions or in such seemingly authoritative publications as the *Norton Anthology*. One letter matters; this is why Noel Polk, responsible editor that he is, stays up nights worrying.

Polk's essay foregrounds what editors have always known but, until recent calls for honest accounting made them fess up, have rarely proclaimed: that many editorial decisions are based on the editor's critical interpretation of the author's work. Polk agonizes over dashes and ellipses because he sees Faulkner as a modernist writer, for whom such matters might matter. This is why he restored the typescript reading of "rotundra" in his edition of *Pylon,* even though the original editors had corrected what Polk eventually agreed, after examining the typescript of *The Mansion* (1959) some years later, was a typographical error, repeated twenty times. Of course, Polk could still be wrong. After all, Faulkner might have meant to write "rotundra" in *Pylon,* for all the reasons that Polk thought of, and simply slipped when typing the word more than two decades later in the typescript of *The Mansion.* Or Faulkner might have thought that the word was indeed spelled "rotundra" and thanked the language gods for a word that so wonderfully captured his "wasteland imagery." I could go on, but my point is simply that Polk could have saved himself a lot of grief if he had kept his critical speculations out of his editorial work.

But of course Polk could not do so because what he did is what responsible critical editors do, especially when facing a doubtful reading. As Philip Cohen asserts in "William Faulkner, the Crisis of Masculinity, and Textual Instability," textual studies and literary theory have always shared "a complex dialectical relationship." That relationship, however, is becoming increasingly vexed. Polk's confidence that he will find the correct word or punctuation—even when the evidence seems to frustrate his quixotic desire for precision—is worlds away from the situation Cohen describes in the opening paragraphs of his essay. However much Polk might vacillate before reaching his decision, he *will* decide one way or the other: his *Pylon* will have "rotundra" or "rotunda," not both. But since current literary theory and criticism privilege textual instability, it is not surprising to find, as Peter Shillingsburg indicates later in this collection, that textual scholarship has moved away from championing the single stable text to advocating multiple versions. This move may be seen either as the welcome recognition that one size does not fit all, that some works may be represented in one text while most cannot, or as a deplorable abjuration of the editor's office. If we agree that language is unstable and that texts are indeterminate, we need not attempt to fix meanings or texts. This is why, I believe, hypertexts are so appealing to some of us, mirroring in their fluidity and malleability our desire for polysemousness, our postmodern delight in disorder. Curiously enough, as Cohen observes, while textual scholars have attempted to change their discipline to accommodate the latest trends in literary theory and criticism, many literary theorists and critics remain unaware of how textual scholarship impinges on what they do. Cohen accurately notes that such critics combine "a postmodern critical orientation with a traditional, if unacknowledged, Romantic-Modernist textual orientation."

Cohen demonstrates that literary theorists and critics can benefit from an awareness of current textual scholarship. His test-case concerns the original version of *Sartoris* (1929), *Flags in the Dust* (unpublished until 1973), which he finds "suffused with Faulkner's obsession with the failure of contemporary masculinity." By examining in detail some of the major excisions made to *Flags in the Dust* by Ben Wasson as he condensed the novel to make it acceptable to its publisher, Cohen shows that this potentially offensive and explosive theme all but disappears from the published *Sartoris*. A careful study of this complicated publication history, Cohen argues, offers crucial evidence to critics, whether they be feminists, new historicists, or cultural historians, interested in the troubled role of masculinity—gender, more broadly—in Faulkner's earlier work. Such a study will also remind us once more that solitary authorship is largely a Romantic, capitalist myth, "that professional authors, like most writers, routinely revise their work, and that many other agents routinely assist them." In short, textual studies and literary theory and criticism are inextricably bound up, though I wonder whether Cohen would have been able to deduce Faulkner's "crisis of masculinity" only from examining the publication history of *Flags/Sartoris* or whether he was able to do so only because of the current critical interest in the topic. But my puzzlement here might only prove Cohen's point about the inseparability of these two ways of intervening in the interpretation of literary works.

That inseparability is the theme of James L. W. West III's "The Scholarly Editor as Biographer." Unlike Cohen, West explicitly identifies his method as inductive rather than deductive. Again unlike Cohen, who waffles somewhat in his allegiance to authorial intentions, West unequivocally declares that "scholarly editing is an exercise in *biography*." But West is no naive disciple of the school of authorial intentions. In fact, the "biography" he is talking about is a "biography" fashioned by the editor—out of historical evidence, to be sure, but largely of the editor's own making. The editor constructs "an author who will approve (posthumously) of the text that is going to be published." In other words, West argues that textual editors, before beginning their editorial tasks, have already constructed biographical grids for their authors into which they will or will not fit the materials before them. For West, scholarly editing has "empirical features" but is not finally an empiricist enterprise: "It relies on intuition and imagination much more heavily than it does on analysis of evidence," he believes. This is a truth, I would suggest, known to textual editors (and biographers) for quite some time—known to Bowers as well as to McGann—though not universally acknowledged until recent disciplinary and institutional changes have made it possible and necessary to do so.

West illustrates his claims by drawing on his experience as editor of Theodore Dreiser's *Sister Carrie* (1900; 1981) and *Jennie Gerhardt* (1911; 1992). He wished to disprove the once-prevalent view of Dreiser as an inept author rescued from his own boorishness and clumsiness by his early editors—a view that privileged the originally published editions of the novels. So he created a Dreiser "more attentive to his texts and more troubled about editorial tampering than earlier biographers and critics believed." He then edited the novels accordingly, restoring the texts as his "Dreiser" would have liked to have seen them published, before all that "editorial tampering" occurred. Luckily for West, as he admits, since Dreiser and his editors were safely dead, nobody with the knowledge and authority to do so could object to his recuperation of Dreiser as a self-conscious artist or to his restoration of the texts that supported this bit of biography. Luckily (again) for West, when he wanted to restore some passages to William Styron's *Lie Down in Darkness* (1951) that the publisher's editor had excised, he was able to consult the author. After initially agreeing to the restoration, Styron decided that the originally published text should stand in West's 1992 edition. In this case, West's biographical speculations were trumped by the authority of the living author who, in a move that would delight McGann and his disciples, chose to go with the social text. But, given advances in technology, why choose at all? As it were anticipating Shillingsburg's comments, West imagines both versions available to readers as electronic texts. West, however, is a man of the book, and he concludes by returning to the problem of which edition to print. Though the matter might be settled for now, how will a future editor of *Lie Down in Darkness* proceed? Biographically, of course, and, since the historical record may be interpreted to support either version, West predicts that such an editor will publish whichever text fits his or her biographical constructions.

Biography, if not precisely in West's sense, is the subject of Charles E. Robinson's fascinating "reflections" on editorial authority and his recent edition of *The Frankenstein Notebooks*. After beginning his essay with several pointed references to the "creative metaphor" encouraged by Mary Shelley's own characterization of her novel as "my hideous progeny," Robinson traces the complex biography of the work from manuscript to printed book. I use the term "biography" because, as we follow Robinson in his exploration of the several stages of composition, we are reminded with peculiar force of the Romantic belief that works of art are living organisms: they are born, they grow, they change. Some of them, we like to think, will live forever, being constantly reanimated by future readers. Whatever our attitude to this conceit, we cannot deny its appropriateness to the specific circumstances of *Frankenstein*, a work obsessed with acts of creation and revision. Robinson details Mary Shelley's original bringing-forth of the work in 1816 and 1817, and examines her continued involvement in revising further drafts, proofs, and printed editions of the work during the following decade and a half. The work was also helped along in its growth toward maturity—before its several publications in 1818, 1823, 1826, and 1831—by the often substantial editorial interventions of Percy Shelley, William Godwin, and "various publishers' readers and printers." Given that there exist "no fewer than ten texts that go into the making of *Frankenstein*," we might well ask: whose work or text are we supposed to be reading?

Robinson's answer to this question is far from simple. While he leans toward granting Mary Shelley authority for her work, he also admits that "all these interventions should help to dispel the still-persistent myth of the solitary artist who has total control over a text." Yet, if Mary Shelley did not have "total control" over her text, there is a sense in which, by accepting or rejecting changes made to her work by others in various drafts and published versions, she can still be seen as retaining her authority. To recall West's model once again, the "Mary Shelley" biographically constructed by Robinson might not have "total control"—a tellingly totalizing phrase—yet she is in charge when it really counts. The loss of control is only a momentary strategy, to be followed by the author's editing of the editors' work. If the work was produced by committee, as the evidence of the notebooks seems to indicate, Mary Shelley was the committee's undisputed chair.

In short, *Frankenstein* was a collaborative work because Mary Shelley wanted it to be one. While Robinson invites us to see evidence of a social text in the multiplicity of hands at work in *The Frankenstein Notebooks,* he also wants us to view the novel as Mary Shelley's, not Percy's or Godwin's or anybody else's. This is why, in his final "reflection," after gingerly sidestepping the issue of a new eclectic edition, he cannot endorse the obvious solution to the problem of how best to present the multiple versions of the work: namely, by putting all the extant texts on the World Wide Web. That future readers might "be able to assemble their own *Frankensteins*" and thus "become authors or at least editors of their own texts of Mary Shelley's novel" alarms Robinson. For him, this potentially endless versioning of "Mary Shelley's novel" poses "the threat that a web of undisciplined texts about a monster might produce texts more monstrous than we already have." Under these dreadful circumstances, without institutional or disciplinary constraints (as we know them today), Mary Shelley's "hideous progeny" might go forth, but it will not prosper. There is a difference between plural texts edited by a responsible editor like Robinson and a hypertextual free-for-all. Robinson thus establishes his own editorial authority by preserving and reaffirming Mary Shelley's (now posthumous) authority over her work, not by disseminating it out of existence.

Issues of authority and biography also concern Peter Shillingsburg, who, in "Editing Thackeray: A History," traces his own development as he has confronted and in many cases influenced changes in editorial theory and practice over the last twenty-five years. Although he began his career as a disciple of the Greg/Bowers school working on the Centennial Edition of the Writings of William Gilmore Simms, Shillingsburg soon discovered that Greg/Bowers intentionalism could not "without qualifications and revisions" solve the sorts of problems that characterized the texts of Thackeray that he wanted to edit. But Shillingsburg is a generous and fair historian. Unlike McGann's polemical *Critique of Modern Textual Criticism* of 1983, the history that Shillingsburg tells does not comfort us with easy dichotomies or teleologies. Editorial theory and practice have not progressed in a straight line from a benighted Bowers to the brilliant possibilities of hypertext. In fact, Shillingsburg attributes to Bowers and his contemporaries a degree of self-consciousness often denied them. In spite of the confidence with which he stated his principles in his many theoretical articles, Bowers was often cautious when confronting specific editorial decisions. The language of his textual introduction to the Wesleyan edition of *Tom Jones,* for example, is far more tentative than we would expect from his assertions elsewhere. Such words as "perhaps" and "apparently" appear throughout. Bowers also admits that he has based many of his editorial decisions on educated guesses, not solid evidence. He has tried to recover Henry Fielding's intentions, but, given the inevitable opacity of the historical record, "the present editor"— here Bowers attempts rhetorically to recover some measure of objectivity— has had to cobble together his own text of *Tom Jones.*[4] In what I interpret as an act of filial piety, Shillingsburg points out that our forebears in textual studies knew far more than we give them credit for—indeed knew far more than many of us do. If we can perhaps see more, it is because we stand on their shoulders.

Shillingsburg is also a realistic historian. With touching honesty and self-deprecation, he anticipates the not-too-distant day when "the Garland Thackeray editions become a disgrace to modern literary scholarship." Although I agree that as our editorial fashions change so must our critical editions, I cannot fully concur that such an exquisitely meticulous edition as Shillingsburg's Thackeray will not be used and appreciated by learned readers many years hence. As Shillingsburg writes a few sentences later, "what matters is the fit between the concepts about textual conditions of works of art and the accomplishments of the editorial work produced." We may no longer pretend that we can produce definitive critical editions, but we are still responsible for making sure that, at the very least, our editions are carefully and accurately prepared as well as faithful to the historical circumstances in which the works were produced. Anything less would be unacceptable, I hope, in any age—unless, of course, we do away with all standards and do whatever we like. But in that case we would not be producing critical texts, however generously we might care to define them.

While often celebrating changes in editorial theory and practice, and while rightly emphasizing the importance of recognizing the needs of readers, Shillingsburg warns us about the potential pitfalls of pursuing novelty for its own sake. McGann claimed to have changed his editorial practice because "the things which I have seen I now can see no more,"[5] but Shillingsburg encourages us to remember and to benefit from all that we have seen. One of the first textualists to recognize both the potential benefits and the potential drawbacks of scholarly editing in the computer age (to borrow the title of his influential book), Shillingsburg concludes on a cautiously optimistic note: "Perhaps in the electronic scholarly edition we have a medium with the dexterity, capacity, flexibility, and agility to incorporate multiple editorial intentions and readerly intentions as well as those of the author and producers of books."

The possibilities of digital or electronic texts excite S. W. Reid, too, in "Conrad in Print and on Disk," an essay similar to Shillingsburg's in its judicious endorsement of old and new technologies. Unlike Robinson, who is horrified by the gothic nightmare of a fully democratic Internet, Reid imagines a well-organized and responsibly prepared Conrad archive, brimming with texts of Conrad's works and pertinent historical documents, possibly enhanced by audio and visual capabilities, all waiting to be accessed by the eager scholar. The electronic documents that he envisages have already been edited, collated, and annotated by capable editors and put on the Web or on CD-ROM for the benefit of scholars, such as the transplanted Oxford Ph.D. whom he introduces in his opening anecdote, who have no access to major research libraries or collections of primary materials. What troubles Reid is the often unacknowledged gap between the technologies available to produce electronic texts and the technologies available to those who wish or need to use those texts. This is why he concludes that Conrad should be available in good print editions as well as in good digital ones. It is salutary to be reminded that the much-ballyhooed universal accessibility promised by our technological cheerleaders does not apply universally and that the humble technologies of yesteryear can still serve us well. A book, in some cases, is more portable than an electronic text.

Although Reid celebrates the potential scholarly benefits of digital texts for those who can access them, he begins and ends his essay by focusing on books. His young Oxford graduate working in South America wishes to write a scholarly book on Conrad's style, only to discover that she is lacking the "reliable editions" needed to complete her project successfully. Reid thus illustrates, as Cohen does in his essay on Faulkner, the crucial links between textual scholarship and literary criticism. As he traces the tangled history of Conrad's works through their many British and American editions, he suggests ways in which authorized readings might be recovered or reconstructed. Yet he also offers a sobering reminder that, with an author who has left us sometimes contradictory statements regarding his "intentions" for his works, the editor must confront nearly insurmountable difficulties in fashioning an authoritative text.

For Reid, as for other contributors to this collection, editorial decisions must be based on the judicious sifting of often contradictory data. While Reid may at times invoke the authority of the author, he does not worship at the altar of authorial intentions: there are too many instances in which we do not know what Conrad actually wrote or intended to write. With patience and hard work, Reid assures us, it is still possible to come up with more "reliable editions" to meet the needs of various readers. But we must remember that "as all transmitted texts are mediated, a definitive text of Conrad's works is a will-o'-the-wisp" and that "as all texts are constructs . . . a critical edition, and especially one with an eclectic text, must be imperfectly constructed." This is admirably put, though it raises one final difficulty. The young woman in Reid's anecdote might one day get her hands on more "reliable texts" of Conrad's works, but, given the inevitable residue of uncertainty present in even the most carefully edited critical text, she might still have difficulties writing her book on Conrad's style because she will be unable to assume, with complete confidence, that the words she is reading on the page or on her computer screen appear there as they were written or intended by Conrad. In other words, as textual editors (as they must) honestly call attention to the imperfections of their editions, certain types of text-based literary criticism might become less viable. Troubled by the linguistic uncertainty revealed by textual scholarship, Reid's Oxonian abandons her naively New Critical topic and becomes a cultural historian.

Whereas Reid argues for the complementarity of digital and print editions of Conrad's works, Charles L. Ross, in his bracing polemic on D. H. Lawrence's "textuality," focuses on the opposition of print and hypertext. Ross minces no words in stating his main point: "As a medium of communication the print critical edition has outlived its usefulness." Curiously, however, given his postmodernist slant, Ross bases his argument on authorial intention. We are invited to infer that if Lawrence were around today, he would like to see his texts presented exactly as Ross imagines them. While in the last thirty years or so we may have learned to stop worrying about the author and love the text, it appears that, even for such a staunch defender of "textuality" as Ross, the author is still very much with us.

Ross contends that "our printed critical editions [of Lawrence], despite all their scholarship, fail to liberate the multiple voices of textuality." This sad state of affairs is especially evident in the Cambridge edition of Lawrence, the principal object of Ross's displeasure. He grants that volumes in the Cambridge Lawrence present in their apparatus raw data for "versioning" of the sort that interests him, but he argues that the "semiosis" of the apparatus—the discrete annotations and the specialized systems for recording variants—collaborates with the "medium of print" to prevent readers from gaining full access to the textual richness of Lawrence's works.

For Ross, then, previous attempts to edit Lawrence have failed because "print's technology of presence resists variety." But the problems are not confined to the unavoidable deficiencies of the medium. The Cambridge editors, by imposing on the works traditional editorial principles, have also ensured that the polyvocality of Lawrence's texts remains muted. Given the edition's goal of publishing "authoritative" editions, the editors set out to fashion a single, stable text. To do so, they engage in biographical reconstructions and interpretive maneuvers that Ross, unlike Cohen and West, finds unwarranted. Thus James T. Boulton and John Worthen intrude their biographical speculations in producing two different—and inadequate—versions of "Odour of Chrysanthemums" (1911; 1969, 1983). Similarly, Helen Baron and Carl Baron fashion "a splendid edition of Sons and Lovers" (1913; 1992) but are blinded to the subjectivity and partiality of their procedures.

In exposing these editorial sins, Ross intends "to demonstrate that *any* editorial rationale construes the 'author' interpretively and that our print editions inevitably enable certain sorts of versioning while hampering others." Of course Ross himself, though he does not admit it, cannot escape his own indictment. For example, when he objects that Mark Kinkead-Weekes "imposes" an interpretation of Ursula's character to solve a textual problem in his edition of *The Rainbow* (1915; 1989), he counters with an interpretation of his own—an interpretation, to my mind, equally as debatable as Kinkead-Weekes's, though perhaps not so politically incorrect. As I have already suggested, Ross construes a "Lawrence" that will sanction his hypertexts. He seems to mistake the apparent freedom from the reification of print promised by digital texts for freedom from all editorial biases. It just so happens that Ross's desire to "liberate the multiple voices" in Lawrence's texts by the technological empowerment of every user of his database—so that each reader becomes, as it were, an author-editor—jibes nicely with our contemporary faith in linguistic instability and textual indeterminacy. While perhaps instilling fear in the hearts of more traditional editors like Robinson, who will see chaos where Ross sees liberation, Ross's scheme speaks to our particular institutional and disciplinary moment. Given the convincing argument that he presents for the advantages of hypertexts over print editions, he might well be prophesying the future of textual studies.

While the millennium may be upon us, the triumph of the hypertext might be farther off. At least that is the contention of the last contributor, Michael F. Suarez, in his examination of our faith in the unbounded power of technology to improve our critical and editorial lives. If Ross celebrates the nearly infinite possibilities of hypertext, Suarez stresses its shortcomings. Take, for example, the much-vaunted capabilities of the computer to enhance our critical prowess. As Suarez forcefully demonstrates, while computers might give us access (as Reid would hope) to otherwise unavailable literary texts, what they actually allow us to do with those texts is fairly narrow. We may use computers as fancy concordances, but the activity is always limited by the specific word or phrase we choose to search for. Other applications are limited by the fact that electronic editors embed only certain codes in their texts and thus allow only certain sorts of searches. Suarez argues that there is still no fully satisfactory electronic substitute for engaging in a close and careful reading of the literary text.

Even if computers cannot yet do much critical thinking for us, there is no denying, as Suarez admits, the power of hypertext to "overcome the limitations" of print "by creating 'webs' of linked documents." But, unlike Ross,

Suarez worries about the informational glut that this capability facilitates. What if, in our efforts to contextualize the work as thoroughly as possible, we lose the text that we are supposedly studying in a maelstrom of hypertextual links? What about the discontinuities in our reading—the "*lectio interrupta,*" in Suarez's wonderful Latinism—caused by all that mouse-clicking? Wouldn't they "diminish the creative process," as well as our perception and understanding of it? What if an electronic editor—Suarez cites the example of McGann and his massive hypertextual project on the works of Dante Gabriel Rossetti—believes that the best way to present the material is to present all of it with minimal editorial guidance, so that readers can pick and choose what they need from the archive? For Suarez, though obviously not for Ross or McGann, this would be an invitation to anarchy, not to mention an abdication of editorial responsibility. As he sees it, by declining "[to establish] a text through the long and demanding process of critical discernment, of carefully weighing complex evidence and deciding in the midst of difficulty, the electronic editor is not empowering users but obliging them to arrive at judgments they most often will have neither the time nor the expertise to make." For Suarez, "this is not freedom, but the illusion of freedom."

Suarez is not a technophobe, however. Like Shillingsburg, from whose work he approvingly quotes, he believes that, if we proceed cautiously and judiciously, hypertext will yield substantial editorial benefits. Following Shillingsburg, Suarez endorses the concept of the "electronic scholarly edition." Given the expansiveness of the hypertextual environment, the electronic editor can move beyond "the extreme case of establishing *the* definitive edition that forever fixes the text and must be the standard for all subsequent interpretive work"—an unexceptionably post-Bowers pronouncement with which virtually every contemporary textual editor, including Ross and the other contributors to this volume, would readily concur. "Such positivism," as Suarez eloquently puts it, "has no place in so humanistic a discipline as literary editing."

Unlike Ross, however, Suarez is not persuaded by postmodern notions of textuality. For him, even "if editorial certainty is impossible, it does not follow that we should undertake no critical editing and surrender to a textual skepticism that leaves us forever in a world of radical indeterminacy."

Textual editors, electronic or otherwise, have responsibilities—to the works they edit, to their authors, to their readers. They must make decisions: choosing not to decide is an abdication of those responsibilities. There is also the danger that machines will rob us of our humanity. At the conclusion of his essay, Suarez movingly reminds us that "the speed of electronic texts can beguile the reality that human understanding takes time." In other words, the dreams of boundless progress fostered by modern technology must be tempered by full and humble acceptance of our humanity, with its inevitable fallibility, limitations, and imperfections.

Given the eloquent and varied testimony of the contributors to this volume, we may assume that the very best textual editors are not likely to take for granted their enormous responsibility as transmitters and preservers of human knowledge or to take the easy way out in attending to their difficult tasks. That is, of course, my hope rather than a prophecy of future developments in editorial theory and practice—a hope predicated on yet another hope, that future textual editors will have the wisdom, tact, and perspicuity of, say, a Noel Polk or a Peter Shillingsburg. While we may be stumbling on the road toward a brave new world of textual editing, we are not there yet. As I have attempted to show, authorial intention, while under fire, continues to inform our thinking about textual matters. It is difficult to let go of a concept with so much explanatory power or with such potential as a whipping-boy. Even Charles L. Ross, the most committed advocate of the new digital order in this collection, operates under the old assumption that he knows Lawrence's authorial intentions far better than the Cambridge editors do. While we may be in the midst of a paradigm shift from print to electronic editions, this change is marked more by continuity than discontinuity. When we think of electronic editions, I would argue that most of us still think of them as versions of print editions: we think of the book first, then we think of the book digitized. If there is an editorial revolution going on, it has not yet overturned the old order with the radical Darwinian or Kuhnian break from the past that McGann might have hoped for when he published his *Critique* in 1983.

Granted, seventeen years is not a very long time, but so much has happened in this time that it might not be unwarranted to speculate that the future of textual studies will, in all likelihood, look very little like the past or even the present. To begin, digital texts are here to stay. While I share some of Suarez's misgivings, I am convinced that the actual benefits of such hypertextual projects as McGann's Rossetti archive far outweigh the potential drawbacks.[6] McGann's site is like a well-stocked research library, where textual editors, teachers, students, and "common readers" can access materials with ease, in the comfort of their homes, libraries, or offices. Changes in the erudition and technological competence of future editors and readers will no doubt influence future developments in this field. What would an "electronic scholarly edition" (to use Shillingsburg's term) look like if educational standards continue to decline and what is deemed "scholarly" continues to be discounted? More broadly, what will happen if funding for the humanities, in the form of research grants or faculty salaries, continues to erode, and the editing of literary texts, however defined, becomes a luxury we can no longer afford?

Questions of this sort perhaps call attention to overarching *fin-de-siècle* anxieties as well as to specific problems in textual studies. But in any case, it seems safe to say that we are only just beginning to discern the contours of a future in which human beings will learn about the world from computer screens rather than from books. While, like Suarez, I find books more "human" than computers, such (I suspect) is not the case with my eight-year-old son, for whom cozying up with a computer monitor is as "natural" as cozying up with a book. While the book might not disappear altogether or be entirely superseded, it will very likely lose its primacy as the deliverer of texts, literary or otherwise. Moreover, the effects of globalization and multiculturalism, as authors, editors, and readers from diverse classes, ethnicities, and sexual orientations stake their claims for representation, might well lead to editorial theories and practices in the next millennium undreamed of in the old Greg/Bowers philology.[7] In short, the future of textual studies is unclear and uncertain, fraught with challenges, dangers, and possibilities, but no less exciting for all that.

Notes

1. For Bowers's editorial principles, see, for example, Fredson Bowers, "Greg's Rationale of Copy-Text Revisited," *Studies in Bibliography* 31 (1978): 90–161; and Bow-

ers, *Essays in Bibliography, Texts, and Editing* (Charlottesville: University Press of Virginia, 1975). Cf. Philip Gaskell, *A New Introduction to Bibliography* (1972; reprint, New Castle DE: Oak Knoll Press, 1995), esp. 339–40.

2. For a concise summary of Tanselle's views, see Tanselle, *A Rationale of Textual Criticism* (Philadelphia: University of Pennsylvania Press, 1989); for more expansive treatment, see Tanselle's two collections of essays, *Textual Criticism Since Greg: A Chronicle, 1950–1985* (Charlottesville: University Press of Virginia, 1987) and *Textual Criticism and Scholarly Editing* (Charlottesville: University Press of Virginia, 1990). Cf. Jerome J. McGann, *A Critique of Modern Textual Criticism* (1983; reprint, Charlottesville: University Press of Virginia, 1992).

3. It is perhaps ironic that the authors' expansiveness on this point recalls more pointedly theorized (and less pointedly intentionalist) arguments about editing and the nonverbal aspects of books; see Jerome J. McGann, *The Textual Condition* (Princeton: Princeton University Press, 1991), 48–68; and George Bornstein, "What Is the Text of a Poem by Yeats?" *Palimpsest: Editorial Theory in the Humanities,* ed. Bornstein and Ralph Williams (Ann Arbor: University of Michigan Press, 1993), 167–93.

4. See Fredson Bowers, textual introduction to Henry Fielding, *Tom Jones,* ed. Martin C. Battestin and Fredson Bowers (Middletown CT: Wesleyan University Press, 1975), lxii–lxxxiv.

5. McGann, *Critique,* 7.

6. For a good introduction to this subject, see *The Literary Text in the Digital Age,* ed. Richard J. Finneran (Ann Arbor: University of Michigan Press, 1996).

7. On the roles of race, class, and gender in current scholarly editing, see essays by Gerald MacLean, William L. Andrews, Brenda R. Silver, Ann Thomson, and Jonathan Goldberg in *The Margins of the Text,* ed. D. C. Greetham (Ann Arbor: University of Michigan Press, 1997), 25–128.

PHILIP COHEN, associate professor and chair of English at the University of Texas at Arlington, has edited *Devils and Angels: Textual Editing and Literary Theory* and *Texts and Textuality: Textual Instability, Theory and Interpretation.* He is currently writing a book entitled *Textual Scholarship, Textual Instability, and the Novels of William Faulkner.*

FREDERICK M. LINK is professor of English at the University of Nebraska–Lincoln and editor of Aphra Behn's *The Rover,* John Dryden's *Aureng-Zebe, The Plays of Hannah Cowley,* and *The Plays of John O'Keeffe.* He has also edited Willa Cather's *Obscure Destinies.*

CHARLES W. MIGNON is professor of English at the University of Nebraska–Lincoln; editor of Edward Taylor's *Upon the Types of the Old Testament;* and textual editor of the Willa Cather Scholarly Edition (Nebraska), in which capacity he has edited, most recently, *Death Comes for the Archbishop.*

ALEXANDER PETTIT, associate professor of English at the University of North Texas, is author of *Illusory Consensus: Bolingbroke and the Polemical Response to Walpole, 1730–1737;* general editor of The Works of Tobias Smollett and British Ideas and Issues, 1660–1820: A Series of Reprinted Books and Pamphlets; and general and textual editor of Selected Works of Eliza Haywood. He is currently preparing an edition of Daniel Defoe's *The Complete English Gentleman.*

NOEL POLK, professor of English at the University of Southern Mississippi, has served as one of four chief editors of the forty-four-volume William Faulkner Manuscripts, edited fourteen of Faulkner's novels, and has agreed to edit the rest of Faulkner's fiction. His books include *Children of the Dark House* and *Outside the Southern Myth.*

S. W. REID is chief executive editor of the Cambridge Edition of the Works of Joseph Conrad, published by Cambridge University Press and centered at Kent State University, where he is professor of English and director of the university's cross-disciplinary Institute for Bibliography and Editing.

ALBERT J. RIVERO, professor of English and director of the Honors Program at Marquette University, has published books and articles on eighteenth-century British literature. A member of the editorial board of The Works of Tobias Smollett, he is working on a critical edition of Samuel Richardson's correspondence and on books tentatively entitled *Duplicitous Representations: Fashioning Fiction from Behn to Burney* and *Empires of Memory*.

CHARLES E. ROBINSON, professor of English at the University of Delaware, is author of *Shelley and Byron: The Snake and Eagle Wreathed in Fight* and editor of *Mary Shelley: Collected Tales and Stories*. He has also edited twenty-seven new William Hazlitt letters, co-edited with Betty T. Bennett *The Mary Shelley Reader*, and edited Mary Shelley's *Proserpine and Midas* and *The Frankenstein Notebooks*.

KARI A. RONNING is assistant editor of the Willa Cather Scholarly Edition at the University of Nebraska–Lincoln.

SUSAN J. ROSOWSKI, Adele Hall Professor of English at the University of Nebraska–Lincoln, is general editor of the Willa Cather Scholarly Edition, author of *The Voyage Perilous: Willa Cather's Romanticism,* and editor-in-chief of *Cather Studies.*

CHARLES L. ROSS, professor and chair of English at the University of Hartford, has edited Lawrence's *Women in Love* and, with Dennis Jackson, *Editing D. H. Lawrence: New Versions of a Modern Author.* He is author of *The Composition of "The Rainbow" and "Women in Love": A History* and *"Women in Love": A Novel of Mythic Realism.*

PETER SHILLINGSBURG, professor of English at the University of North Texas, is author of *Scholarly Editing in the Computer Age* and *Resisting Texts* and general editor of Works of W. M. Thackeray.

MICHAEL F. SUAREZ, S.J., is associate professor of English at Fordham University and a member of the University of Oxford's Faculty of English Language and Literature. The winner of Oxford's Gordon Duff Prize for bibliography, in 1995 he delivered the Graham Pollard Memorial Lecture before The Bibliographical Society (London). He has edited Robert Dodsley's *Collections of Poems by Several Hands* and is co-editing (with Michael Turner) Volume 5 (1695–1830) of *The Cambridge History of the Book in Britain.*

JAMES L. W. WEST III is Distinguished Professor of English and a fellow in the Institute for the Arts and Humanistic Studies at the Pennsylvania State University, where he also directs the Penn State Center for the History of the Book. He is general editor of The Cambridge Edition of the Works of F. Scott Fitzgerald and one of the textual editors of the University of Pennsylvania Dreiser Edition. His *William Styron: A Life* was published in 1998.

Index

Abbott, Craig, 2
accidentals, 3, 12, 33–34, 47, 52–62, 133, 180, 183; capitalization, 33; punctuation, 13, 14, 16, 34, 42, 44, 55–58, 182–84; spelling, 13, 33, 48, 59. *See also* substantives
Anderson, Sir Robert, 128–30
annotation. *See* emendation; essays; notes
archives, 123, 140 n.12, 150, 174; Blake, 179 n.31; Cather, 48, 183; Conrad, 190; Lawrence, 150–54; Rossetti, 9, 19, 21, 172–73, 194, 196
Aristotle, 174, 179 n.32
authoritativeness/authority, 4, 9, 20, 25, 65, 77, 123, 150, 191–92; in Cather, 31, 34, 37, 48; editorial, 91, 172, 187; of print versions, 141, 143–45, 192; proprietorship and copyright law, 117–18, 141–42; in Shelley, 187–88; in Styron, 89
authors and authorship, 2, 7, 10, 54, 77, 155, 159 n.35; collaborative, 8, 22, 65–66, 76, 82, 84, 92, 107, 142, 157, 188; cultural and social factors in, 8, 9, 42, 76–77, 82, 115, 118, 170; plurality of voices in, 18, 22, 141–42, 192; post-Romantic, 8, 16, 26 n.12, 65–66, 77, 97, 118, 182, 185, 187; relations with editors, 14, 16, 32, 62, 86–87; revisions, 30, 31, 44–46, 66, 84, 116, 128, 142–45, 154, 180, 187; self-editing/self-censoring of, 92, 94, 97, 144–46, 150–54. *See also* editing, textual: biographical fashioning of; intention: authorial

Baron, Carl, 145–46, 192
Baron, Helen, 145–46, 192
base-text, 2, 3; clear vs. annotated, 11, 35, 124 n.7, 144

Beck, Warren, 60
Beckford, William: *Vathek,* 174
Benda, W. T., 34
Bentley, Richard, 97, 105–6
Bobbs-Merrill, 88–89
Bodleian Library, 94, 98
Bolter, Jay David, 172
books, physical features of, 182; bindings, 33, 141; design and manufacturing, 32, 34, 42, 48, 66, 116, 164; fonts, 18, 95, 122, 136, 140 n.13; frontispieces, 33; illustrations, 31, 33, 34, 48, 66; page formatting, 31, 122; paper stock, 31, 34; typography, 31, 33, 34, 165; wrappers, 34
Bornstein, George, 27 n.23, 65, 197 n.3
Boulton, James T., 142–43, 192
Bowers, Fredson, 3–12, 18, 20–21, 27 n.15, 34–35, 112–16, 142, 180–83, 186, 188–89, 194, 196
Brontë, Charlotte, 7, 8
Burrows, Louie, 22, 23, 142
Butler, Marilyn, 25 n.3, 110 n.18. *See also* editing, textual: of women authors; editors: women as
Byron, Lord, 107, 181

Cambridge University Press, 22, 122, 129, 139 nn.3,4, 141–47, 150, 192, 195
Cather, Willa, 11, 13, 15–17, 19, 28 n.26, 30–51, 182–83; Autograph Editions, 43–44, 46, 48, 182; *Cather Archive,* 48–49, 51 n.23; correspondence, 31, 38, 42–43, 47; knowledge of flora and fauna, 12, 40–41, 50 n.17; quotations and allusions in, 36–37, 42; revisions by, 30, 31, 44–46; Scholarly Edition, 10–12, 23, 31–49 passim; as self-editor, 33; serial versions, 35, 43, 45–47, 182; sources for places

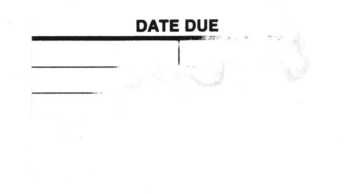

DATE DUE